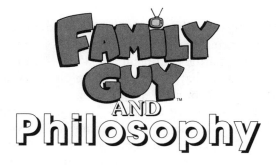

The Blackwell Philosophy and PopCulture Series
Series editor William Irwin

A spoonful of sugar helps the medicine go down, and a healthy helping of popular culture clears the cobwebs from Kant. Philosophy has had a public relations problem for a few centuries now. This series aims to change that, showing that philosophy is relevant to your life – and not just for answering the big questions like "To be or not to be?" but for answering the little questions: "To watch or not to watch *South Park*?" Thinking deeply about TV, movies, and music doesn't make you a "complete idiot." In fact it might make you a philosopher, someone who believes the unexamined life is not worth living and the unexamined cartoon is not worth watching.

South Park and Philosophy
Edited by Robert Arp

Metallica and Philosophy
Edited by William Irwin

Family Guy and Philosophy
Edited by J. Jeremy Wisnewski

The Daily Show and Philosophy
Edited by Jason Holt

Forthcoming

Lost and Philosophy
Edited by Sharon Kaye

24 and Philosophy
Edited by Jennifer Hart Weed, Richard Brian Davis, and Ronald Weed

The Office and Philosophy
Edited by J. Jeremy Wisnewski

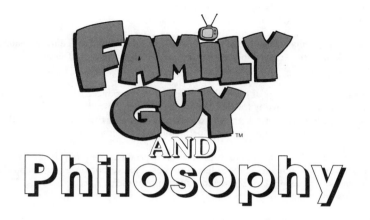

Family Guy and Philosophy

A Cure for the Petarded

Edited by J. Jeremy Wisnewski

Blackwell
Publishing

© 2007 by Blackwell Publishing Ltd

BLACKWELL PUBLISHING
350 Main Street, Malden, MA 02148–5020, USA
9600 Garsington Road, Oxford OX4 2DQ, UK
550 Swanston Street, Carlton, Victoria 3053, Australia

The right of J. Jeremy Wisnewski to be identified as the author of the editorial material in this work has been asserted in accordance with the UK Copyright, Designs, and Patents Act 1988.

This publication is designed to provide accurate and authoritative information in regard to the subject matter covered. It is sold on the understanding that the publisher is not engaged in rendering professional services. If professional advice or other expert assistance is required, the services of a competent professional should be sought.

First published 2007 by Blackwell Publishing Ltd

1   2007

Library of Congress Cataloging-in-Publication Data

Family guy and philosophy : a cure for the petarded / edited by J. Jeremy Wisnewski.
    p. cm. — (The Blackwell philosophy and pop culture series ; 3)
    Includes bibliographical references and index.
    ISBN 978-1-4051-6316-3 (pbk. : alk. paper)
    1. Family guy (Television program)   I. Wisnewski, Jeremy.

    PN1992.77.F27F36 2007
    791.45'72—dc22

                                                                    2007024720

A catalogue record for this title is available from the British Library.

Set in 10.5/13pt Sabon
by Graphicraft Limited, Hong Kong
Printed in the United States of America
by Sheridan Books Inc.

The publisher's policy is to use permanent paper from mills that operate a sustainable forestry policy, and which has been manufactured from pulp processed using acid-free and elementary chlorine-free practices. Furthermore, the publisher ensures that the text paper and cover board used have met acceptable environmental accreditation standards.

For further information on
Blackwell Publishing, visit our website at
www.blackwellpublishing.com

CONTENTS

Contents

1 That's right, freakin' #F. What are you, some kind of mathematician?

ACKNOWLEDGMENTS:
These People are Freakin' Sweet

This book owes everything to the Griffins. They're freakin' sweet, and a lot of energy has gone in to showing just *how* sweet they are, even philosophically. Peter Griffin looked at every chapter before confessing that he only liked books with pictures. Stewie was pleased with the book until he read the chapter praising Lois. Brian did some delightful copy-editing. He was particularly pleased to find out that he was a person. Chris can barely speak, let alone read. Meg – well, Meg just doesn't matter.

Seth MacFarlane gets big thanks for getting the Fox Network to let us use images from the show for the cover of the book (we've been thanking him for years for *Family Guy*). Don Keefer, a philosophy professor at the Rhode Island School of Design, really came through for us by contacting Seth (I'll use his first name as though we're buds . . . I can dream) and telling him about the book. Thanks Don!

I also want to direct some *Family Guy* love to Bill Irwin and Jeff Dean. They've both been great to work with, and have made my labors with *Family Guy* even more enjoyable than I imagined they would be. Bill Irwin had a hand in improving every contribution, and his good work shows through. Mike Veber, Carl Rose, Henry Jacoby, and Stefanie Rocknak proved their dedication to the show (ok . . . maybe they were just proving their dedication to philosophy) by reading parts of the book. Peter G. Res read the manuscript with a keen eye for errors, and a real dedication to the project. (He's the self-dubbed "*Family Guy* bitch.") Meghan Lonergan (a Meg that matters) deserves thanks for helping with the index. Finally, big thanks go to P. Sue Dohnimm, who came into existence right when I needed her to. I'd also like to thank the Academy.

Whoa. That can't be the end.

I wouldn't be much of a family guy if I didn't thank my wife, Dorothy Wisnewski, for enduring my near-religious watching of the show, even when it meant that I had to ignore what were undoubtedly more important things (giggity-giggity).

I also want to thank my daughter, Audrey Wisnewski, for no reason whatsoever. She didn't contribute one damn thing to the book, aside from being adorable (she's only two, for Christ's sake – what do you want from her?). If you don't like it, go read some other acknowledgments, pal! These here are mine, and I'll do with them what I want!

YOU BETTER NOT READ THIS, PAL:
An Introduction to *Family Guy and Philosophy*

J. JEREMY WISNEWSKI

You've got some nerve, buddy. What the hell were you thinking, picking up and then actually *reading* a book that dares to put together venerable old philosophy with that scandalous bitch *Family Guy?* Did you think it would be funny to dignify the association by reading this introduction? How dare you! The Audacity! (the 'a' is capitalized because it's so infuriating that you're actually *reading* this! Stop it!)

What?! You're *still* reading! Obviously, you've got no sense of decency – but I suppose we knew that the instant you picked up this book. I mean, the very idea that there could be something philosophical about fat, idiotic men and their farts – or about homicidal babies, dogs that talk, and perverse sexual obsessions. That Seth MacFarlane's a lot like you – he's got *nerve*. The characters he's created, and the writing he's done – it's just downright vulgar. He has dogs wanting to screw women, and babies screwing babies, and Quagmire screwing anything. It's like there's a screw loose.[1] And he's always making fun of things like disability, homosexuality, religion, consumerism, America, and Fox television. *He's got nerve,* just like you.

But we're not so different, the two of us. I've got nerve too, pal. I'm willing to bring philosophy and *Family Guy* together, and then to put my name on the resulting concoction! And I'm willing to risk my good name to do this! (I'll confess that I'm not risking much, given my own rather indiscreet history.) When I told a friend – someone not so different from you -- about *Family Guy* and philosophy, she

1

laughed out loud, and then she said: "I can't decide if the show is really deep or just a bunch of gratuitous stupidity" (that's a direct quote, as you may have noticed from the use of quotation marks). I started to respond by saying something about the importance of bringing accessible philosophy to the masses, of using the everyday world of popular culture to actually *do* philosophy with other people, and so on. But instead I just smiled. Gas will do that to you.

I'm now prepared to give *you* the response, since you're *still* reading this book: *Family Guy* is *both* really deep and really stupid. It occasions real insight into the human condition, and into the world at large. It's also full of some really dumb gags – gags so dumb that you're forced to love them with everything that you are. *Family Guy* presses us on questions about who we are and what we're committed to, and it does all of this knee-deep in some of the most ridiculous television ever seen. As offensive as *Family Guy* is, it is offense that we desperately need – it is offense that demands us to account for ourselves, that demands we at least acknowledge that some of the things we hold sacred may not necessarily be so. And maybe, just maybe, philosophy can be good even if it investigates the aesthetics of the fart joke.

So *keep* reading. You've made it this far – and I promise you there's insight to be had here. As much as I wanted to further sully my not-so-good name, my philosophical companions have made this virtually impossible here. They're a smart bunch, as you'll soon see, since you're obviously incapable of following my directions to stop reading.

Oh, and one more thing (but don't take this the wrong way, pal): if you find yourself thinking about beer, or TV, or farts, absolutely all the time, this book could make you smarter. If it's possible to cure the petarded, we've got the medicine in the pages that follow.

NOTE

1 I apologize for this pun. Despite my shame at having written it, I will not delete it. Now stop reading this footnote!

PART I

THOSE GOOD OLE' FASHION VALUES ON WHICH WE USED TO RELY

1

KILLING THE GRIFFINS:
A Murderous Exposition of Postmodernism

J. JEREMY WISNEWSKI

This is not an essay. It's a prelude to homicide.

I am going to kill the Griffin family. I will even kill that baby and especially that ridiculous dog. I will do this for one straightforward reason: it's the only way we can be saved.

Saved? Yes. *Family Guy* will be the end of the civilized world. It will be the death of value. *Family Guy* oozes the postmodern, and the post-modern will be the end of us all. *Postmodernism* is a movement that has developed over the last several decades in philosophy, architecture, literature, and elsewhere. This movement emphasizes the absence of any real structure to the world or our lives, and of any overarching meaning to our activities. It systematically calls into question our most serious ideas: Truth, Progress, Freedom, Rationality, and the Individual.[1] Instead, postmodernism sees the world as disjointed, with pockets of power relations and politics and nothing to unify it all. Yes, there is reason (with a small 'r'), but he's just a little fella, and can't do much by himself. At most, he pops up here and there – and he's never divorced from a particular context. The postmodern world is a ruptured world – and *Family Guy* just oozes these ruptures.

And so, the Griffins must die. It's the only way to save us from becoming cynical conservatives. That's right. I'll say it plainly and with gusto: *Family Guy* is *conservative*. You see, my friends, I am so left that the left doesn't even want me. As a good leftist and socialist, I have discovered that *Family Guy*, that glob of the postmodern, is a vehicle of conservative politics. To prevent *Family Guy* from exerting its corrupting, conservative-making influence on our youth, I must kill the cartoon. It's the only ethical thing to do.

Family Guy is Real

It's not as difficult to kill a cartoon as you might think. Paint thinner is a choice weapon – but there are other ways as well. (The Fox network thought it knew how to kill *Family Guy*, but it was wrong as usual.) I prefer the direct approach: I will simply find the Griffin family, and squash them under my official Communism© Boots. I can do this, dear reader, because *Family Guy* is dangerously *real*.

I first knew there was a problem when I saw the season one premiere ("Death has a Shadow"). The show featured the following: G. I. Jew, who wielded a bagel, a joke about not standing up to a tank at Tiananmen Square, Peter irresponsibly letting dangerous toys pass his inspection, God being embarrassed by a sermon, Stewie trying to mind-control or kill Lois five times, Kool-Aid, *The Brady Bunch* (with Aunt Jemima), and, worst of all, *Joanie Loves Chachi* (the audacity!).

I was disgusted, and hence instantly taken in by the show. It was this, I later realized, that made the show so dangerous.

The next two episodes ("I Never Met the Dead Man" and "Chitty Chitty Death Bang") were no less insensitive: there were jokes about being racist (Dianne Simmons, the news co-anchor, remarks "Tom, I just plain don't like black people" when she thinks they aren't broadcasting), about World War II (the German sausage vendor, the spitting image of Hitler, takes over the polish sausage vendor, who is located beside him – and of course he doesn't stop there), and about the control that television exerts over our minds. Indeed, it is this that allows Stewie to attempt to destroy broccoli ("Their puerile minds are once again distracted by that flickering box. Time to be bad!"). And if all that weren't bad enough, there were references to Batman, Raisin Bran, *Star Trek*, *Scooby-Doo*, *Willy Wonka*, *Chips*, and (I think) *The Wonder Years*.

It was a television blitzkrieg. I was being assaulted by images of the past, meshed together with those serious events that have collectively composed our history – and *nothing was real*. Or, perhaps better put, nothing was more real than anything else. Scooby-Doo and Hitler, Tiananmen Square and Willy Wonka: it was all the same – it was all scenery for folly, a backdrop of the cultural imagination.

And it was here that I realized that *Family Guy* was real – or, again, as real as anything else. (And perhaps then, as I lay weeping on the floor, curled in a fetal position, I realized that they needed to be stopped. What is real can be murdered, dear reader.) It was as real as Disneyland – and that is as real as things get these days. As the French philosopher and social critic Jean Baudrillard (1929–2007) remarks, "Disneyland is presented as imaginary in order to make us believe that the rest is real, whereas all of Los Angeles and the America that surrounds it are no longer real." He might well have been talking about *Family Guy* and the families that loiter the developed West. Baudrillard continues, "it is no longer a question of a false representation of reality (ideology), but of concealing the fact that the real is no longer real."[2]

The real is no longer real. That about says it all. You see, Disneyland knows it is artificial. Everything is designed to produce certain experiences – the castles, the rides, the characters. We, on the other hand, do not know what's real. We think that the *real* is outside of us, but it's all just more scenery. The characters on *Family Guy* present us with an image of familial relations that is designed to seem absurd, and this leads us to think that *our* families are somehow more real than the cartoon images displayed before us – that our families are somehow *not* absurd caricatures – the mere filling out of generic cultural variables and preexisting social roles. But we are wrong about this. We occupy the same space as *Family Guy*, only we are not in Technicolor, and we are not as aware as *Family Guy* is of our situation. Our families are modeled after television images and cultural icons such as those spoofed on *Family Guy*. We are as indebted to Fred and Wilma Flintstone as the Griffins are. But there is one *big* difference between us and the *Family Guy* family: *at least the Griffins know that they are cartoons.*

Peter: Everybody, I got bad news. We've been cancelled.
Lois: Oh no. Peter, how could they do that?
Peter: Well unfortunately Lois, there's just no more room on the schedule. We've just got to accept the fact that Fox has to make room for terrific shows like *Dark Angel, Titus, Undeclared, Action, That 80's Show, Wonder Falls, Fast Lane, Andy Richter Controls the Universe, Skin, Girls' Club, Cracking Up, The Pits, Firefly, Get Real, Freaky Links, Wanda at Large, Costello, The Lone Gunman, A Minute with Stan Hooper, Normal Ohio, Pasadena, Harsh Realm, Keen Eddy, The Street, American Embassy, Cedric the Entertainer, The Tick, Louie,* and *Greg the Bunny.*

7

> *Lois:* Is there no hope?
> *Peter:* Well, I suppose if all those shows go down the tubes, we might have a shot.
> ("North by North Quahog")[3]

The Griffins also know the power that the corporations exert over their existence – something few of us care to acknowledge. After having what looks like a World Wide Wrestling Federation Death Match, the Griffins reflect on what they've been broadcasting.

> *Peter:* TV is dangerous. Why the hell doesn't the government step in and tell us what we can and can't watch – and shame on the network that puts this junk *[namely, Family Guy]* on the air.
> *Lois:* Uh, Peter . . . Peter maybe . . . maybe you shouldn't say anything bad about the network.
> *Peter:* Oh, why? What are they going to do? Cut our budget? *[Peter then moves to the other room, his entire body going from right to left, a clear indication that there wasn't enough money to finish the animation]*
> ("Lethal Weapons")

And so we watch, thinking that we know so much, that we are so much more than what is portrayed on the screens before us. It is in this way that we are subdued – and it is for this reason that the Griffins must die. You see, we are made to feel secure by the Griffins – strange as this sounds – because we are hoodwinked into thinking, with relief, "well, at least we're not like that – we must be ok."

Oh dear readers, I am not ok, and it isn't simply because I forgot to take my medication.

Family Guy is Serious

Modernism is the philosophical movement typically associated with the 17th and 18th century intellectual climate of Europe. The philosopher and mathematician René Descartes (1596–1650) is often cited as the father of modern philosophy. Rather than submitting to traditional views ordained by the church, Descartes insisted that we must use rationality to discern the true nature of reality – and in doing this, he contended, we would vastly improve the world. This ideal was perhaps best instantiated by the Prussian philosopher Immanuel

Kant (1724–1804). Kant claimed that the use of reason was enabling human beings to come into their own – to develop, morally and socially, into something far better than we have ever been before.

These stories of progress – of using Reason to grasp Truth and attain Freedom – are at the very center of modernism. This story of how society and human beings will improve their lot in the universe is what French philosopher Jean-François Lyotard (1924–98) calls a meta-narrative. It is a story that makes sense of every other story – a story that allows us to see the world as a fundamentally unified place with real significance. *Post*-modernism, on the other hand, concerns the death of such stories. It is infatuated with disunity. Whereas the modernist looked for the unity of things, the postmodernist looks for *difference* (or *différance*, if you're French). The postmodernist aims to show that the unity of the world is another piece of human conceit. The "postmodern," Lyotard coyly claims, is "incredulity toward meta-narratives."[4]

To say that *Family Guy* is incredulous is just to put lipstick on a pig. No need to church it up here. *Family Guy* is downright obnoxious about meta-narratives. In this way, the show *exemplifies* the postmodern.

If you talk to the people who live around you, there are certain things they will likely believe – and these beliefs will likely help to organize their days: they will likely believe that human beings should not have sex with animals, that one should be respectful of religions, that alcoholism should not be encouraged, that cartoon pornography should not be on prime-time network television, and that we shouldn't joke around about things like World War II, homosexuality, homelessness, sadomasochism, racism, anti-semitism, violence, sexual harassment, political oppression, and so on.

And of course, *Family Guy* does all of this: Brian frequently goes on dates with human females (bestiality). Stewie's sexuality is constantly in question, and there are frequent jokes about homosexuality ("Hey, excuse me, is your refrigerator running? Because if it is, it probably runs like you . . . *very* homosexually").[5] Peter is clearly an alcoholic. Peter and Lois engage in what appears to be lively bondage and S&M sex. In fact, they even have a safety word – it's *banana*, in case you ever need to know ("Let's Go to the Hop"), and the seeming disrespect shown to all religions reaches a fever pitch in *Family Guy*. I'll permit myself one of my favorite examples:

9

> *Peter:*   Yeah, I'm looking for toilet-training books.
> *Clerk:*   Yes. We can help you there. *Everybody Poops* is still the standard, of course. We've also got the less popular *Nobody Poops But You.*
> *Peter:*   Well, see, we're Catholic, so . . .
> *Clerk:*   Then you want *You're a Naughty Child And That's Concentrated Evil Coming Out the Back of You.*
> *Peter:*   Perfect!
> ("Brian in Love")

And perhaps politics gets it worst of all. When Peter founds his own country (Petoria, in "E. Peterbus Unum"), he is irritated at how he is treated by the United Nations. Upset, he seeks some advice from an Iraqi diplomat, who convinces him that invasion is the only way to go.

> *Diplomat:*   They *[the other UN representatives]* don't respect you.
> *Peter:*   What do you mean?
> *Diplomat:*   Listen to me. I used to be the laughing stock around here until one day my country invaded Kuwait. Now I have a seat in the third row! Look – the only way to get something you want around here is to find something and just take it.
> *Peter:*   Wait a second . . . if everyone around here respects you, how come you're still eating by yourself?
> *Diplomat:*   I don't shower.
> *Peter:*   Oh . . . that's what that is . . . *[pause]* Take what I want, huh?

Following the advice of the diplomat, Peter proclaims Joe's pool the newest province of Petoria ("Joehio"). But the mockery of world politics can't stop there – not without at least making light of a few of the world's most notorious abusers of human rights! The dictators of the world are invited to Peter's country (read: his backyard) so that Peter can show Lois they have some supporters.

> *Peter:*   Hey Slobodan, you made it!
> *Slobodan Milošević:*   I didn't know what to bring so I made coleslaw. *[He begins waving his arms]* It's made out of people!!! *[laughs]* Just kidding. Hey – is Momar here yet?

To show us that it ain't a party with only one dictator, we see Sadam Hussein and Momar Khadafi having a grand ole' time discussing how they enjoy *Seinfeld*, not to mention murdering their respective peoples:

> Sadam: . . . then Jerry guessed that her name was 'Mulva.' *[both laugh]*
> Momar: That show was funny. It really reminds me of my friends. You know, the way we just hang out . . . before I kill them for worshipping the wrong God.
> Sadam: And I love that Kramer guy. He comes in the room like this. *[tries to impersonate Kramer]* I can't do it but you know . . .
> *[We then see Stewie reprimanding Fidel Castro for running around the pool.]*

Incredulity at meta-narratives indeed! *Family Guy* undermines all meta-narratives – but it also undermines *everything else* as well. I will not defend any meta-narratives here. I will, however, suggest that joking about everything under the sun is a good way to get burned. After a few seasons of *Family Guy*, what do we have left to take seriously? We are thrown into a world where everything is equally real and fictitious, where everything – even the most serious stuff we can imagine – is potential for punchline. Nothing is sacred; everything is profane. And all I can do in response is laugh. Famine, poverty, oppression, big chickens, the Fonz, and diarrhea. This is just the state of the world. If Randy Newman is going to sing, so be it. There's nothing we can do anyway. The postmodern liberates us from our concerns – but this means that it also liberates us from our *causes*. In the absence of any real goals, we are left to become cynics – albeit cynics who get to see babies try to kill their moms, dogs who are alcoholics, neighbors who overcompensate for injury or who are sexually obsessed, and, of course, fathers who are blithering idiots.

This is a family that shouldn't get too close to the paint thinner, at least if good murderous Marxists like me are around.

Family Guy Must Die! Long Live *Family Guy*!

Perhaps Peter and his horde of miscreants don't need to die. Perhaps the po-mo don't need to be no-mo. Perhaps I just need to remember to take my medication.

Is it really so bad to make people cynical? To get them to sit on their butts and accept whatever the world throws at them, believing that nothing can be done about it?

11

Hell yes it's bad!

But perhaps postmodernism, much like *Family Guy*, has gotten a bad rap for little reason (pun intended). After all, the view that postmodernism leads to inaction doesn't quite map on to the action of some of the most notoriously postmodern theorists. The philosopher and historian Michel Foucault (1926–84), for example, participated in the students' revolts of 1968, advocated prison reform, and spoke out on other social issues to boot. Was he simply inconsistent, or is there something peculiar about postmodernism that allows action *and* cynicism? If such an avenue was open to Foucault, perhaps *Family Guy* can live after all. Meta-narratives and medication be damned. Let's see how the fancy-lad Foucault pulled it off, and maybe I won't need to kill any cartoons after all.

Foucault claimed, in good po-mo fashion, that the notions of Freedom, Truth, and Rationality were simply the products of another story about the world designed to provide us with comfort, but ultimately without any basis in the way the world is. Indeed, as he conceived it, the very notion of "knowledge" was the result of systems of description that were ultimately optional, and often oppressive. Knowledge claims served to situate people in relations of power rather than to emancipate them; what we claim is true, far from setting us free, actually often enslaves us.

What is interesting about this, though, is that it occasions a rethinking of many of our social institutions. When we say someone is "mentally ill," for example, we are not just making a claim that is true or false. We are *also* insisting that this person should be regarded (and treated) in a particular way. Once we've recognized this, though, we can assess the evaluative dimension of knowledge. Quagmire, for example, is a sexual deviant – a pervert. In making this claim, I am implying that Quagmire is in some sense *ill*. The guy's just not right – and he should be regarded (and treated) in a way that represents his condition (perhaps an attempted reconditioning must take place, as in "Blind Ambition").

But to be a pervert, or a deviant, really just means to do things that are normally not done. Brian too does things that are normally not done (he is obviously into bestiality, for example, as in "Brian the Bachelor" or "Perfect Castaway"). So too did Socrates, Jesus, Buddha, and Gandhi. (That's right, I'm calling Jesus a pervert.) The mere fact that someone acts uniquely does not mean they should be regarded as strange, or as grotesquely abnormal, or as "deviant," in the nasty sense of that word employed by many hoity-toity types. But the way we describe people nevertheless situates them in grids of power relations.

By calling into question our knowledge claims, and by getting us to see that our knowledge claims exert power over people's lives (who wants to be a deviant, anyway?), Foucault actually *provides* a response to "power/knowledge" (the two always go together, Foucault claims). He does this despite the fact that "a society without power relations can only be an abstraction."[6] Foucault *does not* offer us a meta-narrative. We will *always* be in some system of control. "Power is everywhere, not because it embraces everything, but because it comes from everywhere."[7] So Foucault is not trying to show the way to a complete liberation from all oppression (that's our friend "Freedom," replete with capital 'f'). There's no such thing. But that doesn't mean we should just sit around feeling sorry for ourselves, either. "To claim that one can never be 'outside' power does not mean that one is trapped and condemned to defeat no matter what."[8] It does mean that we have to pick our fights locally – and that there's no grand story about God or Calling or Country that will justify what we do. We just have to fight for causes that we embrace, whether it's an end to poverty, the resurrection of *Family Guy*, an end to the FCC, or an increase in tolerance.

Let's not give *Family Guy* too much credit here – at least not before we have to. Can it really pull off what fancy-lad Foucault managed? Foucault enables us to be both postmodern and active. One doesn't need a big meta-narrative to engage in a little critique. But does *Family Guy* engage in critique, or does it just poke fun? Perhaps there isn't a difference here that makes a difference (or a *différance*, if you're *still* French). After all, sometimes a little fun-poking of big and nasty meta-narratives is *exactly* what we need to avoid doing serious damage.[9] Maybe this is enough for even good leftist socialists like me to say "Bring on the incredulity! We need some of that!"

Peter:	As we all know, Christmas is that mystical time of year when the ghost of Jesus rises from the grave to feed on the flesh of the living. So we all sing Christmas carols to lull him back to sleep.
Bob:	Outrageous! How dare he say such blasphemy! I've gotta do something!

Bob's friend:	Bob, there's nothing you can do.
Bob:	*[Sighing]* Well, I guess I'll just have to develop a sense of humor.

("A *Family Guy* Freakin' Christmas")

Taking religion a little less seriously might well save some lives, even if it does create some cynics along the way. And I'm pretty sure that's a good trade. Or, again, in a country as divided as ours is, maybe we should stick our tongues out at the politicians with a little more gusto.

George W. Bush:	*[as a young man]* All right, let's do this. Let's kick some ass.
Soldier:	Uh, George, the war's over.
George W. Bush:	What?
Soldier:	Yeah, it's done.
George W. Bush:	Get out of here! Are you serious?
Soldier:	Yeah.
George W. Bush:	Aw, man, aw, man, I just got your messages and . . . I . . . I, aw, I'm sorry.
Soldier:	George, it's been over for a while.
George W. Bush:	Really?
Soldier:	Yeah, it's 1981.
George W. Bush:	It's, uh . . . oh, oh, wow. Oh, so I'm way late. Oh, boy.
Soldier:	Yeah.
George W. Bush:	Uh, well, you want to do something else?
Soldier:	I got some blow.
George W. Bush:	Son of a bitch, took you this long to tell me? Break it out, man!

("PTV")[10]

The idea that our leader can be trusted is just too much for a good communist like me to stomach. The idea that the US government has figured out *the* way to run a society also gives me stomach pain. Perhaps incredulity (or, I'll say it, being downright obnoxious about these ideas) is exactly what the doctor ordered. And damnit, maybe Foucault and *Family Guy* aren't that far apart after all.

So there you have it. Either I've convinced myself to rethink my craving for cartoon blood or I'm just a big commie pansy. *Family Guy* need not fall prey to my murderous wrath after all – not yet, anyway. The sort of cynicism the show breeds won't make us all con-servatives – at least not if we remember Foucault's lesson: we can be cynics about the big stories, so long as we still have a little fight in us when it really matters.

Or maybe I'm just kidding myself. Maybe I'm already one of the victims of *Family Guy*, too postmodern to take anything seriously.

Or maybe I've just developed a sense of humor.

NOTES

1   These are so serious that they must all be capitalized, and then their seriousness must again be acknowledged in a footnote.

2   Jean Baudrillard, *Simulacra and Simulation*, translated by Sheila Faria Glaser (Ann Arbor: University of Michigan Press, 1994), pp. 12–13.

3   And of course this is the opening dialogue in *Family Guy*'s second television premiere, after a spell in the television cemetery.

4   Jean-François Lyotard, *The Postmodern Condition: A Report on Knowledge*, translated by Geoff Bennington and Brian Massumi (Minneapolis: University of Minnesota Press, 1984), p. xxiv.

5   Peter makes this joke in "Lethal Weapons."

6   Michel Foucault, "The Subject and Power" in *Michel Foucault: Beyond Structuralism and Hermeneutics*, ed. Hubert L. Dreyfus and Paul Rabinow (Chicago: Chicago University Press, 1983), pp. 222–3.

7   Michel Foucault, *The History of Sexuality*, translated by Robert Hurley (New York: Vintage Books, 1990), p. 93.

8   Michel Foucault, "Power and Strategies" in *Power/Knowledge* (New York: Pantheon Books, 1980), p. 142.

9   As author Sam Harris reminds us, "Only 28 percent of Americans believe in evolution; 72 percent believe in angels. Ignorance in this degree, concentrated in both the head and the belly of a lumbering superpower, is now a problem for the entire world." *The End of Faith: Religion, Terror, and the Future of Reason* (New York: W. W. Noton, 2005), p. 230.

10 And to see Osama Bin Laden get some incredulity, make sure to watch the opening segment of the episode.

2

FAMILY GUY AND GOD:
Should Believers Take Offense?

RAYMOND J. VANARRAGON

While *Family Guy* has a significant fan base, you don't have to look far to find that not everyone likes the show. As exhibit A, consider the Parents Television Council (PTC). On their website (www.parentstv.org), they declare that *Family Guy* is an "unbelievably foul animated series," a show that "bases its humor on scatological and sexual references (including masturbation, incest, bestiality, necrophilia)," and in which "institutions such as the church and family are held up to ridicule on a near-weekly basis." Further, the PTC ranks *Family Guy* the second worst show for family viewing on prime time broadcast television (for the 2005–2006 season),[1] and regularly gives *Family Guy* episodes the "worst TV show of the week" designation. Viewers of the PTC website can read a description of the winning (or perhaps *losing*) episode and, if they so desire, watch a video clip from it. (Watching the clip is not recommended, however: the clip comes with the warning, "Graphic content!!! Do NOT push play if you don't want to see the explicit video!!!")

The Parents Television Council has a point. *Family Guy is* an offensive show, and it mines for laughs nearly every culturally sensitive topic imaginable. It would take a book to catalog all of the offenses. Rather than write a book, however, I intend in this short essay to focus on *Family Guy*'s treatment of religion. *Family Guy* regularly lampoons religious practitioners, doctrines, and objects in a way that goes beyond almost anything else found on broadcast television. And this raises a question for religious believers, especially those who, like me, are fans of the show. What should we do?

16

Should we take offense? Should we follow the advice of the Parents Television Council – an organization that appears to have religious backing – and turn off the television, or at least change the channel to more wholesome fare? To answer these questions, we'll begin by comparing *Family Guy*'s treatment of religion to the treatment of religion on *The Simpsons*. Then we'll consider some reasons that might be given in defense of *Family Guy*, or more particularly in defense of believers who persist in watching the show. Some of those reasons are legitimate, I think, even though the dangers of watching should not be overlooked.

Family Guy versus *The Simpsons*

Let's start with *The Simpsons*, where references to God and religion come fast and furious. I'll mention just a couple of examples that I think capture something about the show's way of dealing with the subject.

The first example involves what we can call "making light of an important Christian doctrine." In the episode, "Miracle on Evergreen Terrace," Bart accidentally destroys all of the Simpsons' Christmas presents, hides the evidence, and blames the disappearance on an unknown intruder. Residents of Springfield pitch in to help the family but feel used when they find out that Bart has been lying. "So, this was all a scam. And on *Christmas*," says Moe. "Yeah," says an indignant Barney, "Jesus must be spinning in his grave!"

Barney implies here that Jesus is still dead, a suggestion that runs directly counter to Christian belief in the Resurrection. For Christians, this belief is no minor matter, either: the Apostle Paul says that if Jesus has not risen, then our (Christian) faith is in vain. This makes what Barney says more than a little odd, since his regular attendance at the First Church of Springfield suggests that he's a Christian too. Indeed, I think Barney's comment is funny in large part for just that reason: it reflects his lovable and earnest ignorance. As we might put it, the joke is squarely on him. Believers can laugh at this right along with everyone else, guilt- and anxiety-free.

A second example involves the supreme being of the major theistic religions, God. In "Homer the Heretic," Homer stays home from church, falls asleep, and dreams of God coming down to speak

17

with him. During their conversation, God concedes that Reverend Lovejoy's sermons aren't that great ("That Reverend Lovejoy really displeases me. I think I'll give him a canker sore.") and helpfully encourages Homer to follow his own path. A couple of points about this scene are noteworthy: first, God is portrayed majestically, voiced with depth and power by Harry Shearer; and second, the writers distance themselves from the suggestion that this really *is* God by making the sequence part of a dream. (Homer, however, explains to Marge and Reverend Lovejoy that the dream must have been legitimate because he usually dreams about naked . . . Marge.)

Family Guy's treatment of religion is not quite so tactful. The show's very first episode, "Death has a Shadow," shows Peter attending church and taking communion. Upon drinking the wine, he exclaims, "Is that really the blood of Christ? That guy must have been wasted 24 hours a day!" (It's interesting that while this scene can be found on the first season DVD, it was cut for the first showing on network television. The scene also shows up in "Fifteen Minutes of Shame" from the second season DVD, and one expects that it wasn't cut twice.)

Peter's exclamation is nastier than anything about religion that I can recall seeing on *The Simpsons*, but it's not so easy to pinpoint why. He draws attention to the mysterious doctrine of transubstantiation, accepted by Catholics, which claims that the bread and wine actually become the body and blood of Christ during the sacrament of communion. (Many Protestants believe that the bread and wine merely *symbolize* the body and blood.) What Peter says can be taken as simply a ham-handed expression of a consequence of taking that doctrine at face value, given by an ignorant buffoon. (And a *drunk* buffoon – the scene is a flashback to a time when Peter got drunk during communion.) But while Barney is also a buffoon, he has a lovable and innocent side that Peter doesn't have, and hence Peter's inadvertent attacks on church doctrine have more of an edge to them. Peter's remark also paints Jesus himself in an unflattering way, as a drunkard. That's different from ignorantly implying that Jesus is still dead, since being dead doesn't seem to involve having any deep personal flaws or failings.

In any case, if there is any doubt about *Family Guy*'s lack of restraint when it comes to religion, consider a few examples of the show's treatment of God. In "Fifteen Minutes of Shame," Meg has

18

friends sleeping over, but things are going badly because her parents have been embarrassing her. "Oh God, kill me now!" she cries. The camera pans over to God, standing on a cloud, aiming a gun down at Meg. Suddenly a nearby phone rings. God puts down the gun and grabs the phone. "Hello? . . . Karen!" – where "Karen!" is said in the sort of voice that Seth MacFarlane or Brian the talking dog might use to try to pick up an attractive woman at a bar. (The writers chuckle on the DVD commentary track about God "getting a call from a hot chick.")

In another more recent episode, God actually *is* at a bar, trying to pick up an attractive woman. He lights her cigarette with a lightning bolt, and she's impressed. Unfortunately, the next lightning bolt gets away from him and incinerates her. "Jesus Christ!" God exclaims, apparently cursing. "What?" asks Jesus Christ, who has been standing nearby but out of the picture. "Get the Escalade," God replies. "We're out of here!"

Well, there is something funny about that, but you can see how some believers might be a wee bit offended by it. While *The Simpsons* had God sounding majestic, *Family Guy*'s God sounds like a decidedly non-majestic, ordinary male – not surprisingly, a lot like Seth MacFarlane (and Brian). In *The Simpsons*, the way God appears in Homer's dream serves as a bit of a buffer to suggest that it isn't really God. There is no buffer in *Family Guy*. And to top it all off, *Family Guy* depicts God as error-prone and lustful, a lot like Jim Carrey's Bruce from the movie *Bruce Almighty*, who, upon being granted the powers of the divine, caused disaster by pulling the moon a little closer to earth in order to spice up a romantic encounter with his girlfriend.

Other holy religious figures are similarly skewered in *Family Guy*. In "A Very Special *Family Guy* Freakin' Christmas," Mary, the mother of Jesus, announces, "I'm the Virgin Mary; that's my story and I'm sticking to it!" (Apparently that line was edited out in some network reruns.) In "Road to Europe," Stewie and Brian fly through the Vatican in a hot air balloon, accidentally snag the pope off of his balcony, and leave him dangling from a statue with his undergarments exposed for all to see. (Later the pope accosts them in the street and calls on God to smite them, but nothing happens.) Clearly, *Family Guy* has no qualms about making such objects of religious devotion look foolish.

Raymond J. VanArragon

The Ethics of Offense

Family Guy's treatments of religion are definitely offensive. But in what *way*? That's easy enough: they are offensive at least in the straightforward sense that they are inclined to offend people, by subjecting to ridicule practices that many people take very seriously and by mocking persons and deities whom many people believe ought to be treated only with the deepest reverence. Moreover, the *Family Guy* writers clearly *intend* to offend, or at least know that offense will result. Implying that Mary told the "virgin" story just to protect her reputation, leaving the pope dangling from a statue for all to see, suggesting that Jesus was a drunkard, showing God attempting (with mixed results) to pick up women – it's inevitable that some believers are going to be bothered. If Seth MacFarlane and his cohorts were to apologize – "We're really sorry; we didn't mean to upset anyone" – we'd all know they were lying.

But so what? What's wrong with offending people, anyway? That's an ethical question, and philosophers may be of some help in answering it. A great philosopher and ethicist who had something to say about this is Immanuel Kant (1724–1804). He talked about the moral requirement to treat people as "ends in themselves," and never merely as "means." What is it to treat people as ends and not as means? Put loosely, to do this is to take into consideration other people's goals and aspirations whenever you deal with them, and never use people solely to fulfill your own selfish ends and purposes. To use people solely as the butt of a joke or to offend their sensibilities for a laugh is to use them as means only, and that, Kant thinks, is always wrong. And if that's what the writers of *Family Guy* are doing, then by Kant's lights they should simply cease and desist.

Is *Family Guy*'s Offensiveness Justified?

So far, then, things don't look good for us believers who are fans of *Family Guy*. But maybe we don't need to give up (and change the channel) right away. Perhaps we can find some *justification* for the show's offensiveness. Offending people is *sometimes* acceptable, after all – it sometimes does not involve using them merely as means. It's

20

hard to be sure about Kant's view on all of this, but most of us think that we can justifiably offend people if what we do will prove sufficiently beneficial to them. A coach who goads a player into working harder partly by insulting him is one example. And we can all think of cases where a person said something that really bothered us, but after cooling off a little we saw their point and benefited from it. With that in mind, perhaps we can defend *Family Guy* by finding some way that its offensive jokes about religion actually benefit believers.

Our task doesn't look easy. How could it possibly benefit believers (or anyone else) to see God depicted as a lust-filled bar patron or Jesus portrayed as a practitioner of mediocre magic tricks? (In the movie *Stewie Griffin: The Untold Story*, old Stewie, who has been doing some time-traveling, tells young Stewie about his trip back to biblical times. There, he reports, he saw Jesus and discovered that "his abilities might have been exaggerated a bit." Immediately we get the flashback to Jesus standing in front of a few unimpressed spectators and using amateurish hand tricks to mimic removing his thumb and putting it back on.) For now, let's put aside our skepticism and try out a few possibilities.

Perhaps one way that this offensive material can benefit believers is by moving them to lighten up a bit, to learn to laugh at themselves. And surely there would be some good in that! The world would probably be a better place if people took themselves less seriously. Still, I doubt that *Family Guy* has this effect on many offended believers. The problem is that in order to push believers to take some of their religious doctrines and pursuits a little less seriously, the show would probably have to employ a measure of gentleness and tact, and demonstrate a certain degree of sympathy for its subject. And *Family Guy* doesn't do *any* of that. (This is the basic way in which *Family Guy*'s treatment of religion differs from *The Simpsons*'. Of course, many believers are offended by *The Simpsons* too; but I think it's easy – or should I say, *easier* – to make the case that they needn't be.)

To see another problem with this defense of *Family Guy*, consider an old adage based on the ethics of Aristotle (384–322 BCE): "Everything in moderation." Aristotle wanted to apply that principle to many things in life, including eating, experiencing pleasure, and feeling fear. A virtuous person, he said, does these things in moderation: she doesn't eat too much or too little, but just the right amount; she doesn't refrain entirely from pleasures or indulge herself excessively, but she finds the happy medium; and she isn't cowardly or fool-hardy but is instead courageous, which is in between those two extremes. Well, perhaps we should also engage in *laughter* in mod-eration, and the worry is that *Family Guy* encourages believers not to do this. Some people seem prone to the extreme of approaching religion only with deadly seriousness and finding no humor in it. *Family Guy* certainly doesn't do that. But by having God, the first Being of the Universe, the Creator of us all and the Source of all goodness, get his head slammed in an oven door by Albert Einstein,[2] *Family Guy* seems to be pushing us towards that other extreme. At least Gary Larson, author of the *Far Side* cartoons, had God pitch a shutout against the defending champion on *Jeopardy* to avoid implying that God was beaten to a question.[3] Is *Family Guy* encour-aging us to laugh at things that we shouldn't joke about? Is nothing sacred anymore?

So maybe *Family Guy* doesn't tend to make believers better people by getting them to lighten up. That justification of the show's offen-siveness regarding religion appears to be out. But could believers enjoy other benefits? Well, a closer look reveals that *Family Guy* in fact raises questions about religion that are worth considering. We already mentioned Peter's remark at communion – "Is that really the blood of Christ?" – that draws attention to the doctrine of transub-stantiation: how can the bread and wine literally *become* Jesus' body and blood? It's at least worth the time of believers who accept this doctrine to ponder what it might mean, and maybe an obnoxious comment from Peter is just the thing to get them to do it.

Another controversy *Family Guy* implicitly comments on has to do with the gender of God. Following much of the Christian tradition, *Family Guy* portrays God as male. But how can God, a non-physical being, have any gender at all? And if God is male, what could that maleness possibly imply? Perhaps *Family Guy* can be seen as explor-ing some of the implications of the maleness of God by joking about God being attracted to women. Or, a related point, by having God behave like the consummate male show-off, *Family Guy* could be poking fun at the way believers tend to think of God as being a lot like themselves, sharing their traits and values. In that way believers are warned of the dangers of creating God in their own image. These issues are raised in a jarring way, but perhaps the good of raising them justifies the offense.

A final point where *Family Guy* raises significant questions for believers occurs when Stewie professes (in the episode "Holy Crap") that he loves the Bible because he finds God to be "deliciously evil." A quick perusal of some Bible stories reveals why Stewie would say a thing like that. No doubt those episodes in the Old Testament where God commands the Israelites to slaughter large numbers of people would be appealing to a person who, like Stewie, is prone to murderous fantasies. Many believers honestly struggle with how those stories should be understood (and maybe those who don't struggle with it should). That seems to be another example where *Family Guy* could prompt believers to think a bit more about the God they worship or the books they accept as holy, even if doing so also causes offense.

Well, that's the best I've got. There is some good that may come from *Family Guy* dealing with God and religion in a way that offends believers. If the offense is ultimately justified, then believers who recognize this can continue to watch with a clear conscience. But really, does anyone think *Family Guy* is as high-minded as all that? And even if it were, how many believers are going to use the show as a source of some helpful food for thought, given that it is delivered in such a heavy-handed, unsympathetic way? The issues *Family Guy* raises really are important, but sadly I think we have to conclude that the benefits believers can get from having those issues raised does not excuse the offense that the writers dole out. Believers who watch the show will have to look elsewhere to defend themselves.

Why Do They Target Religion, Anyway?

Maybe we can try again by looking at these matters from the point of view of the writers. As we said, they're probably not benefiting believers when, for example, they have Peter start a religion whose object of worship is the Fonz and whose services and rituals mimic those of Christianity. (Just run a check of the internet to see how some believers have reacted to that one.) And no doubt they're not *trying* to benefit believers. I suspect that the writers' main motive is to make a funny show, and in my view they have proven quite good at that.

But why do they target religion and religious believers? Well, I think any believer can admit we're easy targets, and sometimes we even deserve it. It's probably a good lesson for believers, and anyone

23

else, to think about how someone who disagrees with them might view their beliefs. (It's much easier to think about how crazy everyone else's beliefs are.) As a matter of fact, many religious beliefs and practices can look pretty strange from the outside. The doctrine of transubstantiation is one odd-sounding doctrine, but there are many others. Another example is the idea of heaven – or at least Peter Griffin seems to think so. In "The Story from Page One," he recalls a time he got people to believe "crazy things," and we are treated to a flashback of him teaching a Sunday school class surrounded by young children. "And if you are pure of heart indeed," he says in a soothing voice, "You'll all go to a beautiful place called heaven." The children look joyful, until Peter ruins the moment: "Ha ha, I'm yanking you; you'll just rot in the ground!"

Other features of religion make it an easy target as well. The way that religious people fight among themselves, the utter conviction that some display on the most arcane topics, even in the face of disagreement and religious pluralism – these are often the subject of scorn among non-believers and great concern among believers themselves. (Not surprisingly, *Family Guy* also pokes fun at religious pluralism. In "Screwed the Pooch," after Lois's father finally accepts Peter as his son-in law, Peter is relieved. "Thank you, Jesus," he exclaims. We immediately get a view from above, where Jesus is standing beside a many-armed deity, apparently a god from some Eastern religion. "It wasn't me!" says Jesus. "Don't worry, I'm used to it," the Eastern deity replies.) Brian expresses a common view about religion when referring to Peter's new Church of the Fonz: "All Peter's done is find another way to exploit people's ignorance," he says. And even if you disagree with Brian's sentiments, you can understand where he's coming from.

So although I'm a believer myself, I can see why the writers for *Family Guy* might choose to lampoon religious practices and persons (God, for instance) that I consider sacred. And I'm not offended by the fact that they do so. It's a free country, after all. Moreover, they aren't forcing anyone to watch. Of course, even if believers aren't offended by the fact that *Family Guy* deals with religion so irreverently, they could still be bothered enough by what they see to politely refrain from watching the show. And yet many don't do this. Can believers in good conscience watch the scenes I've described so far and *not* be bothered by them?

The Absurdity of *Family Guy*

Perhaps I can best answer that question by saying why *I* am not bothered by them. The reason, I think, is that the characterizations of religion – the portrayals of God, Jesus, the pope, the Virgin Mary – are so absurd that I don't even associate the God to whom I pray with the character on the screen. When *Family Guy* has Jesus tell everyone at a party, "OK everybody, for my next miracle I'm going to turn water into funk" (whereupon a disco ball appears and Jesus, now adorned with big hair, busts a few dance moves), or when they show the trailer for *The Passion of the Christ II* (with the title, "Crucify This!" and the tagline, "Let he who is without sin kick the first ass," and a plot apparently involving Jesus teaming up with Chris Tucker to fight the bad guys), I don't think, "Oh no, that's my Lord they're mocking!"[4] Or when God rushes out of a bar to get to the Escalade . . . that's not anything like the Creator I worship in church on Sundays. And when I laugh, I'm certainly not laughing at God (or Jesus, or the pope, or whomever). Instead, I'm laughing at the crazy product of someone's imagination wherein God, who is in reality glorious and magnificent beyond description, is portrayed as inept and lust-filled. How absurd – an absurdity that tickles my funny bone and, apparently, the funny bones of many other people as well.

That is not to say that there are no religious risks one takes by indulging in this sort of humor. A legitimate concern is the possibility that this sort of irreverence might seep somehow into one's own religious life and that as a result one might lose touch with what really *is* sacred and holy. Watching Monty Python's movie *The Life of Brian* years ago had that sort of effect on me: for some time afterwards I had trouble reading the Beatitudes (from the sixth chapter of the New Testament book of Matthew) without hearing those befuddled people in the back of the crowd: "Blessed are the *cheese*-makers?!" For what it's worth, I have noted no such problems with *Family Guy*. The show has no connection at all to my religious life, so far as I can tell. But the concerns of believers about the effects of the show on young people – that it helps promote an unhealthy cynicism about religion, for instance – are not entirely groundless. Believers, like everyone else, have to be careful about what they and their children watch.

I expect that most believers who are fans of *Family Guy* watch for the same reason that I do: on the whole, the show is funny, clever, and unusual. Perhaps the religious content doesn't benefit believers; but then perhaps it doesn't harm them either. And maybe that's enough to justify our choice to watch, and not to take offense.[5]

NOTES

1   The worst show? *The War at Home*, another show broadcast on Fox on Sunday evenings.
2   This was part of a running gag in "The King is Dead" from season two, where Einstein, a fraud, assaults people and makes off with their discoveries and inventions. At the time of the unfortunate oven door incident, God had just succeeded in inventing the shrinky-dink.
3   Larson discusses this cartoon in the collection *Prehistory of the Far Side*.
4   There's an analogy here with absurd violence in popular entertainment. In the movie *The Naked Gun*, when the unlucky Nordberg (played by O. J. Simpson) gets shot multiple times, puts his hand on a hot stove element, and steps in a bear trap, no one thinks, "Oh no, that must really hurt!"
5   Thanks to William VanArragon, Janel VanArragon, and especially Jeremy Wisnewski for helpful comments on earlier drafts of this essay.

3

QUAGMIRE:
Virtue and Perversity

SHAUN MILLER

Quagmire is a pervert. He has a foot fetish, and when he's not fantasizing about Lois, he's fantasizing about sex with someone (or something) else. His goal in life is to have as much sex as he can with as many partners as possible. Most of the things he does and thinks about are downright crude. I admit it all freely. But I also think it's not that bad. If you're going to be a pervert, Quagmire's the way to go. And I'm going to try to demonstrate this with the help of another pervert, the philosopher Aristotle (384–322 BCE).

It's All Greek To Me

We'll start at the beginning, which I hear is a good place to start: life is a series of actions. When we engage in an intentional action, like watching an episode of *Family Guy*, we do so for a reason (that's just what we mean by *intentional* in philosophy). We turn on the television and settle in to watch Peter be an idiot, to see Stewie try to kill his mother, or to watch Brian deal with his demons. You may not think so, but in watching *Family Guy* we instantiate the very essence of human action. We engage in *teleological* activity. So what does that mean smarty pants? It means that actions are fundamentally oriented toward the attainment of certain goals.

The characters on *Family Guy* operate in the same way. Quagmire goes to kids' sporting events not to watch the players, but to drink beer, "check out the soccer moms," and maybe even score a goal of his own – giggity-giggity ("Mind over Murder"). As a pilot he earns money, which he uses to fix up his bachelor pad, throw some swingin' parties, and go to the Drunken Clam. Quagmire's action, like all intentional action, is explained with reference to particular goals: Quagmire goes to the Drunken Clam to hang out with Peter, Cleveland, and Joe.

If we step back, we can even ask why Quagmire wants to achieve the particular goal he is currently working toward. Quagmire is going to the Clam to hang out with some friends. But why would anyone want to do that? What is the *telos* (the goal) of this action? Like all other actions, even this one is oriented to some end. Quagmire wants to hang out with his friends because they're good company. And it doesn't stop here. Why does Quagmire want to spend time with good company? He wants good company because good company is pleasurable. Why aim for pleasurable things? Because it makes him happy. And why be happy? And here we reach the bedrock (yabba dabba doo) of all of our action. There is no real answer to this question. Happiness is basic: it is a goal in itself. As a basic goal of our action, then, it can be used to explain Quagmire's (or our) activity. Quagmire goes to the Drunken Clam, ultimately, because he wants to find happiness. The same thing is true with fixing up the bachelor pad and throwing swingin' parties – or anything else, for that matter.

The recognition of happiness as the basic *telos* (it still means goal) of human existence is one of Aristotle's most fundamental insights: the goal, the aim, the purpose of life is to be happy. Working, going to the doctor, watching an episode of *Family Guy*, these all aim at the same goal: what the Greeks called *eudaimonia,* and what we call, a bit more loosely, happiness.

Quagmire, it seems, is happy. His life is one long sexual adventure, albeit with the occasional mishap. Indeed, "Giggity-Giggity-Goo" could serve as the theme song of the happy life – if we understand *happiness* loosely enough. In modern usage, happiness is a feeling (and what feeling is it? It's the feeling Peter has when he watches "Kiss Saves Santa" in "A Very Special *Family Guy* Freakin' Christmas" – namely, a feeling of pleasure). As is obvious, though, happiness in this sense is merely subjective pleasure or contentment. We can't control it directly. It just happens, sometimes by luck, and sometimes by pharmacology. But even if we *are* happy in this sense, that doesn't mean we've attained all of our goals, or that we no longer seek what Aristotle (and other Greeks) called *eudaimonia.*

Eudaimonia – the fundamental goal of all human action – is not, as it turns out, a feeling at all (sorry Quagmire).

Eudaimonia does not happen by luck or chance, but by *choice*. It's not about *feeling* a certain way; it's about *being* a certain way. Eudaimonia involves doing the things that lead to well-being, flourishing, and success – not just giggity-giggity. And functioning well, in the Greek sense, is to attain *arête*. (What's with all the freakin' Greek? Is he trying to say that Quagmire goes giggity-giggity in the Greek sense? *Not that there's anything wrong with that.*) The term *arête* is usually translated as *virtue*, but it makes more sense if we translate it as *excellence*. When we speak of virtue, we typically think of something remote (like the 19th century), rather than something that we see all the time. We also tend to think of virtue as something that only applies to human beings. If someone started talking about a virtuous toaster, we would think they were speaking Greek.

And they would be. The Greek term *arête,* like the English word excellence, can apply to instruments, substances, animals, weapons, baskets, drawings, trees, texts, toilets, *yada yada yada.* If you were going into battle, you'd want a horse with "virtue," and you would have weapons that had "virtues." Likewise, when you sit down to watch TV, you want to see a virtuous show (sound Greek? After all, you want to see an *excellent* show). Virtues are everywhere. For a human being to attain *eudaimonia*, that human being must achieve *arête* (need a dictionary yet?).

Character and Habits

So, what allows us to function well – to achieve *arête*? Aristotle's answer is surprisingly straightforward: character. The key to becoming a virtuous person is to develop the right sort of character – the right sorts of tendencies and characteristics. To have the right tendencies is to act in the right ways, at the right times, to the various circumstances you find yourself in. And this is precisely what we mean when we speak of a person as having an excellent character (that person behaves just as one should behave in any given circumstance).

Of course, with this key to excellence, we've also found the key to all the blemishes of humanity. While our character can be constituted by excellent tendencies and characteristics, it can also fall afoul of excellence; it can be constituted by nastiness and bile (so to speak). If we develop the wrong habits, vices (the opposite of virtues), we will certainly become the wrong sorts of people, vicious (the opposite of virtuous).

Now, apply this analysis to Quagmire. It's probably no surprise that Quagmire's not a paragon of virtue. Though Quagmire is certainly aiming for pleasure and happiness, he is a far cry from aiming at *eudaimonia*. Having a constant giggity-goo lifestyle does not guarantee a happy life – but it *does* almost guarantee the formation of the kind of character that cares more about carnal giggities than attaining the good life (in Aristotle's sense). For Aristotle, *eudaimonia* requires developing the right kind of character – one that guarantees that one's actions will always manifest excellence. We develop this character by engaging in *correct* actions – by continuously acting *as though* we were already the person we we're trying to become. Aristotle states: "we learn by doing, and people become, say, housebuilders by building houses or harpists, by playing the harp. So, too, we become just by doing things that are just, temperate by doing things that are temperate, and courageous by doing things that are courageous" (1103b).[1] So while we're learning these skills, we may fumble at first, but over time we gain success. Once a habit is ingrained in our character, it is second nature to us – it *is* us. Our character defines not only what we do, but who we are. Indeed, who we are presents itself in what we do. To attain *eudaimonia*, then, is to attain a certain kind of character – namely, one that is virtuous. We don't get our character automatically. It comes through the development of habits acquired in training and practice. The habits we develop can be either good or bad. The good habits perfect our nature, while the bad ones (obviously) don't.

It is our job as rational beings to learn to tell the difference between these two kinds of habits – a task that is anything but easy. To help us determine, in particular cases, what actions to perform (and thus what habits to support), Aristotle points to the Golden Mean. (Quagmire couldn't tell you what the Golden Mean is, though he probably could tell you what a golden shower is.) Although the Golden Mean is not named after Goldie Locks, the goal is much the same. Both Aristotle and Goldie Locks like things "just right," not too much, not too little. Our actions and emotional reactions can be extreme in either of two directions. They can be excessive or deficient, morally speaking. The goal is to get our actions and reactions to the world just right.

Perhaps surprisingly, "The Cleveland-Loretta Quagmire" presents us with paradigm cases of *both* kinds of moral failure, excess and deficiency. When Quagmire has an affair with Cleveland's wife, Loretta, Cleveland doesn't get angry. In fact, he apologizes *to* Loretta.

Cleveland:	Loretta, is it true what they're saying? Were you really having carnal relations with another gentleman?
Loretta:	I'm a woman Cleveland! I need some passion in my life. I need a real man. And Lord knows that ain't you.
Cleveland:	Well I admit that after a long day at work, I don't always come home with that "Riunite on ice . . . that's nice" mentality. And for that I apologize.
Loretta:	Apologize?! I cheat on you and you apologize to me? Cleveland Brown, you are pathetic.
Cleveland:	I disagree but I respect your candor.
Loretta:	Goodbye Cleveland.

Loretta then kicks Cleveland out of the house. His last gesture is to say "I love you" right before she slams the door in his face. And we can understand Loretta's anger. She's angry because Cleveland, in almost inhuman fashion – *isn't* angry. And there are some things you *should* get angry about. If your life-partner betrays you with a friend – if you are a victim of deceit – you *ought* to be bothered.

Even Peter recognizes this, and Peter is a complete idiot. Brian and he pretend to be Loretta and Quagmire, and begin rolling around on the floor, simulating the throes of passion. When Cleveland reacts to this, we see another extreme of emotion: Cleveland becomes almost homicidal. Once again, as Cleveland stands over Quagmire preparing to throttle him, there's something off about Cleveland's action. Yes, he has a right to be angry – and he *ought* to be angry – just not *that* angry.

Cleveland's failure was a moral failure. He failed to respond in the right way to the world around him, and he did so in two divergent ways. First, Cleveland wasn't angry enough (he had a deficiency of anger, we might say). Next, he was way too angry (he had an excess of anger). What Cleveland failed to do, on the Aristotelian view, is react with exactly the right amount of anger. To be an excellent human being, perhaps surprisingly, will sometimes require you to

31

be outraged – but only when outrage is appropriate. When we achieve the right level of emotional response, we have acted according to the mean.

But how do we know where the mean lies? This is where our intelligence comes in (sorry, Peter). We must use intelligent judgment to find the appropriate way to respond to different situations – to find the mean. Quagmire may need a little courage (sometimes liquid courage) to talk to the ladies, but he needed a lot of courage to apologize to Cleveland for sleeping with Loretta. In fact, Quagmire agrees to a boxing match. Now that takes courage! It's true that fear is part of human life, but some handle fear in a good way. Others cower before mice, and still others charge mindlessly into an avalanche of flatulence. Those who have the virtue of handling fear are courageous (they have the virtue of courage), while those who do not are (like most of us) imperfect human beings – too cowardly or too rash. The courageous person assesses the situation and takes proper action. He or she hits the perfect mark, the Golden Mean, between rashness and cowardliness, demonstrating what might be called "moral intelligence."

These same considerations apply to other virtues that Aristotle examines: generosity, self-confidence, honesty, wit, modesty, and justice. In each case, one must decide what is appropriate – and what is appropriate will depend on the situation at hand. The virtues don't apply in a cut-and-dry way to everything and every situation. In fact, they couldn't: the mean itself is different for *each person*, not only for each situation. As Aristotle says, "by a mean that belongs to the thing, I am speaking of what holds a position equally apart from either of the extremes, which is one and the same thing for everyone, but the mean in relation to us is what neither goes too far nor falls short, and *this is not one thing nor the same thing for everyone*" (1106a 30–33, my emphasis). We must judge in particular situations, and every situation is particular. There are different amounts of courage when Joe fights a criminal, when Quagmire spies on women, and when Peter is fighting a giant chicken. To have practical judgment is to recognize what each situation requires.

So, there's been a lot of talk of virtue, and a little talk of perversion. Given how much I enjoy perversion, we've really got to get clear on what might be wrong with it. Even though Quagmire is obviously not virtuous (because he doesn't aim for *eudaimonia*, but merely for pleasure), is he really vicious? What exactly is wrong with wanting to score with chicks?

Let's consider the virtue of temperance. Many people indulge in food, imbibe drink, and engage in sexual relations. Some handle these pleasures in a good way. Others, like Flanders (from that other Fox show) and a few Buddhist monks, are insensitive to pleasure. Still others, like Peter and Homer, overindulge. Temperance involves handling these pleasures in the right way: one doesn't drink so much that one becomes incapable of anything else (as Peter frequently does), one doesn't eat until one cannot handle another possible bite (as Peter has been known to do), and one doesn't obsess about sex to such an extent that one's life would be meaningless without it (while Peter is fond of bondage games, he's got enough beer and food to live without sex).

Those who have the virtue of handling their pleasures properly have the virtue of temperance. Quagmire isn't a drunk or a glutton, but he is totally at the mercy of his sex drive. He understands everything in terms of the pleasures of sex. Consider these examples, pulled from the cesspool that is Quagmire's libido:

> *Quagmire:* I felt guilty once, until she woke up!
> ("One if by Clam, Two if by Sea")

> *Quagmire:* *[finding a cheerleader tied up in the bathroom]* Dear Diary,
>   Jackpot.
> ("Peter Griffin: Husband, Father . . . Brother?")

I'm not suggesting for a second that one should be a prude. Sexual pleasure is good, but being able to think about nothing else is not good. This is precisely Quagmire's problem – and what is wrong with his perversion (as reluctant as I am to admit that there's anything wrong with perversion). As Aristotle puts it, "the dissipated person desires all things that are pleasant, or those that are most pleasant, and is led so much by desire as to choose these things in preference to all others; and this is why a dissipated person is pained both by missing out on pleasures and by desiring them, since desire involves pain, though it seems absurd to be pained on account of pleasure" (1119a 1–5).

Except for the fact that it would be a ridiculous anachronism, I'd say Aristotle must have been thinking of Quagmire when he wrote this. Quagmire is pained by the absence of sexual pleasure. The person who has mastered temperance, on the other hand, feels no distress when he or she is not in the throes of pleasure. Again, Aristotle sets us straight about the difference between the virtuous person and Quagmire: "the temperate person is so called for not being pained at the absence of or abstention from what is pleasant" (1118b 32–33). Quagmire is a slave to his desires, and this is his fundamental problem. (Or one of them, anyway.)

Learning from Quagmire

Despite all this, Quagmire isn't a bad guy. Of course, like most of the rest of us, he's also no virtuoso of the virtues. Quagmire, rather, is somewhere in between – trying to react in the right way to things around him, and trying to keep himself out of trouble. And in the realm of *Family Guy*, this is hardly unique to Quagmire. Virtually every other character manifests the same tendencies. Stewie just wants to kill Lois, Peter just wants to watch TV and drink beer, and Lois just wants to be a good mother. Like Quagmire (and the rest of us), they often miss the mark. This doesn't make them (or us) awful people. It makes us human.

Quagmire may not be virtuous, but he does have some redeeming qualities. He cares about people close to him. In "I Take Thee Quagmire," when he marries Joan, he realizes he made the mistake of getting married and wants to get out. Joan, however, says she will cut herself if he leaves her. If Quagmire were truly vicious, he wouldn't care. He would go back to his promiscuous ways, leaving Joan by herself. Instead, he stays. He doesn't want to see Joan get hurt. (Of course, when Death comes to take Quagmire, and Joan volunteers to take Quagmire's place, Quagmire doesn't mourn for a minute. That would waste time to get giggity-giggity going.)

Not convinced yet? How about this: in "Love Thy Trophy," Stewie is sent to a foster family and everyone in the neighborhood comes up with a plan to get him back. Quagmire's part is to distract the social worker by sleeping with her. Still seems too selfish? How about this: although sleeping with Loretta is a vicious act since it betrays his friendship with Cleveland, Quagmire *was hesitant* to sleep with Loretta. And let me follow that up with this: Quagmire is incredibly *honest* about his love for life (and for giggity-giggity). Quagmire *admits* his passions. In this sense, at any rate, we all wish to *be* Quagmire. We wish that we could be so bold (thus the courage), and so free to explore our desires for pleasure without the constraints of those social norms that stop us at every turn. Quagmire is *beyond* social norms: he loves what he loves, and he does not attempt to hide these from anyone (even when he should!). He's being the most virtuous pervert he can be, and that's what makes him admirable.

Ok. Even I'm not convinced.

Maybe Quagmire doesn't have any redeeming qualities. There are moments where he is just plain perverted. He sticks a jacket sleeve down his pants and asks Lois to put her jacket on ("Stuck Together, Torn Apart"). He lets Lois borrow his car after searching for many near-pornographic seconds through his robe for his keys ("When You Wish Upon a Weinstein"). He's known for giving dates roofies ("Stuck Together, Torn Apart"). He drugs the bachelorette, but he stops short, knowing that the cameras are on him (he still manages to steal her flip-flop) ("Brian the Bachelor"). He's even willing to have a three-way with his mom ("Brian the Bachelor").

Oh to hell with it. What does Aristotle know anyway? I'm gonna stick with the pervert. How much could an ancient Greek philosopher who invented logic really know about this stuff? Long live perversion![2]

NOTES

1 This is taken from Aristotle's *Nicomachean Ethics*, translated by Joe Sachs (Newburyport, MA: Focus Publishing, 2002). All other citations occur in the text.

2 I would like to thank many people for helping me by reading my drafts and looking over any corrections needed. Any faults are my own. I'd like to thank Doug Miller, Jessica Daniel, Christie Chelaru, Jamie Price, and Jeff Moore. Special thanks goes to Nicole Miller and Julie Lebo for helping me finding good Quagmire examples and how it fits with this essay. Another special thank you goes to Steve Campbell for helping me clarify Aristotle's ethics. I want to especially thank J. Jeremy Wisnewski for helping me with drafts and revisions of this essay.

4

FRANCIS GRIFFIN AND THE CHURCH OF THE HOLY FONZ:
Religious Exclusivism and "Real" Religion

DAVID KYLE JOHNSON

In the opening to every show, Peter and Lois complain about violence in movies and sex on television. The Griffins, though, suggest we are all lucky that there's a "family guy" like Peter – someone who is a defender of the "good old-fashioned values on which we used to rely." Apparently, or at least according to the theme song, Peter is a champion of *family values*. But anyone who watches the show knows better! Not only does Peter love media sex and violence (recall Peter's love for *The A-Team*, his addiction to the "pornographic marriage counselor," and his campaign against TV censorship in the episode "PTV"), but his devotion to family values is completely lacking. He tells sexist jokes at work (for example, in the episode "I am Peter, Hear Me Roar," Peter suggests that "women have breasts . . . [s]o you have something to look at while you're talking to them"); he's a drunkard (recall Peter drinking his *real father* Michael Seamus "Mickey" McFinnigan – who is the town drunk in the Irish village of McSwiggin – under the table at Wifey McBeaty's Tavern in "Peter's Two Dads"); he is not religious at all (in "Holy Crap," he suggests that there is a book of the Bible where Jesus swallows a puzzle piece and a man in a big yellow hat takes him to the hospital); and he's a sexist/bigot (again, in "I am Peter, Hear Me Roar," he suggests that women aren't people but objects made for men's amusement by Jesus Christ). Peter is nowhere close to being the "family guy" suggested by the show's title.

36

Peter's legal father, Francis Griffin – grandson of Willie "Black Eye" Griffin and nephew of Adolph Hitler (see "Untitled Griffin Family History") – is a different matter. Francis is a staunch Catholic and a defender of family values. Unlike Peter, Francis may indeed be a "family guy."

Yet, because he makes *unjustified judgments*, no one likes Francis (except perhaps Peter, who is devoted to him because he is his son). In the episode "The Father, The Son, and The Holy Fonz," Francis condemns Peter and his new religion – The Church of the Holy Fonz – as "unreal" and an "abomination." In "Holy Crap," the first episode in which Francis appears, he expresses his religious beliefs – without argument – to everyone in earshot. Francis forces his standards of moral behavior on anyone he can, and he verbally condemns and demeans anyone who disagrees with, or acts contrary to, his standards. (For example, in acts of "kindness," Francis suggests that Lois – a Protestant – "won't burn in hell after all . . . [but will] . . . just go to purgatory with all the unbaptized babies" and calls Meg a harlot and tells her that God will give her leprosy for holding hands with a boy.) Francis believes that Catholicism is the only true faith (he is a *religious exclusivist*), and he is therefore entitled to "evangelize" others in this brutal manner.

In this chapter we'll argue that Francis's exclusivist claims and evangelism are unjustified and immoral. Evangelism, the process of spreading one's religious beliefs to others, isn't *always* immoral – but when it takes the form that Francis defends, it doesn't get much worse. One of the reasons that Francis-style evangelism is so nasty is that it excludes other (perhaps real) religions (like the Church of the Holy Fonz) without any real reasons. As we'll see, distinguishing the *real* religions from the *unreal* ones is much more difficult than the old codger lets on.

Holy Crap

Francis is despicable in his *Family Guy* debut, calling Lois a Protestant whore (a label he had posted on Peter's car on Peter and Lois's wedding day) and calling all of his co-workers sinners. Beyond that, Francis declares flash photography in church earns you a ticket to hell and beats up a Fox cameraman who wears a hat in church. Foretelling

37

the end of a *Dike Van Dike* episode, Francis prophesies that "Laura burns the roast and *God kills her for parading her bum around in those pants!*" Finally, assuming that Chris – because he is a teenage boy – masturbates every time he is in the bathroom for more than two minutes, Francis makes Chris go days without a bowel movement.

> Chris: *[exits the bathroom]* Sorry grandpa, you might want to give that a minute or two.
>
> Francis: I know what you were doing in there, and it's a sin! If you ever do it again, you'll burn in hell!
>
> Chris: But I do it everyday; sometimes twice.
>
> Francis: Mark my words lad: you may think you're alone in there, but God's watching. *[Francis exits]*
>
> Chris: God's watching me do number two? Oh man, I'm a sinner and God's a pervert.

Francis's behavior is fueled by the view that his religious beliefs and moral convictions are true, and that anyone who believes differently or has different convictions is mistaken. But this isn't so strange. As the philosopher Alvin Plantinga points out, to hold a belief or conviction is to believe that it is true; and to believe something is true is to believe that its opposite is false; and to believe that its opposite is false is to believe that those who believe its opposite are mistaken.[1] For example, if I believe "Brian can talk" then I must believe that "Brian can't talk" is false and consequently must believe that anyone who believes he can't talk is mistaken. Thus, part of believing something is believing that those who disagree are wrong. But no one can be morally blamed for this, can they? If they can, then no one is morally permitted to believe anything! Thus, we can't morally blame Francis for simply believing something is true and believing that those who disagree are wrong – unless we're willing to blame ourselves for the same thing (and *I'm* not willing to do *that*).

So what is morally wrong with what Francis does? I will simply say it (though, unlike Francis, I will offer arguments for my view below): Francis lacks adequate justification for his religious beliefs but, nevertheless, tries to *shove them down* everyone's throat. His religious condemnation and conversion techniques – what Francis might call his methods of evangelism – are immoral.

In response to this, Francis might insist that he does have sufficient justification for his beliefs. He would probably cite as sources of justification the Bible, the tradition of the Catholic church, and perhaps even personal religious experiences. But the problem is that these sources don't provide adequate justification. There are millions of religious people, all with many religious beliefs contrary to Francis's Catholic beliefs, and all these people have scriptures, traditions, and religious experiences of their own. Additionally, thousands of years of unresolved conflict have shown that there is no definitive way to prove who is right. This is a problem – and not just for Francis.[2]

The problem here is an inductive one. Inductive arguments are based in observation and prediction. For example, suppose that Quagmire told me that he didn't try to seduce my daughter, but then I find out that he told four other fathers the same thing and then openly admitted that he only told one of us the truth. Am I justified in believing that Quagmire didn't try to seduce my daughter? No! Since Quagmire lied 80 percent of the time, he is not a reliable source of the truth. The probability that trusting him will lead to a false belief is high, and thus a belief based on his testimony is not justified. None of the fathers – even the one whose daughter he didn't try to seduce – is justified in believing what Quagmire says in this case.

Similar reasoning applies to religious beliefs. Take the five major world religions: Judaism, Christianity, Islam, Hinduism, and Buddhism. These religions have distinct and mutually exclusive doctrines.[3] That is, no two of these religions could be true at the same time. Still, we have no way of proving which one (if any) is true.[4] Each religion bases its beliefs on Scripture, Historical Tradition, and religious Experience ("SHiTE" for short).[5] But, since only one of these religions can be true, we know that at least 80 percent of the time SHiTE leads to false beliefs.[6] So the inductive evidence suggests that *our* own SHiTE did not lead us to true beliefs – our religious beliefs are not justified. Just like Quagmire, SHiTE is not a reliable source of truth. The probability that trusting SHiTE will lead to a false belief is high, and so a belief based on it is not justified. No one – even a person who happens to belong to the one true religion (as perhaps Francis does) – has justified religious beliefs.[7]

Some philosophers, like William Clifford (1845–79), have argued that holding any belief without sufficient evidence is immoral. Clifford's argument runs as follows. Suppose you own a ship on which people are about to take a voyage. You could check the ship to ensure that it is seaworthy, but instead you simply choose to believe, without evidence, that it is seaworthy and send it on its way. It seems clear that you have acted immorally. If a belief-based action could harm someone if the belief were false, then you better have good evidence that the belief is true.[8] Clifford suggests that all beliefs influence actions, and thus all beliefs could lead to actions that harm others. Consequently, if we believe anything without evidence, we are doing something immoral. Thus, Clifford suggests, it is a moral imperative to refrain from believing something unless we have sufficient evidence. So Francis Griffin is behaving in an immoral fashion by simply holding his religious beliefs without sufficient evidence.

William James (1842–1910) would disagree, arguing that sometimes refraining from belief is impossible. If there isn't sufficient evidence either way, belief without evidence is inevitable. James argues that, in such a situation, you have the moral right to choose which way you believe, even though you will believe without evidence. James suggests that most religious beliefs are like this. For instance, refraining from believing anything about the existence of God (being an agnostic) is the same thing as believing that God does not exist (being an atheist). Since it turns out that neither "side" has sufficient evidence, one has the right to hold (or reject) belief in God even without evidence.[9] James would suggest that Francis is morally permitted to hold his religious beliefs, even though they are unjustified.

Clifford and James both make good points.[10] But I believe the answer to our question – what is morally wrong with what Francis does – lies in the middle ground. One has the right to hold religious beliefs, even without evidence, under the circumstances described by James. But, as Clifford suggests, it is immoral to risk harm to others with actions based on beliefs that lack sufficient evidence. Consequently, one has the right to hold one's religious beliefs, even though one might lack evidence for them, but one does not have the right to harm, or even risk harm, to others with actions based on those beliefs. If this is right, it is clear why Francis's actions are morally wrong. Even though it is morally acceptable for him to hold his religious beliefs, it is not morally acceptable for him to harm others because of those beliefs. And – whether it be the physical harm of hitting cameramen, the internal harm of keeping Chris from pooping, or the emotional harm of making Meg afraid to hold hands with boys and condemning Lois to purgatory – Francis's actions cause harm. They are thus immoral, given that they are rooted in an insufficiently justified religious belief.

But I think Francis's moral wrongdoing goes even deeper. Francis – in a kind of backhanded way – is also trying to convince others of the truth of his religious beliefs. But again, this is a moral mistake. Although one has the right to choose to believe something without evidence, one does not have the right to try to "correct" others who oppose that belief. Yes, if one has sufficient evidence for a belief, one would be morally justified in trying to convince others of the truth of that belief. We would not have a moral objection if Brian tried to convince Lois that Stewie is trying to kill her, since he would have well-documented, convincing evidence. But without sufficient evidence, such efforts are intrusive and immoral.[11]

This conclusion does not require us to give up our religious beliefs. As James suggests, we still have the right to accept certain religious beliefs even without sufficient evidence. We must, however, also recognize that our religious beliefs are poorly justified.[12] Consequently, we must recognize that we do not have the right to try to forcefully convince, convert, or condemn those who do not share our beliefs. In most cases, we'll need to just keep our SHiTE to ourselves. If someone comes to us, seeking religious advice or debate, that is a different matter; if someone is open to your SHiTE, share it. But unwanted or forceful evangelism – especially if you are trying to *switch* a person from their religion to yours[13] – is immoral.[14] What is moral is (a) disagreement with other religions – you can still hold your religious beliefs and think that others are wrong – but also (b) an attitude of religious acceptance where we tolerate and respect the religious beliefs of others.[15]

The Holy Fonz

The senior Griffin's intolerable intolerant behavior continues in his second *Family Guy* appearance. In "The Father, The Son, and The Holy Fonz," Francis makes Lois sit at the kids' table because she is a Protestant, and he demands that Stewie be baptized – because the baby will burn in hell otherwise. Francis even admits to embracing a "believe what I say or I will hurt you" approach to Christian evangelism. Perhaps most painful of all though is Francis's condemnation of Peter's new religion: The Church of the Holy Fonz.

41

As Peter struggles to find a religion, Francis suggests that he look in his heart and turn to the person that has "always been there for him, offering wisdom and truth." After searching his heart, Peter starts a church that worships Arthur Fonzorelli – the Fonz – from *Happy Days*. Francis, after attending a service, calls it an abomination and declares that it is not a "real religion." By this, Francis is not merely suggesting that the doctrines of *Fonzieism* are false. Francis is making the more serious charge that – unlike other religions that Francis merely disagrees with – Fonzieism is not a religion at all.

Most people would agree with Francis's assessment: Fonzieism is not a *real* religion. But even though Francis's assessment is probably correct, once again, it doesn't look like it is justified. In fact, the problem may go even deeper. It may be that *nothing* can justify such an assessment.

Francis suggests that Fonzieism is not a real religion because its worship service only consists of people "singing songs and listening to a bunch of tall tales." Brian, however, brings up a good point when he argues that this doesn't seem to be a good reason for thinking Fonzieism isn't a real religion. Singing in worship services is common and the scriptures of most religions do contain quite a few tales that are "tall."[16] Brian is in fact suggesting that this aspect of Fonzieism makes it more like a real religion, not less.

In reply, Francis might suggest, despite what Brian thinks, the stories and doctrines of the Bible are true. So it really is because the tales and doctrines of Fonzieism are fiction that Fonzieism is not a *real* religion. But, even if we ignore the problem of establishing that the stories and doctrines of the Bible are true, this is still a bad argument. If Francis thinks that true tales and doctrines are what makes a religion *real*, since Francis doesn't think that any other religion is true, Francis would have to think every other religion is *unreal*. But, like most people, he does not think this.

It doesn't look like *having true tales* is a good criterion for distinguishing *real* from *unreal* religions. So let's give it another try. One might argue:

> "It is the fact that we know the tales of *Happy Days* to be fiction that makes it a non-real religion. Even though we can't prove the truth of the tales of other religions – Christianity, Buddhism, Judaism, etc. – we also don't know that they are false. And it is the possibility that their tales are true that makes these religions real."

However, even if we ignore the fact that scientific evidence calls into question the legitimacy of many stories from many religions, this is still a bad argument. Many people from many religions do not take all the stories of their scriptures literally. Many Christians consider many biblical stories allegorical or exaggerations. They suggest these stories have "true lessons" but admit that they could not have actually happened – they are "truthful fictions." (Some followers of other religions employ similar reasoning.)[17] But, even though Francis might disagree with such people, I doubt he would be willing to dismiss them as *non-religious*. Even though non-literalists claim that the tales of their religion are *truthful fictions* – just like Peter would admit that the tales of *Happy Days* are *truthful fictions* – they are still religious people. So it doesn't look like "a religion must have tales that could be true" is a good criterion for distinguishing between *real* and *unreal* religions either.

One might suggest that Fonzieism is not a real religion simply because Peter just made it up. But Peter didn't just make it up.[18] Rather, he founded the Church of the Holy Fonz because he had a religious experience; he looked into his heart and concluded that founding Fonzieism was the right thing to do.[19] In fact, the way in which Fonzieism was founded is similar to the way Joseph Smith founded Mormonism. Both Peter and Joseph were trying to figure out which religion they should belong to and both had a religious experience that motivated them to start their own religion. Even though you may not be a Mormon, unless you are willing to dismiss Mormonism as an *unreal* religion, you cannot dismiss Fonzieism as an *unreal* religion simply on the basis of the way it was founded.

Lastly, one might suggest that Fonzieism is not a real religion because it doesn't worship a deity or deities. But, ignoring the inevitable argument that Peter would submit on behalf of Fonzy's divine status, the fact that Buddhists don't worship a deity or deities quickly eliminates this as a legitimate response.

So what are we left with? Perhaps only our intuition. There doesn't seem to be a criterion by which we can establish that Fonzieism is not a real religion. But some would argue that we can still justifiably label it as such. How? Consider the classic philosophical pile/heap problem. Take a pile of sand, say 10,000 grains. Such a small pile is not a heap. Now, slowly add one grain at a time. Eventually you will have a collection of sand as big as a sand dune; and clearly that collection is a heap of sand. Question: At what point did the pile of sand become a heap of sand? Was it after 1,000,000 grains? 100,000,000? No one knows. And in fact, it seems to be no one knows because there is no objective criterion for delineating piles from heaps. A conclusion that one might draw is this:

> "There is no objective criterion that delineates piles from heaps, but this does not mean that we can't label certain things piles and certain things heaps. Some things are clearly heaps and some things aren't. It just means that there will be some cases where it is unclear whether something is a heap, and in those cases there may be no fact of the matter about whether there is a heap or not."

A person, like Francis, who wants to call Fonzieism an *unreal* religion might embrace this conclusion and likewise suggest:

> "The fact that I cannot identify what makes Fonzieism an unreal religion does not mean it is a real religion. There may in fact be no objective criteria which delineates real from unreal religions – which does mean there will be some "borderline cases" where there is no fact of the matter about whether a certain thing is a religion – but there are still clear cases of things that are not real religions, and Fonzieism is one of them."

But there are a couple of things that we might say in reply. First, we might simply deny the intuition, admitting there are clear cases of things that are not religions, but Fonzieism is not one of them. Clear cases of non-religions are things like social clubs, fans clubs, and gaming clans. It is not intuitively clear that Fonzieism is not a real religion; it is intuitively clear that it is a "borderline case."

Second, one might suggest the above conclusion is the wrong conclusion to draw from the pile/heap example. The fact that there is no objective delineating criterion does not mean that there are borderline cases; it means that there are no objective facts about whether things are piles or heaps. "That is a heap" is a way in which a human might describe a piece of the world, but it does not represent an independent property that piece of the world has. If we say something is "clearly a heap," it is probably true that most people would describe it as a heap. But if someone does not, they are not making a mistake,[20] but merely describing the world differently. The mistake is thinking that there is an objective criterion that makes a collection of sand a heap or not. In the same way, one might suggest, there aren't any facts about whether things are religions or not; there are only ways people describe the world. And if someone deviates from the norm – perhaps by calling Fonzieism a *real* religion – they are not wrong but merely different. It's not a mistake to describe Fonzieism as a *real* religion, nor is it a mistake to describe it as an *unreal* religion. The mistake is thinking that there is an objective criterion that makes something a religion or not.

I must be clear: the conclusion here is *not* that Fonzieism is a *real* religion. The conclusion is actually twofold: (a) If Fonzieism is an *unreal* religion, identifying what makes it so may be impossible; (b) it may be impossible because there is no objective criterion by which one can establish something is a religion. Thus there may be no justified way to establish that Fonzieism is not a *real* religion, and so one who claims it is a real religion may be justified in doing so.

The Holy Mission

There is a practical lesson to take from this chapter. When it comes to religion, we need not be concerned about converting others to our religion, whether other religions are *right*, or whether other religions are *real*. What we need to be concerned with is our own attitude toward religion and the religious acceptance of others. It is wonderful to hold and be devoted to your religious beliefs, and it is even all right to think that those who disagree are wrong. But, in the absence of definitive proof, we must tolerate and respect the beliefs of others and their right to hold those beliefs, even if we would describe their religion as "unreal." But regardless – and whether Fonzieism is *real* or not – perhaps we are best off following Fonzie's example of bravery and acceptance. *Please rise . . . and now sit on it . . .* for a reading from the Letters of Potsie to the Tuscadaros:

> Yeah, and did Fonzy downstairs cometh from his apartment from above the garage, and sayeth he "Reassemblith will I the pieces of my motorcycle, though I suffereth from temporary blindness. And yeah, for I am holy, befriendith will I, Sticks Downy, the only Negro in the state of Wisconsin." Amen.

The Fonz be with you.

NOTES

1 See Plantinga's "A Defense of Religious Exclusivism"; chapter 7 in James Sennett, ed., *The Analytic Theist: An Alvin Plantinga Reader* (Grand Rapids, MI: Eerdmans, 1998).

2 Philosophers so far have not really addressed the problem. They agree that the fact that there are devout members of other religions and no way of definitively proving one religion true and others false seems to threaten the justification of one's religious beliefs, but they do not suggest why or how this fact does so. For a good example of this, see Plantinga (1998).

3 There is some overlap, mostly regarding ethical claims, but this is irrelevant. I am concerned mainly with doctrinal claims here.

4 Of course, it could be that they are all wrong. But for argument's sake I will be generous and assume that one gets it right.

5 I use the acronym "SHiTE" (pronounced *shīt*) only because I have been forced to. I do not wish to insinuate that scripture, religious tradition, or religious experience are *shit*; I merely wish to argue that they are not sufficient as a basis for a belief's justification. I pleaded to use more respectful, alternate acronyms but, in the end, because "SHiTE" was the editor's suggestion – and the editor is a totalitarian dictator – "SHiTE" is now stuck to the proverbial heel of this chapter.

6 This actual number here would depend on which religion is true, and how many people subscribe to that religion. But regardless of which religion is true, a large majority of the time, SHiTE would lead to false beliefs – and that is enough to justify the conclusion that SHiTE is likely to lead to false beliefs and thus that SHiTE can't sufficiently justify beliefs.

7 Take into account that each religion has many differing sects, and at best only one sect in one religion has it right, and the problem multiplies by leaps and bounds. If each religion has four sects, but only one religion's sect has it right, SHiTE would only lead to true belief 5 percent of the time.

8 It would have been acceptable to risk the lives of the passengers on the stability of the ship if there was sufficient evidence that the ship was stable.

9 James is not suggesting that believing without evidence is always acceptable; certainly if there is sufficient evidence against a belief, one is not justified in holding it.

10 To view the original work of Clifford and James, along with some commentary, see A. J. Burger, ed., *The Ethics of Belief* (Roseville, CA: Dry Bones Press, 2001).

11   Some might think that Francis is not trying to convince others to hold his beliefs; he is not interested in conversion, he is just interested in condemning those who do not share those beliefs. But, if trying to *convince others* of an insufficiently justified belief is immoral, it should also be clear that condemning those who do not share that belief is especially immoral. So, whether his actions are rooted in a motivation to convince or to condemn, it should now be clear why Francis's actions are immoral.

12   This holds for atheists as well.

13   Since you have no evidence that your SHiTE leads to truth and theirs doesn't, you have no right to try to talk them out of their beliefs and into yours.

14   Christian evangelicals, I am sure, will be especially disturbed by this conclusion. But I think that it is important to note that many religions – even certain sects of Christianity – don't put an emphasis on converting others to their beliefs. Many find spiritual/intellectual enlightenment and outreach to others to be the rightful focus of religious devotion.

15   In this section, I am arguing against the moral permissibility of deliberate and intentional unwanted belief coercion. But I think there is a notable exception. Given that the reason that such coercion is immoral is because it risks harm to others, if avoiding such a coercion would risk greater harm to others, belief coercion would be morally justified and even perhaps morally obligatory. If someone does (or plans to do) physical harm to others because of their religious beliefs, I believe it is morally permissible to try to change their religious beliefs; they have the right to believe what they wish, they do not have the right to harm others. (Given this exception, one might argue, not making attempts to convert people can condemn them to hell and thus – since this would harm them – coercion would be justified. But since belief in hell is a religious belief – one that lacks sufficient justification like all the rest – the belief that the person will be harmed is unjustified as well, and thus the coercion is still not morally permissible.)

16   According to Brian, the tales of the Bible – such as the creation story, Noah's Ark, and Daniel and the Lion's Den – are just as fictional and even more unbelievable than the tales of *Happy Days*.

17   Take for example the tale of Buddha's four signs. The tale suggests that, while in his twenties, Buddha sees for the first time four signs in succession: an old man, an ill person, a funeral procession, and finally a sage (who is free from anxiety of age, illness, and death). This prompts Buddha to undertake the quest for enlightenment. Most Buddhists do not take this story literally; they do not suppose that he wasn't exposed to age, illness, or death until his twenties and don't suppose

that he was exposed to them all in immediate succession. They treat it instead as a story that illustrates Buddha's motivation and goal for reaching enlightenment.

18 It is true that some people do make up religions. I believe on the internet you can find many religions made up by people for the purpose of selling ordinations to other people who want to be an ordained minister (often so that they can make a few bucks marrying people). It seems that if a religion is "made up" in this way – where the founders of the religion don't even believe in the religion's doctrines – the religion is not real and is not so for that reason.

19 This is not the first time that Peter has had a religious experience involving the Fonz. In the episode "The Son Also Draws," the Fonz appears to Peter as his "Spiritual Guide" in an Indian "Vision Quest." This adds even more credibility to the claim that Peter is not simply "making it up." Repeatability with such consistency in religious experience is rare.

20 They don't believe something contrary to the way the world is.

PART II
LUCKY THERE'S A FAMILY GUY! (AND WHAT A FAMILY!)

5

LET US NOW PRAISE CLUELESS MEN:
Peter Griffin and Philosophy

JERRY SAMET

Philosophy is Not Funny

Philosophy is not funny. Philosophers are, by and large, serious. The themes they discuss are serious, they discuss them seriously, and they expect their discussions to be treated seriously. There are, of course, exceptions to this generalization,[1] but even when philosophers are jokey, there is an underlying seriousness of purpose.

Still, philosophers do seriously ask what makes things funny (the nature of the funny, the essence of funniness, what the Funny Itself is, etc.), the varieties of funniness, the place of the funny in the overall scheme of things, the ethics of the funny, and so on. These are not only serious but very difficult philosophical issues. We are still a long way from having a satisfactory account of what makes things funny, for example, and even further from a recipe for creating funny things. But that's about to change. So read on.

Giotto (Not Funny Either)

The art historian Bernard Berenson (1865–1959) tells us that the greatness of the 14th-century Florentine painter Giotto lies in the fact that Giotto's paintings are in some way "more real" than the things they depict.[2] This explains why we enjoy them so much. The paintings allow us to see the world more clearly, with less distraction. We have a sense of exaltation that we are having a "deeper" or more direct encounter with reality, and we love the painting that makes all this possible. At the risk of oversimplifying: the increased pleasure in looking at the picture makes us feel better about ourselves, and this positive feeling of enhanced self-worth is now associated with the painting which caused it. It follows that we can enjoy and value the painting of the object more than the object itself. Berenson's analysis, as we will see, applies equally well to Peter Griffin.

The Peteresque (Funny)

To see the connection, I want to now turn from Art to Music, specifically to a song Peter Griffin, the family guy of *Family Guy*, sings in an episode entitled "When You Wish Upon a Weinstein."[3] At the start of the episode, Peter has been scammed out of his wife Lois's savings. He finds out that Jewish lawyers and accountants have made his friends rich, and he longs to "get a Greenstein or a Rosenblatt of my very own" to essentially manage the intellectual and financial life of his family. Peter does get a Weinstein of his own for a while, but when he loses him, he decides to improve Chris's school performance by having him convert to Judaism. Peter thus takes Chris to Las Vegas to get him a while-u-wait style Bar Mitzvah. Lois foils this plan and the episode resolves in a "you're fine as you are" scene. This longing for "a Jew of his own" is expressed in a wistful meditation, sung to the tune of "When You Wish Upon a Star":

> Nothing else has worked so far
> So I'll wish upon a star
> Wondrous dancing speck of light
> I need – a – Jew
> Lois makes me take the rap
> 'Cause our checkbook looks like crap
> Since I can't give her a slap
> I need – a – Jew
> Where to find
> a Baum or Steen or Stein
> To teach me how to whine
> And do my taxes
> Though by many they're abhorred
> Hebrew people I've adored
> Even though they killed my Lord
> I need – a – Jew
> ("When You Wish Upon a Weinstein")

There are things that we all know – things that we sense without having to be told, things that we know not to say, things we (think we) would never even think. The "we" does not include Peter Griffin. As the song makes clear, Peter doesn't seem to know that one cannot simply "get a Jew" in the way one gets a lawyer. He enthusiastically embraces the stereotype of Jews as smart and especially good with money, and urges his family to embrace it as well. He is furthermore not embarrassed about his misogynistic desire to slap his wife Lois for faulting him about the checkbook, and he seems to be under the illusion that slapping her, if only it were possible, would solve the checkbook problem, and obviate the need for a Jew. Finally, he cheerfully embraces the anti-Semitic image of the Jew as Christ-killer, but has no problem overlooking this fault because of the positive side of the ledger.

Anyone who has not seen *Family Guy* cannot begin to understand what an idiot Peter is. Part of the genius of the show's writers is that they are able to constantly outdo themselves in creating new layers and forms of stupidity for Peter to embrace.[4] I've chosen to focus on this song not because it is especially representative; it isn't. Peter's idiocy is vividly on display in every episode, and almost defies summary. But this moment brings together a number of strands in a neat little soliloquy. From this multi-dimensional array of idiocy, I want to focus on one particular aspect of Peter's cluelessness. Peter hasn't a clue about all sorts of things, and this is part of what makes him funny. The philosophical issue we face is why cluelessness in real life is not reliably funny, but works to such advantage in *Family Guy*.

The Essence of the Peteresque: Cluelessness and Philosophy

Peter is clueless – he is a genius at not grasping the bigger picture. He rarely grasps the smaller picture either, but we all lack knowledge of certain things. Peter is most different from us in that he so rarely and so reluctantly seriously *reflects* on his life – or on life, period. His moments of reflection (e.g., "Why am I such a financial failure?") typically do not involve measured deliberation. There is no weighing of evidence, and no stepping back and imagining the world from

53

other perspectives, or from the perspective of those around him. When Peter does step back from the particularities of his experience and achieves some general insight ("I'm not good with money"), the insight has no effect on his life or self-understanding. Rather, the insight is merely an instigation to some ridiculously idiotic course of action ("Find a Jew"). We (or most of us, anyway) are not like this. We develop action plans based on our understanding of our needs and individual natures. This understanding, this higher-order awareness of ourselves, is critical in making us who we are and tying together our experiences into a life. It is hard to see this in Peter. When he reflects, what results is simply action aiming at desire-satisfaction. Reflection never *elevates* Peter beyond his idiocy, it merely redirects that idiocy.

Peter's cluelessness, the virtual absence of serious reflection in his life, connects us to one of the oldest themes in Western philosophy: the Socratic claim that the unexamined life is not worth living. Given that philosophy is, for better or worse, all reflection, Peter is the anti-philosopher, a paradigm case of the life not worth living. The irony in the Socratic claim is that one who reflects, who examines life, and tries to decide what makes life worth living, can hardly come to any other conclusion but that the *un*examined life is not worth living. To judge that a life has value seems to require a perspective on it, and that perspective is obviously only available to someone who steps back from the stream of immediate experience and reflects. The unexamined life cannot be properly evaluated without examining it, and to enter into such an evaluation is to lose the quality you want to examine.

Looked at in this way, *Family Guy* provides a valuable philosophical service. It depicts a life with little or no reflection. Of course, we live that life most of the time, and we ought to. Whatever commitment we have to Socratic examination, we understand that reflection has its place and time. For most of our lives, we need to learn *not* to reflect, to be "in the moment."[5] And Peter certainly knows how to do *that*.

Art can freeze life and extract it from its normal stream, so that we can examine it, and paradoxically, grasp our own experience in a deeper way. Giotto was able to give his contemporaries a glimpse of life that they experienced as "realer than real." We have *Family Guy*. As strange as it sounds, Peter Griffin gives us a glimpse of life and experience that we would not otherwise have. But what life is that? Does it somehow give us a special window on what it's like to be an idiot? Why would we want such a window? And why would it be funny to have such a special insight?

Peter has something to tell us about an element or layer of our own cognition and affect – a kind of core animal responsiveness. You don't want to hear this (none of us do) – but you too are like Peter. You are (at least in part) a stimulus-response machine dealing moment-by-moment with an impinging environment. Of course, unlike Peter, you can modulate and inhibit all sorts of responses and associations that get played out in Peter's actions (at least, I hope you can!). Peter feels the need for a Jew, enlists the first Jew who knocks at his door to satisfy that need, and proceeds to tackle the Jew when he tries to escape.

We are typically not conscious, or only dimly conscious, of the Peteresque elements of our cognitive lives, but we do see them played out overtly in children. Any parent who's had to leave a clinging toddler at day care will be familiar with elements of this last tackle-the-Jew scenario. I am not suggesting that Peter is simply our "inner toddler." There are layers of stupidity and idiocy in Peter's behavior that we would be stunned to find even in a toddler, and much of what is funny about the character goes beyond his childlike cluelessness. Still, unlike normal adults, Peter is overly responsive to the here and now, to his immediate emotions and needs, to current stimuli, to free associations, and so on. He cannot step back and modulate his behavior in terms of overarching goals or principles.

Why is Cluelessness Funny? A Suggestion

Reflecting on the anti-Socratic life is not in itself funny. The existentialist Jean-Paul Sartre (1905–80) seemed to find such awareness nauseating and depressing. Why then is Peter's cluelessness funny? Here's a shot at an answer: we can sometimes get a kick out of animals – especially our pets – just by observing them going through their unexamined lives. This is especially true if we can imaginatively "trade places" with them. Consider two recent examples that make this more vivid:

- *The Onion* (online comedy newspaper) ran a picture of a little kitten with the headline: "Kitten Thinks Of Nothing But Murder All Day."[6]
- A short video of a kitten stuffing itself into a small glass bowl.[7]

The first is funny because, cute as they are, kittens might well be thinking of murder – of mice, of flies, of aluminum balls, and so on. Their unreflective, instinctual preoccupations with prey do not in any way compromise their innocence. The second works because of the sheer pointlessness of the kitten's attempt to stuff itself into the bowl. We wonder what it hopes to accomplish with this silliness, but of course realize that it is not out to accomplish anything at all. It is simply responding to the bowl in a way that is more elemental, and we simply find it funny to watch the unselfconscious effort and persistence.

Cluelessness can be *cute*, and *endearing*. But why is that? Part of why Peter appeals to us is that he helps us see more of *what we are*, and at the same time, *what we happily are not*. Our attention is directed to the automatic and unreflective aspects of our make-up, but we are also enlarged in our realization that we are *not* Peter. The philosopher Thomas Hobbes (1588–1679) calls laughter *sudden glory* "caused either by some sudden act of their own that pleases them or by the apprehension of some deformed thing in another."[8] Hobbes goes on to excoriate those who laugh at the deformities of others. Normal adults typically do not find the deformities of others funny. Even if we factor in the pleasure of novelty and the satisfaction that we are not similarly deformed, such deformities in others evoke our sympathy and sadness (and no doubt set in motion other trains of thought and feeling). In the end, the positives are weighed down.

But comedy can depict deformity – in this case Peter's cluelessness – in novel and realistic ways without the attendant normal concerns that arise when we experience real cluelessness. The virtually infinite range of Peter's cluelessness allows us to glory in how much "bigger" we are than Peter, and think: "there but for reflection go I."

Why Philosophy Is Not Funny

The connection to the Socratic ideal also casts some light on our starting point: the seriousness of philosophy. The Socratic ambition, which remains very much alive, is to develop a complete, comprehensive picture of life and the world.[9] Philosophers traditionally sought to provide the biggest picture in which every aspect of life finds its proper place and is properly understood. In the contemporary philosopher Thomas Nagel's apt phrase, philosophy is (part of) the search for "the view from nowhere." Philosophy's *seriousness* is directly related to the scope of this ambition. The philosophical seeker must always be ready to ascend to higher levels of reflection and abstraction, and inevitably, to leave behind the particularities of the world and our experience of it.

But what's funny, what makes us laugh, is much more often than not the sheer particularity of experience or something that brings that to the fore. And if Hobbes is right, it is *our* response to the particularity. There's nothing funny *per se* in the novel ways that Peter is so severely limited. It is only funny to me because I can look down at Peter and marvel at the difference. The pleasure is essentially connected to *my* conception of *myself* as somehow enlarged. For those in the grip of philosophy's totalizing ambition – those with the desire to provide an account of every aspect of everything in the world; those who want to say what the world really *is* – the personal level, which is where humor lives, falls away. For the rest of us, almost all the time, the pleasure of life is in the living, not in the abstract examining. It is not accidental that the lightness or jokiness we find in philosophers (like Nietzsche and recent French philosopher Jacques Derrida (1930–2004)) goes hand-in-hand with the loss of confidence in the majestic totalizing conception of philosophy that dominates much of the Western tradition.

Philosophy can be *about* humor because it is about everything. In this respect, philosophy and humor share an important feature. In the same way that humor can provide the material for a philosophical discourse, philosophy – and everything else for that matter – can itself be the subject matter for humor. One can, if one is clever enough, make fun of anything. So both can take anything as their subject matter. In a philosophy book about *Family Guy*, philosophy has the upper hand and makes humor into philosophy. But if you have a sense of humor, you can't help but imagine gag-writers turning the tables ("Philosophers unable to understand *Family Guy*"). Each can try to get in the last word. The fight between Peter and the Philosopher – between the light and the serious – is one that can teach us quite a bit about ourselves. But perhaps the most important lesson to be learned is this: even at our most serious, there is something laughable about what we do, and even at our most comical, there is something profound to be discovered.[10]

NOTES

1   Friedrich Nietzsche (1844–1900) is one, and some of the Pre-Socratic philosophers (philosophers living and writing largely in the 7th and 6th centuries BCE) were probably joking some of the time. A number of contemporary French philosophers have been, much to the annoyance of their analytic English-speaking counterparts, less-than-fully-serious, even annoyingly playful and light-hearted.

2   *Italian Painters of the Renaissance* (New York: Meridian Books, 1957), p. 74. Subsequent citations will occur parenthetically.

3   This episode was originally censored by the network and therefore not aired as part of the initial run of the series, but it has since been shown and is available on the DVD compilation of Season 2.

4   And as they point out in one of the audio commentaries, still make it possible for Peter to pick on his still-more-idiotic son Chris.

5   The failure to "be in the moment" – the over-examined life – is the essence of Larry David, the main character of *Curb Your Enthusiasm*.

6   www.theonion.com/content/node/51603.

7   www.youtube.com/watch?v=kOOVCpW8jP0.

8   Thomas Hobbes, *Leviathan* (Indianapolis: Bobbs-Merrill, 1958), Part I, ch. 6.

9   Socrates might have settled for less – viz., an understanding of how one ought to live. But the tradition he fathered immediately developed and inspired the grander goals.

10 I profited from many useful discussions of these issues with Ted Munter, Daniel Ackerman, Debbie Zaitchik, and Ezra and Hannah Samet.

6

LOIS:
Portrait of a Mother
(Or, Nevermind Death,
Motherhood is a Bitch)

STEPHANIE EMPEY

Narrator: In the television comedy world, the people are entertained by two separate yet equally important types of shows: traditional sitcoms that get laughs out of everyday situations, like trying to fix your own plumbing or inviting two dates to the same dance, and animated shows that make jokes about farting. This is the latter.
("Fast Times at Buddy Cianci Jr. High")

Family Guy tells us that there are two types of shows: sitcoms and animated shows that rely on farts to get laughs. The writers claim the show fits in the second category, and they supply many fart jokes to convince us (I counted four in this episode).[1] But who do they think they are dealing with? We are *philosophers*. We're sharp tacks. Ok, maybe we are not the sharpest tacks – after all, we kicked, screamed, and clawed our way into graduate school where we racked up tens of thousands of dollars in debt to pursue a career in a field that is typically less lucrative than chimney sweeping. But all that aside, we are *sharp*; and we are not convinced that *Family Guy* is just potty humor (at any rate, *I* am not convinced). *Family Guy* is funny – but its humor is not only in the fun it makes of flatulence, but also in its references to the everyday. And for the very same reason, it is instructive.

I remember very clearly when I first learned that there were philosophers writing about mothering. I thought, "Really? You can do philosophy on *that*?" Apparently, you can "do" philosophy on just about anything (you *did* read the title of this book, didn't you?).

59

Now, this stuff on mothering is seriously important and I would hate to see it lose credibility by being associated with *Family Guy* – but I'm a risk-taker by nature. And so, this is an essay on mothering. In particular, it is an essay about one mother, Lois.

Lois, the Griffin family matron, is an oft-neglected character. She's perhaps only half-visible to the average viewer.[2] We tend to overlook her except as the would-be murder victim of her youngest child, or the object of the family dog's lustful fantasies. But we shouldn't be so quick to look past this gentle woman. She's got a lot to teach us about the plight of the American mom.

Mothering as a Discipline

Philosophers – you should just know this up front – philosophers love definitions. I learned this very early on in my education. You may believe you know what mothers do, but you don't *really* know until you've had a philosopher tell you. And I'm just the philosopher to set you straight about motherhood. Mothering, you see, is a *discipline*. It is a systematic (and potentially transformative) answer to the demands reality makes on us.

And boy does reality make demands. We must eat, sleep, dodge cars, work, help others, meet deadlines, bathe, and behave in fairly predictable ways. Much of what we do is a response to the demands of the real world (the world around you, not the TV show). Disciplines like science, religion, psychology, philosophy, mathematics, and mothering all emerge as a means of dealing with this world around us and the demands it makes on us.

Mothering is like math? Yes, damn it. Mothering is like math. It mirrors the practices of science, mathematics, and religion in that it is a disciplined response to the demands presented by reality (in this case, the reality of a child). The demands of the child are almost endless: from keeping your child alive (and growing!) to enabling her to become a member of society.[3] Just about any (good) parent knows that having a child changes everything – and especially the number (and types) of demands made on us.

Mothering is the particular stance one adopts towards the child (even if he's Stewie). It's a disciplined response to meet that child's demands for preservation, growth, and acceptability (even if he's a matricidal psychopath). It both requires and gives rise to thought, and it can culminate in the development of skills and character traits not necessarily developed elsewhere. Consequently, mothering is a discipline, and for those who engage in it thoughtfully and deliberately, it can transform them (to the same extent that actively participating in science, math, or philosophy can change the way you think, and what you value). As a discipline, mothering has its own method (attention, care, even manipulation); and it has its own standards of truth. (Truth concerns *this* child, as no two children will be the same. And that goes double for Stewie.) It is an intellectual practice as much as any other.

Cultivating Virtues

When we engage in disciplines, we can do so well or poorly. (For evidence of this, consult my secondary school math scores.) In engaging in the discipline of motherhood, a mother can develop virtues of character that are indispensable to her both in her home and in the world at large. Three virtues that stand out are prudence, tolerance, and peacefulness. A mother can cultivate these virtues and others, provided she mothers thoughtfully and intentionally. She must recognize opportunities to develop and practice these virtues, and she must take the opportunities. Lois does so with wit and ease.

Prudence is the exercise of care, caution, and good judgment, especially in the care and management of resources and with a regard for the future of those resources. Given the goals of mothers to preserve the lives of their children (yes, even Stewie), and given the uncertainty of the future availability of resources necessary for meeting these goals, mothers are uniquely positioned to cultivate prudence. Lois's prudence is illustrated best when Peter purchases volcano insurance with the Rainy Day Fund, a jar of money Lois has meticulously stockpiled for family emergencies (in this case, to replace the glasses Stewie breaks when he finds Meg watching him sleep: "Why you sick, sick little moo cow. Well, you shall watch no more" *[Stewie slaps Meg]*):

Lois: Peter, did you take the money from the family jar?
Peter: Who, me? Yes, me. Couldn't be. Then, who? Yeah, I did it. I bought us volcano insurance.

Lois: Volcano insurance? That's ridiculous!
Peter: Oh, that's the same thing you said when you talked me out of getting that cloud insurance. Look at them up there, just plotting,
picking their moment.
("When You Wish Upon a Weinstein")

As Lois demonstrates by her use of the family jar, mothers may
have a unique understanding of the importance of creating and safe-
guarding reserves. Mothers use resources creatively, develop ways to
make resources stretch, or find alternatives. Meanwhile, we're facing
global warming, the widespread disappearance of natural resources,
polluted air and waterways, the destruction of natural habitats, and
increasing pressure on fossil fuels. It doesn't take much of a stretch to
see how a mother's prudence might have benefits that extend beyond
her household.

Tolerance implies restraint. When we are tolerant, we restrain ourselves from interfering with another's freedom to hold views that dif-
fer from our own, or to engage in behaviors we would not ourselves
endorse. When we are tolerant, we refrain from using force to bend
another to our will.[4] A mother is responsible for preserving the life
of her child and ensuring he grows and matures into a flourishing
adult. Of course, children put themselves in danger nearly every day
(does Chris really need to tickle his brain with the bayonet of a toy
soldier?!? Could we have guessed that Meg would join a cult?!?). It
would be great if children always helped us meet their demands. But
they don't. (In the case of Stewie, they actually try to kill us!) Growth
itself requires testing boundaries (both in the physical environment
and in relationships), and this puts children in constant danger (think
of the danger Stewie faces when he enters Peter's testicles to kill his
new brother before he can be conceived in "Emission Impossible"; or,
the danger to Chris when he runs away and the Peace Corps drops
him from a plane into a village of indigenous people in "Jungle Love"
. . .). Children break things, get dirty, push our buttons, and break
rules (as when Stewie breaks a lamp over Lois's head to get her off the
couch in "There's Something About Paulie": "Wakey, wakey worthless domestic; time to make me an edible gruel"). They challenge us,
disappoint us, irritate us, and exhaust us (as Brian discovers in "North
by North Quahog," "I swear to God, these kids are going to make me
put a bullet through my head"). It is tempting for us to use our power,
even violently, to force their compliance. But this is not an option for

a mother, whose commitment to preservation and growth makes violence, which stunts and injures, antithetical to her higher goals.[5]

Tolerance is thus an essential virtue – and good mothers like Lois have it in spades. Mothers use non-violent methods every day to entice others to comply: persuasive rhetoric, guilt and shame, incentives, rewards, and so on. A mother faces conflict involving her children (in her personal relationships with her children, between her children, and between her and others' children). If she is motivated to foster the growth of her own children, and if she is interested in maintaining healthy relationships with those around her, she must formulate ways to mediate conflicts that protect individuals and their ties.

In addition, mothers must rely on outsiders (doctors, social workers, school officials). Because her children are often at their mercy, she cannot afford to alienate them. As most parents know, the interests of an outsider will sometimes conflict with a mother's (and her children's). Mothers must find solutions to conflicts in this arena that will preserve these valued relationships and shelter her children from retribution. Peacefulness is thus essential to successful mothering.[6]

Lois demonstrates tolerance and peacefulness in just about every episode. She accepts abuse from nearly every member of her family, though most notably from her husband and youngest son. In two striking examples, however, she is pushed over the edge and erupts in violence. In both instances, she is brought back by an appeal to her motherhood.

In "A Very Special *Family Guy* Freakin' Christmas," Lois suffers through the greed of her teenagers, Stewie's refusal to play baby Jesus (until the promise of plutonium entices him to play nice), Peter's donation of *all* the family gifts to charity, a fire in the living room (which destroys the TV, couch, and Christmas tree), and the total annihilation of Christmas dinner. Still, she maintains her cool until a shortage of paper towels sets her off. ("Shut your fat mouth. You all think Christmas just happens, you think all this good will just falls from the freakin' sky – well it doesn't! It falls out of my holly jolly butt! So you can cook your own damn turkey, wrap your own damn presents and, while you're at it, you can all ride a one horse open sleigh to hell!") She storms the town center – stopping only to terrorize Frosty – and climbs the Christmas tree to rob it of its star. Only upon seeing Stewie on stage playing the infant Christ does Lois return to her senses – a moment before being hit with a tranquilizer dart.

In "Lethal Weapons" Lois uses violence to end a dispute between Brian and Meg.

> *Chris:* [*To Meg, who is raking*] Hold it Meg, those two are mine.
> *Meg:* What?
> *Chris:* That's Randy, and that's Fred. Randy is the messy one, Fred's very neat. When you get them together, hoo-hoo – hold on to your sides!
> *Meg:* Nice to meet you both! [*Crinkling them in her hands she reduces them to leaf dust*]
> *Chris:* [*Gasp!*] Murderer!
> *Lois:* Stop it, both of you! Starting now you two are going to love each other! [*Lois forcefully shoves them together*] Now stay that way!
> *Chris:* It's going to be weird to potty.

But, when her violence results in the total emasculation of her husband and a sudden (yeah, right) display of aggression from her infant son, Lois realizes she must change her ways. Lois discovers Peter slumped over the table, unconscious from a blow to the head delivered by Stewie (as payback for eating his crackers).

> *Lois:* Oh no! Peter! Stewie, what did you do?
> *Brian:* Looks like he freed the beast all over the back of Peter's head.
> *Lois:* Oh my God, this is my fault! This is my fault! I brought violence into this house. I'm the worst mother in the world!
> *Stewie:* Ah, I got it all on tape.

Lois experiences violence as a contradiction to her role as a peaceful mother. She recognizes that the discipline of mothering involves certain virtues. These same virtues (prudence, tolerance, and peacefulness), it turns out, are essential to a democratic society.

But let's be careful. I'm not saying that women are more capable of being virtuous than men (they *are* more capable, but I'm not saying that). The most powerful consequence of defining mothering as a stance, a social practice, or discipline, is that mothering is immediately *divorced* from gender. The practices of this discipline, the thought that accompanies those practices, the virtues that may be cultivated within it, are open to all. Although women typically mother they are not the only ones who can mother, or who should. Nothing illustrates this idea better than *Family Guy* where mothering is not only genderless, but also ageless, and even species-less![7]

Lois Griffin is the paramount example of an American mom. With the exception of a few mothering *faux pas* (like when she takes Meg to Narragansett Beach for Spring Break and helps her escape arrest after she publicly exposes herself in "A Fish out of Water"; or, when she reads Meg's diary aloud to the entire family in "Stuck Together, Torn Apart" – because no mother is perfect), Lois exhibits all of the methods of the mother while meeting the demands of her children. Unfortunately for Lois, however, this means that she confronts obstacles to participating fully and equally in social institutions, including the family – just like other American moms.

Vulnerability and Injustice

Despite the fact that anyone can mother, women are most likely to do so. At a young age girls form the expectation that they will become mothers, and this can heavily influence the kinds of choices they make about the future. For example, women commonly pass up educational and occupational opportunities because of the plan to become a mother.[8]

Some women are lured by feminist promises that they can "have it all." Alas, they are shocked to discover the absolute impossibility of conforming both to their corporation's standard of an ideal worker (50–60 hour work-weeks, after-hour meetings and weekend conferences, travel, and relocation)[9] and the model of the "intensive mother"[10] (the current established model of motherhood). The mother is expected to invest copious amounts of time and energy into meeting her children's developmental needs: enrolling them in, and transporting them to, numerous extracurricular activities; attending games and performances; assisting them with homework and school projects; being an active member of the PTO; volunteering in classrooms, for school plays, and to chaperone field trips; baking, sewing, crafting, and so on. Did I mention driving? And then there's driving. And, oh yeah, driving. (The boundary between butt and driver's seat blurs. . . .)[11]

Vulnerability to poverty results for many mothers because, either in anticipation of marriage and motherhood or because of what happens after, they are unable to pursue and maintain careers that would make them economically secure on their own. The demands of motherhood have resulted in a mass exodus of mothers from high-paying, high-profile jobs; and they have prevented others from pursuing the education and opportunity that would enable them to get those jobs in the first place. Married mothers are economically dependent upon their husbands and by death or divorce can be plummeted into poverty. Unmarried mothers, on the other hand, may spend a lifetime in poverty dependent upon social systems that never provide security or stability, and which erode self-esteem.

We cannot underestimate the power of this kind of vulnerability, it once drove Lois to consider leaving Peter. Forced to approach her mother for money to buy Meg a new pair of glasses, Lois is presented with an interesting proposition:

> *Lois:* Mother, you know how I hate asking for money but . . . Mother, Peter is an *excellent* provider. No, Mother, I do not think I would be better off married to a chimp. I don't care how well that chimp across the street is doing . . . really? Well . . . Yeah, ok, I guess you can tell him I said "Hi" – but don't make me sound desperate.

Peter, with the help of Max Weinstein (the Jew he prayed for), eventually succeeds in recovering Lois's money. Lois's response might imply that she has been trying to secure another source of support:

> *Peter:* Guess what? I got back the money for Meg's glasses . . . I balanced our checkbook, too. . . .
> *Lois:* Well, I'm going to call my mother right now and tell her to tell that chimp across the street "ooh, ooh, ooh, shriek, shriek." *[I must confess that I don't know what this means, I studied French, not Chimp . . . stupid, stupid, stupid. . . .]*
> ("When You Wish Upon a Weinstein")

Beyond their vulnerability to poverty, mothers face another injustice in that they must choose between two avenues of human flourishing, which are not necessarily mutually exclusive, and between which those who do not mother do not have to choose: mothering and meaningful paid labor.

Because her primary responsibility is supposed to be her family, any meaningful work she might attempt to engage in outside of the home is undervalued. Often her work is seen as a hobby and as secondary in importance to her husband's; it is not to be taken seriously. The common assumption is that a woman derives her primary sense of self, her purpose and esteem, from her work within the home and not from her outside projects.

> *Peter:* I know you can't understand what I'm going through, Lois. I mean, all the stuff that makes you happy – you know, like cooking and cleaning – it's right here in the house just waiting for you. You are one lucky . . .
>
> *Brian:* Uh, uh . . . stop . . . now.

When the artistic director of the Quahog Players theater group suddenly dies and Lois is offered the position, she is positively thrilled ("All of those years of paying my dues as musical director under that old hack have finally paid off!"). Peter, who is excited about an opportunity at *his* job, is totally uninterested in Lois's news.

> *Lois:* Guess what?
>
> *Peter:* Me first! Mr. Weed said whoever comes up with the best idea for the Christmas toy this year gets a huge bonus . . . this is my chance to prove how valuable I am to the company. Oh, sorry Lois, what's your news?
>
> *Lois:* Well, I. . . . *[Peter walks out]*
>
> ("The King is Dead")

After several failed attempts to find his own artistic outlet, Peter proceeds to hijack Lois's play, replacing himself as director and rewriting the play entirely. The significance to Lois of her job and its labor is totally lost on Peter, who cannot figure out why Lois is so upset. Lois responds that she "wanted to create something beautiful" but that Peter "completely destroyed that." Lois attempts to "create art," to serve a higher purpose, to do something meaningful – but she is deprived of this opportunity by her husband, who does not take her seriously or value her work.

Mothers, like Lois, are unable to participate equally in a workforce that would provide them with economic security and the kind of meaningful projects that are part of a flourishing human life. So why does this happen? And what can we do about it?

The Problem and a Possible Remedy

Lois has a dream. Her dream is to be a professional pianist, to play to a packed stadium of adoring fans, to be showered with applause and roses at the end of her performances, and to have the appreciation of her husband ("Mind Over Murder"). Maybe there's a way she *can* have it all (except for the appreciation of her husband – no one can make any guarantees when it comes to Peter).

Institutions like government, education, family, religion, and economy exist to help us meet shared social goals. Two criteria help us evaluate the merit of our social institutions. One is how *well* they help us meet our goals. The other is how well they are coordinated. When institutions are coordinated individuals can participate in the activities of one institution without being prevented from participating in the activities of other institutions. When individuals cannot participate in more than one institution, we have good reason to think that something has gone wrong – that our institutions aren't allowing us the freedom they should.

And here we see the real problem for mothers. They are unable to participate in both the family and the economy because the designs of these institutions are incompatible. To participate in one is to make sacrifices in the other.

The separation that makes it impossible to participate in the economy *and* the family is not inevitable. Prior to industrialization, work, family, education, and even religion were combined under one roof. Families (consisting of a couple, their biological children, and others' children who apprenticed there) worked together to produce goods and provide services. Education was accomplished in the home; and religious training occurred there as well. This suggests that the separation of these practices into competing and mutually exclusive institutions is not necessary and may be reversible.[12]

Peter is insensitive to the difficulties facing Lois, who struggles to combine her paid work (piano teaching – did you remember that she worked???) and her family obligations. Upon his return from a fishing trip with the guys, and after completely undoing all of the housework Lois had accomplished during his absence, Peter presents a dead fish for Lois to prepare for dinner ("All you gotta do is gut it, clean it, scale it, and cook it"), dodges helping Lois clean his mess, and escapes changing Stewie:

Lois: *[Sounding irritated]* All right, I'll do *that* too. Can you *at least* take Chris to his game?

Peter: Ah geez Lois, I just spent all morning on a boat with my friends drinking beer, telling jokes, and screwing around. How 'bout a little me time?

Lois: Honey, I'm begging you, just drop Chris off at his soccer game and come right home; I need you to look after Stewie while I'm teaching piano lessons, *please!*

Peter: All right, all right. *[Chuckling]* You know I spoil you.

And yet, *Family Guy* presents us with one way we might combine the economic and the familial spheres (as well as a way an idiot might make this venture fail). After his arrest (for punching a pregnant woman he thought was a man), Peter is desperate to see his friends on the outside, and is inspired by the ghost of the Pawtucket Patriot to build a bar in the basement. Initially, this means more work for Lois as she sweats in the kitchen washing beer mugs. Nearly fed up, she descends to discover Chris working the door and Stewie completely polluted. She threatens to shut Peter down when she discovers her piano being used as a buffet, but Peter (in a rare display of quick wit) tells her he brought it down so that she might sing for the men. She's a huge success and packs the bar every night.

By bringing a bar into the basement, thereby combining the practices of different institutions in one location, Lois is able to engage in meaningful paid work and meet the demands of motherhood (Stewie isn't exactly thrilled about it – we see him struggling to get out of the baby bouncer as he swings from a door frame). Voila! Institutional coordination, *Family Guy* style.

For the Griffins, unfortunately, it is not sustainable. Peter's jealousy leads him to organize the wives of his clientele against Lois. I cannot help but feel sorry for Lois as she defends her actions against the accusations of the other struggling mothers: "Peepshow? I just do this for fun. Look, all day long I scrub and cook and take care of my kids and nobody cheers, no one even says thank you. But when the band starts playing and the music is flowing through me I feel, I don't know, special. I guess you all think that's pretty silly."

Silly? No, Lois. We don't. We know motherhood is a bitch.

69

NOTES

1   And here they are:

1.   *Peter:* Oh, sorry, I just farted. [Immediately following the opening narration quoted above, and before the music begins]

2.   Matt Damon finishes *Good Will Hunting*. Ben Affleck is supine on the couch behind him:

Ben Affleck: You think we can put both our names on that?

Matt Damon: What?! You've done nothing but eat Breyers and smoke pot for the last six months!

Affleck: Oh, that's ridiculous. Come on, I . . . I helped.

Damon: Oh, yeah? Ok, Uh, write a line. Just, just right now, just pitch me a line right now.

Affleck: Okay *[farting sound]*. How 'bout that?

Damon: That wasn't a line, you just farted.

3.   When the Griffins are seated around the kitchen table and Chris reveals that his crush is Mrs. Lockhart – his teacher.

Lois: Mrs. Lockhart? Your teacher?

Peter: Whoa, whoa, whoa, whoa, whoa, whoa, whoa, whoa, whoa, whoa, whoa, whoa . . . Lois, this is not my Batman glass.

Lois: Peter, are you listening? Chris has a crush on his teacher!

Meg: Eew, gross!

Stewie: You know what else is gross? *[farting sound]* Aaaaah, broke a damn blood vessel! *[Stewie's entire right eye is blood red.]*

4.   Finally, when the family suspects Chris of murdering Mr. Lockhart.

Lois: Chris, honey, we know what you did and I have to say, honestly, I don't approve.

Chris: What I did? Oh, that I lied about my age to get into Indian Bingo?

Peter: Uh . . . no.

Chris: That I had hard gas and pooed myself?

Peter: Close, but still no.

Stewie: How is that close?

I dedicate this footnote to Le Pétomane (1857–1945), who made a name for himself with an act at the Moulin Rouge in which he played a flute, reproduced the sound of cannons and thunder, and extinguished candles from a distance – all with his butt. To learn more about Le Pétomane, check out Wikipedia. A moment of silence for this great fartiste . . . *[farting sound]* . . . uh-ohhhh.

2   I was in Target recently and noticed a bunch of talking Stewie pens at the register. It turns out they were being hoarded by the checker who,

upon noticing my interest, swiped a pen from my hands and, together with the others laying loosely about his station, quickly stashed it from view. He informed me that he had not been quick enough to procure for himself a Brian or a Peter. I was told there had been no Lois pens. He couldn't even remember the names of the other two . . . uh . . . oh yeah, Chris and Meg. Clearly, I am more deserving of the pens.

3 The demands of a child are sometimes characterized as consisting of preservation, promotion of growth, and ensuring her acceptability to her social group. The first of these three demands, preservation, is thought by Sara Ruddick to begin at the moment conception is known to the mother and pregnancy is accepted. The second demand the child makes upon her mother is for the promotion of "physical, emotional, and intellectual growth." Thirdly, a mother is responsible for raising her child to become an adult readily accepted by their social group. See Sara Ruddick, "Maternal Thinking" in Joyce Trebilcot, ed., *Mothering: Essays in Feminist Theory* (Totowa, NJ: Rowman and Allanheld, 1983), p. 215.

4 Andre Comte-Sponville, *A Small Treatise on the Great Virtues* (New York: Henry Holt, 1996), p. 159.

5 This is not to say that mothers do not engage in violence against their children. Developing virtues through mothering is *possible*, not necessary. For instance, when mental health issues or extreme environmental stress is a factor (like spousal abuse or severe poverty), mothering as a thinking and deliberative discipline may well be absent.

6 See Sara Ruddick, "Preservative Love and Military Destruction: Some Reflections on Mothering and Peace" Joyce Trebilcot, ed., *Mothering: Essays in Feminist Theory* (Totowa, NJ: Rowman and Allanheld, 1983), pp. 231–62.

7 For instance, Brian exhibits both preservative and attentive love (the techniques of the mother) in "Road to Europe" when he accompanies Stewie on his quest to join the children of Jolly Farm, a children's television show Stewie believes to be real. When their plane lands somewhere in the Middle East, the two embark on a desperate journey of survival. Brian steals a camel that dies in the desert. As darkness falls and the night promises freezing temperatures, Brian must cut open the belly of the camel to preserve Stewie's life – he notices a Comfort Inn just after Stewie crawls inside. When they finally make it to the Jolly Farm set, Brian allows Stewie to discover the terrible truth on his own, demonstrating concrete knowledge of Stewie as an individual, and respecting his intellectual need to find out for himself (attentive love).

And again, in "North by North Quahog," when Lois and Peter take a second honeymoon to resurrect their sex life, Brian and Stewie must co-mother Chris and Meg. Brian knows he's in trouble when Meg runs screaming for help from Chris, who chases her with his boogie finger ("What good is mining nose gold if I can't share it with the townspeople?". Stewie offers his assistance, which amounts to some assertiveness training for Brian:

> *Chris:* I don't have to listen to you, you're a dog; you don't have a soul.
> *Brian:* Ow.
> *Stewie:* Don't take that – raise your voice to them!

Later, when Chris is caught drinking at the school dance, Brian and Stewie meet the child's demand for acceptability, disciplining Chris in the hopes of one day transforming him into an acceptable adult (not likely . . .):

> *Stewie:* Did you think you were cool? Did you think you were grown up, hmmm?
> *Chris:* I didn't actually drink any of it, besides Jake Tucker gave it to me.
> *Stewie:* Well, we are going to have a talk with Jake's parents tomorrow after my burping.
> *Brian:* In the meantime, you're grounded Chris.
> *Chris:* Oh, come on, that sucks.
> *Stewie:* Do you want us to pull over?
> *Chris:* I don't care what you do!
> *Stewie:* Oh, we'll pull over, we'll pull over. *[To Brian]* Pull over.
> *[Cut to Chris, bare bottomed, hollering in pain as Stewie spanks him.]*

Later, the two scheme to achieve justice for Chris who has unfairly taken all the blame for the Vodka:

> *Brian:* There's gotta be a way to get back at Jake Tucker for what he did to Chris.
> *Stewie:* *[Drawing a big breath]* I know, I know, I know! Let's plant drugs in his locker.
> *Brian:* Oh my God, that's a great idea!
> *Stewie:* Yeah, thought you'd like that.

Ideally, a mother's preservative love would find a better strategy, but this *is Family Guy.*

8 Susan Moller Okin, *Justice, Gender, and the Family* (New York: Basic Books, 1989), especially ch. 7, "Vulnerability by Marriage."
9 Joan Williams, *Unbending Gender: Why Family and Work Conflict and What to Do About It* (New York: Oxford University Press, 2000).

10 Sharon Hays, *The Cultural Contradictions of Motherhood* (New Haven: Yale University Press, 1996).

11 There is also the cooking thing. Apparently some of us are expected to do this whether our family intends to eat it or not – as in, "From Method to Madness" – when Peter's rescue of a nudist results in a dinner invitation, Lois expresses relief at not having to cook, to which Peter responds, "Oh, no, no, no, go ahead and cook anyway Lois and we'll throw it out – I don't want you to get rusty."

12 Let's be sure to look for *new* ways of making these institutions compatible! I'm not advocating a return to pre-industrialization! If we were to return to those times, I wouldn't be able to watch *Family Guy*.

7

MMMYEZ:
Stewie and the Seven Deadly Sins

SHARON M. KAYE

Stewart Gilligan. The youngest member of the Griffin family. He's crabby, he's rude, he's selfish. He can be violent and even homicidal. Why is this *enfant terrible* so funny? Well, why is anything funny? There are two opposing theories of humor. According to one, we laugh at the absurd because we know that it's not true. According to the other, we laugh at the absurd because we know that it *is* true. Stewie certainly is absurd. Taking a traditional view of infancy, according to which babies are sweet innocents, one might suppose that he provides evidence for the first theory of humor. But the little Griffin actually vindicates the second theory: his humor depicts reality, only dimly recognized.

I cite as my primary authority for this thesis St. Augustine, 5th-century philosopher and church father. Augustine is responsible for inventing the famous Doctrine of Original Sin, according to which we are all born with evil in our hearts. It may seem strange to take seriously such an ancient author with such an obnoxious claim, especially given that he also holds the dubious honor of being the first in history to document the phenomenon of musical farting.[1] We have to remember, however, that the Doctrine of Original Sin is the only successful answer to a very disturbing question. If there is a God, then why does he let the innocent suffer and die? Answer: no one is innocent. We either accept this answer, or we admit that there is no God.

Independently of its theoretical role in propping up the teetering edifice of Christianity, the Doctrine of Original Sin is grounded in personal experience. In his *Confessions* Augustine memorably tells the Tale of the Pear Tree. One night, when he was just a boy, he and

74

a bunch of friends snuck into the neighbor's orchard and climbed a pear tree. The pears were beautiful and would no doubt fetch a good price at the market. Not being hungry, but wishing to wreak havoc, the boys snatched every last piece of fruit off the branches, tossing them into a nearby pig sty. Bearing his soul years later as an adult, Augustine swears he was evil from day one.

How many of us have repressed similar memories? I myself would never have recalled viciously biting my best friend at the tender age of three had my older sister not taken it upon herself to remind me at regular intervals throughout the next thirty years. [Cut away to scene of author as preschooler, teeth clamped on neck of red-headed boy. Boy screaming, flailing arms. Sister standing nearby; looks, points, laughs.]

Stewie is evil. Worse still, no one else seems to notice or care. His mother Lois has an epiphany, but only in a dream soon forgotten ("Mr. Griffin Goes to Washington"). Frightening as this situation is, it is an accurate depiction of the modern-day family. We are all in collective denial that our little darlings are rotten to the core. The Middle Ages may have been backward in some ways, but at least they knew the truth about children, and treated them accordingly.

In the Middle Ages, the notion of the Seven Deadly Sins emerged, first proposed by St. Gregory the Great in the 6th century, then elaborated by St. Thomas Aquinas in the 13th, and finally popularized by Geoffrey Chaucer and Dante Alighieri in the 14th. Lust, Gluttony, Sloth, Avarice, Anger, Envy, and Pride: together they provide a simple framework for cataloging our transgressions. The medievals illustrated the Seven Deadlies with relish, developing standard symbolic representations for each. For example, lust is typically represented by a goat or a cow – who knows why.

At any rate, Stewie Griffin single-handedly illustrates all seven Deadlies so masterfully it would have made the medievals weep. Let's examine each in turn.

1st: Lust

Lust is an intense or unrestrained sexual craving. According to Aquinas, lust is wrong because it leads to all sorts of disorderly conduct, such as fornication, masturbation, adultery, incest, rape, homosexuality, and bestiality.[2] Aquinas does not discuss proper conduct toward vegetables or minerals. Although many moderns would question his insistence on throwing so many interesting activities out with the bath water, we can all grant that sexual cravings can certainly be problematic. [Cut away to scene of author alone in her kitchen at eleven o'clock on a Saturday morning, eyeing a banana.]

Sigmund Freud (1856–1939) was the first to theorize infant sexuality. According to his account of the Oedipal Complex, every boy falls in love with his mother and comes to view his father as a rival for her love. Subconsciously wishing to marry his mother, he subconsciously wishes to kill his father until he learns to identify with his father and finds someone else who resembles his mother to marry. Needless to say, our bawdy little monkey makes Freud look like a charming sentimentalist. He hates his mother with diabolical intensity (evident, for example, in his web page address, "killlois.com," his email address, loismustdie@yahoo.com, and in the refrain he teaches his friend Eliza Pinchley, "The life of the wife is ended by the knife"); meanwhile, Stewie barely tolerates his father, "The Fat Man," with resigned disgust.

Given that his hatred has universal orientation, we should not be surprised to find his sexuality equally indiscriminate. Reflecting on his conflict with his mother, he muses, "I sometimes wonder if all women are this difficult. And then I think to myself, 'My God wouldn't it be marvelous if I turned out to be a homosexual?'" (*Untold Story*). Stewie's teddy bear, Rupert, who is his best friend and an obvious projection of his own subconscious, is gay. On the other hand, Stewie seems to swing the other direction as well. For example, he kills time at a funeral assessing the female turnout one by one like a true connoisseur. "I'd do her, do her, wouldn't do her, . . . lose the pigtails and we'll talk" ("Mr. Saturday Night"). And on the third hand, when drunk, Stewie crosses the species line, enthusiastically slurring "You're sexy!" to Brian the dog. Perhaps it was not just a matter of simple grooming Stewie had in mind when, dead sober, he asked Brian to shave his coin purse (*Untold Story*).

We know in any case that Stewie exhibits the physical signs of lust. For example, when he accidentally sees a group of cheerleaders changing in their locker room, he murmurs, "It appears my wee-wee's been stricken with rigor mortis" ("Peter Griffin: Husband, Father, Brother?"). Likewise, upon hearing Lois instruct Meg in the art of revenge, he remarks, "All this talk about eye-gouging has gotten me all frisky! No, really, I've got half a pack of Rolaids in my diaper" ("And the Wiener Is"). Moreover, he discovers autoerotica in the swimming pool – "Helloooo Mr. Water Jet!" ("He's Too Sexy for his Fat"); he experiments with transvestitism in front of the bathroom mirror – "Look at you there. You're a filthy girl, aren't you?" ("Emission Impossible"); and he is already showing signs of fetishizing. "I smell a messy diaper. God, why does that turn me on?" ("Lethal Weapons").

Despite the fact that his imagination is active in every direction, Stewie never actually gets much action. In fact, he meets his future self at the age of thirty-five only to find that he is still a virgin (*Untold Story*). Nevertheless, lack of doing does not make for lack of wanting. "Oh, Cupid, hath thou pierced me with thine sweet searing arrow. Stomach, cease thy lustful quake" ("Dammit Janet"). Stewie has a dirty stomach and a dirty mind; this alone makes him guilty of the sin of lust.

2nd: Gluttony

Gluttony is an excess of eating or drinking. It seems like the official sin of America given that we are the fattest country in the world. According to Thomas "The Ox" Aquinas, however, who was well known to be able to wine or dine any other monk under the table, gluttony is not necessarily a deadly sin. If you die without divine forgiveness for a deadly or "mortal" sin, you have an irreparable defect in your soul and therefore cannot be admitted at the gates of heaven. A venial sin, in contrast (from the word *venia*, meaning pardon), is corrected the moment it is ceased, and therefore does not impede eternal life. Eating and drinking to excess is venial unless it causes you to disobey God's commands.[3] [Cut away to scene of Aquinas eating liver with some fava beans and a nice Chianti.]

There is no doubt that Stewie loves food. One might be tempted to call him a gourmand rather than a glutton. He delights in obscure delicacies such as Sunny D, kitty litter, and paste. "I say, Rupert, this paste is quite delicious. It's almost worth the bowel obstruction" ("Fore, Father"). And his ability to appreciate the pleasures of the palate seems to exceed that of most, as is evident in his reaction to blueberries – "Oh, oh my G . . . oh, that's better than sex!" ("Love Thy Trophy") and fig newtons – "OH GOD! THERE'S AN ORGY IN MY MOUTH!" ("The Story on Page One").

But Stewie is not above using his appetite for nefarious purposes. For example, he fakes an orgasm over one of Lois's dinners just to make it harder for Chris to suffer through his diet ("He's Too Sexy for His Fat"). He often uses food to control people. "I say mother, this hotdog has been on this plate for a full minute and it hasn't cut itself . . . By all means take your time!" ("Peter, Peter, Caviar Eater"). Finally, he can be a dangerous drunk, such as the time a belly full of Mai Tai helps him incite O. J. Simpson to murder his wife ("Peter Griffin: Husband, Father, Brother?").

But the most condemning evidence of Stewie's gluttony emerges when Lois makes a futile attempt to wean him from breast milk. "Those jugs are mine until all the milk dries up. Then you can have the remains!" ("I take thee, Quagmire – Tonight"). Weaning undeniably brings out the antichrist in children. Have we not all witnessed it? Augustine did, and it was the first clue that eventually led him to the Doctrine of Original Sin. Augustine writes: "Thus, the infant's innocence lies in the weakness of his body and not in the infant mind. I have myself observed a baby to be jealous, though it could not speak; it was livid as it watched another infant at the breast."[4]

Stewie is Augustine's poster boy. When Lois refuses to unbutton, he goes so far as to jump another woman's breast, handily knocking her infant out of the way. The look on his face is enough to send chills down American Dad's spine. Clearly Stewie is a glutton's glutton.

3rd: Sloth

For all his faults, no one can call Stewie Griffin a couch potato. His apocalyptic schemes keep him quite busy and push him to impressive heights of ingenuity. The only time he displays a textbook case of laziness is when he becomes so fat that he is reduced to a listless torpor, unable even to successfully insult an innocent passerby ("He's Too Sexy for his Fat"). True, S. G. does have a penchant for television and would no doubt throw a fit if we neglected to call him when *Kojak* starts. One almost feels, however, that he would be a better person if he engaged in such harmless pursuits more often.

If sloth were reducible to indolence, then our tiny hero would be off the hook, disqualified from the claim to perfect corruption. Yet sloth is not reducible to indolence. In fact, St. Gregory originally used the Latin term *tristia*, meaning sadness, for this sin, and, according to Thomas Aquinas, the relevant meaning of sloth is "oppressive sorrow." Sloth is the vice that opposes the virtue of joyful charity.

Pouting? Yes.

Aquinas asserts that if you pout about something good, your act is evil in itself, but even if you pout about something bad your act is evil in its effect. Aquinas surveys various effects of pouting that have come to be known as the Daughters of Sloth: despair, faint-heartedness, sluggishness, spite, bitterness, malicious indignation, wandering after unlawful things, idleness, drowsiness, uneasiness of the mind, curiosity, loquacity, restlessness, and instability.[5]

With this analysis, it becomes evident that Stewie is thoroughly guilty of slothfulness after all. He regularly pouts about good things. He was inconsolable, for example, when he discovered that he was unable to play the asphyxiation game because his football-shaped head was too big to fit in a plastic bag ("Breaking Out is Hard to Do"). Even more importantly, Stewie is the undisputed heavyweight world champion master of one of sloth's daughters, namely, malicious indignation. Malicious indignation occurs when you lash out at someone who has offended you. Stewie is very sensitive about his infant status and does not appreciate being reminded of it. His malicious indignation is often directed against Lois. For example, when Lois says Stewie can't help Chris with his math homework because he's "just a baby," Stewie responds, "And you're a regular Rhodes scholar. Where was it you graduated from again? The University of Duh?" ("When You Wish Upon a Weinstein"). Lois always tries to speak gently to Stewie, in one instance asking, "Why don't you play in the other room?" But to Stewie, her tone is inexcusably condescending. He replies, "Why don't you burn in hell?" ("Death Has A Shadow"). Lois often tries to compensate for Stewie's joyless apathy. When she makes a card for Peter from Stewie, Stewie interprets her actions in the worst possible light. "Did you forge my name? How dare you! Is this backwards 'S' supposed to be cute? I'm going to crap double for you tonight!" ("A Picture Is Worth 1,000 Bucks"). Moreover, when sufficiently provoked, Stewie also strikes out with malicious indignation at complete strangers:

Man on airplane:	Oh great, I always end up sitting next to a damn baby.
Stewie:	What? What did you just say?
Lois:	Stewie, stop fussing.
Stewie:	Not now, Lois. *[Slaps man on head]* Hey big man, turn around. If you've got something to say, say it to my face! Oh, you can't hear me now. That's it. I was going to watch the movie, but forget it. For the next five hours, you're my bitch. Wahhhhhhh!

("Brian Does Hollywood (2)")

This last example epitomizes Stewie's special brand of sloth. He pouts so intensely, and so aggressively, that he is willing to sacrifice lazy pastimes to do it.

4th: Avarice

Avarice is reprehensible acquisitiveness, an insatiable desire for wealth. Stewie's greed does not come out very often, but when it does, it is a humdinger. In the episode "Brian Doesn't Have Stewie's Money," Stewie goes gangsta when Brian is unable to pay back some money he borrowed. Enough said. You just have to see it to believe it.

5th: Anger

Anger is a strong feeling of displeasure or hostility directed toward some real or supposed grievance. Given that we defined malicious indignation, one of the daughters of sloth, as lashing out against someone who has offended you, we may wonder whether there is really any difference between these two sins. Being the crowned prince of anal retentive classification, Aquinas informs us that the essential differentiating feature of anger is revenge.[6]

Aquinas actually has a lot to say in favor of vengeance, arguing in good medieval fashion that it is an integral component of justice. Given that the God of the Old Testament is Mr. Hard-Ass-Scowl-Face-I'll-Get-You-Little-Turds, it would not be prudent for anyone, much less someone vying for sainthood, to be overly critical of anger. But Aquinas seems so bent on glorifying it that one begins to wonder whether it should really be considered one of the Seven Deadlies. [Cut away to scene from *Sesame Street*. Boxed screen showing seven kids, each engaged in one of the seven deadly sins. Singing: One of these kids is not like the others. One of these kids just doesn't belong. Can you tell which kid is not like the others, by the time I finish my song? Did you guess which kid was not like the others? Did you guess which kid just doesn't belong? If you guessed this one is not like the others, then you're not a ding dong . . .]

Nevertheless, revenge can be just as evil as anything else, especially in the chubby little mitts of Stewie Griffin. In *The Untold Story*, Stewie learns that going to hell involves servicing Steve Allen in a red hotel room. This preview of his fate prompts him to lament his hateful nature. But Brian corrects Stewie: he's not hateful, he just needs to control his anger. Brian is right; in this moment we approach genuine insight into Stewie, who of course represents humanity as a whole. From the very beginning, deep down inside, we are all pissed off to be here instead of someplace better.

Just like in real life, however, on the show no one (other than the alcoholic dog) recognizes the truth. This is never more evident than when Stewie takes violent revenge against Peter ("you tottering, femme-sucked dewberry!") for eating his graham crackers.

Dr. Kaplan:	Now, Stewart, I want you to take this Mommy doll and this Daddy doll and show me how they act together.
Stewie:	Yes. Very well. All right. *[In the voice of the male doll:]* "You see, Margaret, after twenty odd years of marriage, your curious indiscretions no longer please me." *[In the voice of the female doll:]* "Really? And I suppose you think I enjoy hanging onto those hammocky deposits of gin sugars you call buttocks?" *[Noticing Dr. Kaplan writing something on his notepad]* What was that? What did you just write there? Give me that! *[Reading:]* "Insecurity? Gender confusion?" I'll give you something to write about! *[Goes wild]* Look at me! I'm insane! I'm Martin Lawrence on a bender!
Dr. Kaplan:	Mr. and Mrs. Griffin, does Stewart have a history of aggression?
Lois:	No. Hitting Peter is the first violent thing he's ever done.
Stewie:	Technically, the first act of violence was that time bomb I left ticking in your uterus. Happy 50th birthday, Lois!
Dr. Kaplan:	It's obvious that your son is learning this behavior from someone.

("Lethal Weapons")

Appropriately enough, the "expert" is totally clueless. Stewie is not insecure, he does not suffer from gender confusion, and he is not learning his violent behavior from someone. Stewie was born with a chip on his shoulder.

6th: Envy

Envy is the resentful desire for another's advantages. Today, fancy pants scholars like to make a hairsplitting distinction between envy and jealousy, but we won't bore ourselves with that here. To be honest, I'm getting kind of sick of Aquinas's mumbo jumbo too. The bottom line is, we have all experienced the ravages of the green-eyed monster. [Cut away to green-eyed monster, lying in a shaft of sunlight; preening himself, stretches modestly; looks up: "What?"]

Stewie's envy is revealed the two times our wee hellion falls in love. In the first instance, when he goes gaga over his babysitter, Liddane, he is livid to find out that she already has a boyfriend, Jeremy. Ready to pounce, he is dragged away, kicking and screaming:

> Ha! I got your hat! Take that hatless! Go back to the quad and resume your hackey sack torney. I'm not going to lie down for some frat boy bastard with his damn Teva sandals and his Skoal bandits and his Abercrombie and Fitch long sleeved open stitched crew neck Henley, smoking his sticky buds out of a soda can while watching his favorite downloaded *Simpsons* episodes every night. Yes, we all love Mr. Plow! Oh – you've got the song memorized do you? So does everyone else! That is exactly the kind of idiot you see at Taco Bell at one in the morning, the guy that whiffed his way down the bar skank ladder. If he wants to throw hands I'll throw hands . . .

Refusing to give up on Liddane, Stewie locks Jeremy in the trunk of Brian's car. Two weeks later, when Stewie remembers that Jeremy is still in the trunk, he notes the consequences with grim satisfaction: "Yeah, he's dead" ("8 Simple Rules for Buying My Teenage Daughter").

In the second instance, Stewie falls in love with his daycare classmate, Janet. It turns out, however, that she just wants Stewie's cookies and dumps him when she finds a different supplier. Not realizing that he has been used, Stewie is so jealous of the new boyfriend that he retaliates by trying to make Janet jealous in turn. He asks another daycare classmate, Melinda, to pose as his new girlfriend:

Stewie: Oh, hello, Janet. Yes, you know Melinda. Yes, it seems she's – What did we figure out, dear? Was it one? No, two. Yes, she's two weeks younger than you. Just look at that butt! That is a tight butt! *[Janet shows no interest]* Damn! Not even a second glance! *[Turning on Melinda]* This is what you call "dolled up"? Listen, why don't you save yourself years of sexual ambiguity and get fitted for a pair of Doc Martens and a plaid flannel shirt? ("Dammit Janet")

Stewie is not a graceful loser in the game of love. Nothing brings out his jealousy more – except sibling rivalry. When Lois and Peter decide to try to have another child, Stewie is beside himself.

Another baby? But . . . but I'm the baby. Why the deuce would they want to replace me? My, my cheeks are pinchable, my bottom is smooth, my laugh is heartwarming. Aha ha ha ha ho ho ho! What's that? I certainly am not overreacting! What the devil do you think happened to Bobby when they added cousin Oliver to the Brady bunch? ("Emission Impossible")

Although he vows to fight his spermatazoic brother to the death, he changes his mind when he learns that the new Griffin could be an ally in his war against the world. This establishes that, although Stewie is subject to envy, one-upmanship is not as significant in his personal eschatology as pride.

7th: Pride

St. Gregory maintains that the severity of the Seven Deadly Sins can be ranked in accordance with the order we have followed – Lust, Gluttony, Sloth, Avarice, Anger, Envy, and Pride – Lust being the least vicious and Pride being the Queen of the Vices. Pride is unreasonable or inordinate self-esteem and is often considered the root or origin of all evil. It transformed the archangel Lucifer into the demon Satan, it puffed up Adam and Eve to their ultimate demise, and it regularly takes its toll on high school prom court nominees across the country. [Cut away to scene of author as high school student calmly explaining to the principal why she wishes to be taken off the prom court list. Principal baffled, suspicious, alarmed, angry; demanding to know what is this Foo cult and its polymorphous power?]

For medieval philosophers such as Augustine, as well as philosophers such as Michel Foucault (1926–84) who dabble in medieval studies, pride is all about power. Just to show what good sports we are, we should allow ol' Aquinas to get in one last word about pride. He asserts that it is "characteristic of pride to be unwilling to be subject to any superior."[7] Hmmmmmmm . . . Does this make you think of anyone in particular? Is he small and pink, with slicked back hair fuzz and an outrageously pretentious British accent?

Stewie Griffin has a serious god complex; it is the not-so-hidden psychological motivation behind his quest for world domination. Although you can hear the ambition in his voice even when he is talking about his diaper, he occasionally expresses it more explicitly. Lois asks Stewie to say "hi" to the new neighbor, Officer Swanson. Ignoring her, Stewie declares "You will bow to me!" ("A Hero Sits Next Door"). Stewie does not so much think of God as a rival but as a mentor. As his piecemeal religious education progresses, he become increasingly enamored with the idea of stepping into God's shoes. Enjoying Bible stories much more than Barney, he ruminates: "Yes, I rather like this God fellow. He's very theatrical, you know, a pestilence here, a plague there. Omnipotence. Gotta get me some of that" and later: "Oh! I love God. He's so deliciously evil" ("Holy Crap!"). There is no doubt that this tyrannical tyke fully plans to rule the world.

Are we ready for Stewtopia? What would it be like? There would be pancakes for breakfast every morning and Raffi would be played on every radio station. Broccoli would not exist. Pickles and sprinkles would be used exclusively for composting. There would be kitties but no dogs. If there were swimming pools, they would be only ten inches deep. But there would be plenty of disco dancing with sunshine and farts for everyone.

Bring it on, baby. It's likely to be better than what we've got now.

Conclusion

I conclude that Stewie Griffin makes us smile, not because he is a fictional impossibility, but because he portrays the truth about children that we daily repress. He makes a legitimate claim to utter depravity because he commits all seven of the Deadlies with panache and verve unequaled by Nero himself. It might be objected that Stewie has moments of pure goodness. Needless to say, it would require a whole other essay to identify such alleged instances and show one by one why ulterior motives cancel them out. In my view, only one moment in the entire history of the show has potential to redeem the Mini Rocket Man. In "The Tuckers," while Peter and Lois are MIA, Brian and Stewie have to take responsibility for the household, becoming temporary parents for Meg and Chris. When Chris is mistakenly accused of a crime committed by another boy, it is up to Brian and Stewie to go to the boy's house to speak with him and his father. It just so happens, however, that the boy in question is Jake Tucker, whose face is upside down. Before going in, Stewie reminds Brian not to call attention to the boy's affliction. Although he agrees, Brian slips mid-sentence saying that something needs to be done for Chris because, "this whole situation has just turned his whole life upside down – face." Stewie is mortified. As he slowly turns toward Brian in disbelief, the expression on his face is poignantly compelling. Is it just annoyance? Or is it scandalized decency? If it is decency, then I take back everything I've said. It is no big deal to sin from time to time if you are a fundamentally decent person.

Come to think of it, forget about everything I said regardless. What happens in this essay stays in this essay.

NOTES

1   Yes, it's really true. See St. Augustine, *On the City of God*, 14.24.
2   St. Thomas Aquinas, *Summa Theologica* II-II, Question 154, www.newadvent.org/summa/315400.htm.
3   St. Thomas Aquinas, *Summa Theologica* II-II, Question 148, www.newadvent.org/summa/314800.htm.
4   St. Augustine, *Confessions* Book 1, chapter 7, www.sullivan-county. com/id3/confessions/augcon1.htm.
5   St. Thomas Aquinas, *Summa Theologica* II-II, Question 35, www.newadvent.org/summa/303501.htm.
6   He writes that "avoidance of good on account of an attendant evil occurs in two ways. For this happens either in respect of one's own good, and thus we have 'sloth,' which is sadness about one's spiritual good, on

account of the attendant bodily labor: or else it happens in respect of another's good, and this, . . . if it be with recrimination with a view to vengeance, it is 'anger.'" St. Thomas Aquinas, *Summa Theologica* I-II, Question 84.4, www.newadvent.org/summa/208404.htm.

7 St. Thomas Aquinas, *Summa Theologica* I-II, Question 84.2, www.newadvent.org/summa/208402.htm.

8

THE *OTHER* CHILDREN:
The Importance of Meg and Chris

P. SUE DOHNIMM[1]

It's a Question of Character

Brian and Stewie are the hands-down favorites of any *Family Guy* popularity contest. The next set of favs will include Peter and Quagmire, and perhaps even Lois. After these five, you might occasionally get a Cleveland or a Joe, a Jasper or an Adam West. But you will never get a Meg or a Chris. If someone says Meg or Chris is their favorite Griffin, get ready to be *punk'd*.

Part of the explanation of their unpopularity is that Meg and Chris are *underdeveloped*. I don't mean just that they're teenagers, or that neither child has yet to develop into a man. I mean, rather, that they seem to lack any kind of robust character; they seem downright plastic. We love Stewie because he's got a very distinct personality (he's a homicidal genius, and a baby), and the same sort of thing applies to other characters as well: Peter is an aloof idiot, Brian is a swank dog with an attitude, Quagmire is a sex-crazed pervert. We can explain who these characters are *exactly*, and in just a few sentences (if not one!).

But Meg and Chris just aren't like that. True, everyone seems to hate Meg, and Chris sometimes seems to be a budding artist – but these characteristics aren't all that distinctive. And it is *distinctiveness* that these other children lack. In philosophy, we often speak about the *essential features* of a thing – in other words, those features that make a thing what it is, that distinguish it from other things – and this is what seems to be absent from Meg and Chris. They seem to lack *essence*.

87

And what is essence? Here's an easy example: a triangle. The essence of a triangle is what makes it what it is – what distinguishes it from rectangles, tables, presidents, numbers, and so on. The essential features of a triangle are fairly easy to identify. A triangle is a bound geometrical object with three sides composed of straight lines, and with interior angles totaling 180 degrees.[2] (See? Establishing essential features is as easy as pi).[3]

Much as things have essential features, we can also talk about *persons* having essential features.[4] When we talk about the essential features of a particular person, we'll likely talk about personality traits – about what sort of characteristics make the person tick, and what things make them unique. These essential features draw us to our favorite characters (and prevent us from loving Meg or Chris). Let's have a quick look at the profiles of these non-Stewies:

Meg: An awkward adolescent with serious confidence issues. She is ridiculed by her classmates and by members of her family. She is a sexually confused, homely girl who is destined to become a man.

Chris: This strange lad is haunted by an evil monkey who lives in his closet. He is a budding artist (or perhaps just lucky). He is also exceptionally well endowed. All the boys in the locker room are jealous. He's like a tripod. He's got a very large penis, if you get my meaning.

These are characters without essential characteristics. All of the things we've just mentioned are merely *accidental* traits (traits that *happen* to be but don't *have* to be) of these two cardboard characters. Consider the two features most associated with Meg: she is unpopular, and she is ugly. If there are any essential characteristics Meg possesses, these would seem to do it. Her unpopularity is featured in nearly every episode of *Family Guy*, as is her ugliness. Both are legendary.

> *Chris:*   *[talking to Peter]* You're just running away from your troubles by being here!
> *Peter:*   What are you talking about? Meg's right here.
> ("Jungle Love")

Meg: Mom guess what! I made the Flag Girl squad.
Stewie: Flag Girl? Ummmm, yes good for you. Now you can be some-
             where else when the boys don't call!
("And the Weiner is")

It initially seems that Meg's unpopularity is one of the things that makes her who she is (that and her moustache). It's hard to think about Meg without thinking of an ugly girl who is often mistaken for a man.

Meg: Hi, Craig. Umm, I was wondering if maybe you would want to, I
        don't know, go out sometime?
Craig: Huh, that's about as likely as me playing by someone else's rules
        besides my own. Which I would never do. I play by my own
        rules, nobody else's, not even my own.
Meg: How 'bout a movie?
Craig: I don't go out with dudes.
("Don't Make me Over")

And even Peter sometimes mistakes Meg for a man.

Meg: I just want to kill myself. I'm gonna go upstairs and eat a whole
        bowl of peanuts.
[Lois and Peter stare in silence]
Meg: I'm allergic to peanuts.
[Peter and Lois continue to stare]
Meg: You don't know anything about me. *[Meg runs upstairs]*
Peter: Who was that guy?
("The Kiss Seen Around the World")[5]

But Meg isn't always ugly. In "Don't Make Me Over," Meg gets a makeover, and is transformed into the leading lady of the Griffin family musical ensemble. Of course, this isn't enough to brush aside the family's sense of who Meg is, and what she's like.

Meg: Look everybody I got a makeover!!
Peter: Aw, Meg I always thought you were beautiful *[begins to laugh
        hysterically]*. Whoa, couldn't do that with a straight face, huh?
        Chris, go burn all of Meg's old pictures.
("Don't Make Me Over")

Meg is still Meg, even when she's both beautiful and popular. So being ugly can't be one of her essential features. (If it were essential, she couldn't be Meg without it.) Even being a girl mistaken for a dude isn't one of her essential features – even if it is a funny and recurrent feature. When Meg becomes *Ron*, she is still essentially Meg (*Stewie Griffin: The Untold Story*). And what does it mean to be essentially Meg? As paradoxical as it might sound, it means to lack essential characteristics (she isn't even essentially a *she*!).

The same applies to Chris: on the two occasions when he rises above mediocrity, showing some artistic promise ("The Son Also Draws" and "A Picture is Worth a Thousand Bucks"), he is still the same pudgy adolescent without much personality.[6] His idiocy seems to be the only thing approaching an essential characteristic.

> *Chris:* There's this game where you put in a dollar and you win four quarters. I win every time!
> ("Chitty Chitty Death Bang")
>
> *Chris:* I never knew anyone who went crazy before, except for my invisible friend, Col. Schwartz.
> ("I Never Met the Dead Man")
>
> *Chris:* When I stick this army guy with the sharp bayonet up my nose, it tickles my brain. Hah hah hah . . . ow. Oh, now I don't know math.
> ("The Kiss Seen Around the World")

Much as Meg defies the easy essentialist characterization of a manly, unpopular girl, Chris resists that character trait that would make him truly his father's son. Chris occasionally shows real acumen, albeit *Family Guy* style. In discussing one of his artworks, Chris shows a capacity for abstract thought that is nevertheless nicely grounded in reality. As Chris deftly remarks, the painting under discussion is "partially an expression of my teenage angst . . . but mostly, it's a moo cow!" ("A Picture is Worth a Thousand Bucks"). There's no artificial inflation of his artistic endeavor, but he does recognize *something* about the source of the need to engage in art, even though this doesn't elevate him to the airy heights of metaphysical speculation. Now, there's no denying that Chris is stupid. But he's not *essentially* stupid. He has moments of amazing lucidity that go well beyond any simple one-liner.

So, what can we learn from any of this? What difference does it make if Meg and Chris don't have the sorts of essential character traits that we find in folks like Stewie and Quagmire? Why does the show even need these two characters? Why am I asking so many questions? There is a justification for the presence of these poster-children for problems – and it isn't simply that they are *funny*. Strange as it might initially sound, Meg and Chris are the *most realistic* characters on the show. They are realistic precisely because they defy any single characterization in the way that the other characters on the show do not. To describe what they are like is much more difficult than it is to describe Peter, Brian, Stewie, or Quagmire. This is *not* because the characters are flat. In fact, just the opposite is true: these characters are multi-dimensional, fluctuating beings – not simply singular punchlines recast in multiple places. This provides them with depth, and also, I daresay, with a pinch of philosophical wisdom.

Character As Explanation

Aristotle's (4th century, BCE) discussion of character is fundamentally a discussion of *good* character. In his *Nicomachean Ethics*, he spends a good deal of time spelling out what it means to say that someone is virtuous (he spends more time spelling it out than Peter spends fighting chickens). As it turns out, virtue is fundamentally a state of character. A state of character, since we're defining things, is the propensity to react in a certain way to the world around you – to do certain things, but also to have certain emotions in particular contexts ("by state of character [I mean] the things in virtue of which we stand well or badly with reference to the passions" (1105b 25)). Thus, we might say that Quagmire has the character of a pervert (he reacts to a hint of genitalia with uncontrollable lust); that Cleveland has the character of a saint (he reacts to everything with incredible calmness of spirit), and that Peter has the character of . . . well . . . an idiot (he responds to everything like an idiot, if you get my meaning).

As Aristotle reminds us, though, it is not enough to say that virtue is a state of character. We must also say "what sort of state it is" (1106a 15). To put it as only Aristotle could, "the virtue of man also will be the state of character which makes a man good and which makes him do his work well" (1106a 23–25). Our current interest in this is not in virtue itself. (Why would *I* be interested in virtue? That's *so* 19th entury.) It is, rather, in the role Aristotle assigns to one's character: a state of character (*hexis*) is what explains why we do what we do. It is what makes us essentially who we are. I'll give some examples, both to help clarify the significance of this, and to insult everyone who's made it this far into the chapter.

Why does a good person do good actions? Because he's good, dummy. Why does a shy person act shyly? Because he's shy, stupid. What does Stewie act so murderous toward Lois? Because he's homicidal, honey. Why does Lois act so nurturing so often? Because she's motherly, you twit. Why does Quagmire act like such a horn-dog?[7]

Aristotle gives us an account of how we can explain our actions that matches up with our common sense. We tend to explain the actions of others in terms of their characters. Such explanations make their actions understandable.

And here we can see the relevance of Aristotle's analysis of character to Meg and Chris. We *cannot* make sense of Meg and Chris in terms of character. Their actions are simply unpredictable. We don't understand what they do precisely because their actions seem to come from nowhere. Consider when Lois home schools Meg and Chris (because Peter has founded his own country, and the children aren't allowed to enter the US).

> *Lois:*   [noticing Chris trying to pass a note to Meg] Chris read that note.
> *Chris:* "I think Mrs. Griffin is hot."
> *Lois:*   Go to your room!
> ("E. Peterbus Unum")

Why would Chris say this? Has he forgotten that Mrs. Griffin is his mother? Or that we aren't supposed to view our mothers as sexual objects? These are trick questions. There's simply no explanation for why Chris does what he does.

> *Chris:* My dad is smarter than your dad.
> *Meg:*   We have the same dad idiot!
> *Chris:* Yeah, but mine's smarter!
> ("Petarded")

Or, again,

> *Chris:* Dad, you should invent the frisbee, that's an awesome toy.
> *Meg:*   Chris, the frisbee is already invented.

Chris: Then how come I never heard of it?
("The King is Dead")

The seemingly random actions of these *other* children reveal an important truth about the human condition: that our characters, in the Aristotelian sense of the term, are not nearly as important as we imagine. If you get a pimple named Doug on your face, as good-intentioned Chris finds out, no character traits are going to save you ("Brian the Bachelor").

Character As Illusion: The Empirical Perspective

The view that character is the source of action has come under fire in recent years by philosophers and social scientists who want to ground our reflections on human existence in scientific research. The results are at least edifying, and at most horrifying. Let's just quickly sketch one of the experiments that calls into question Aristotle's notion of the importance of character.

In one important experiment, psychologists decided to watch people use the phone at a phone booth (remember those?).[8] To make things interesting, they sometimes put a dime in the coin return slot. Every time someone used the phone and checked the coin return slot, they sent in an actor to spill paperwork in the path of the exiting caller. The caller was confronted with a choice: either stop to help pick up the mess, or go on his or her way.

If Aristotle is right about character, we would expect one's actions in this situation to stem from one's character. But after this experiment (and others like it), this doesn't appear likely. In fact, the shocking result of these observations was this: in almost every case where the caller helped pick up the dropped paper, the caller had found a dime in the coin return slot of the phone. Likewise, in nearly every case where a caller *did not* find a dime in the coin return slot, they *did not help*.

Ok, ok, ok. It could have been coincidence. It might be that everyone who found the dime (and helped) also happened to have a virtuous character. And maybe everyone who didn't find a dime had a lousy character. But the odds weigh against this explanation. Consider the distribution of cases:

	Helped	*Did not help*
Found dime	14	2
Did not find dime	1	24

Let's face it, a dime just isn't a lot of money – but it looks like enough to allow us to predict, in most cases, whether or not someone will help a person in need! 14 of the 16 people who found a dime actually helped, while only 1 of the 25 who did not find a dime did the same! It's of course possible that this is all coincidence. But it's much harder to say this when the evidence keeps suggesting the contrary. And what does the evidence suggest? Well, it suggests that our actions can be effected by very small situational variations: a dime we find, a song that we heard, the scent in the air, the presence of an authority figure, whether or not we are in a rush, and so on. So much for firm character!

And it is here that we can begin to see why Peter, Stewie, Quagmire, and most of the rest of the cast of *Family Guy* might just misrepresent the way human beings actually are. We can predict the behavior of Quagmire, for example, with extraordinary ease. If Quagmire has the opportunity to pork someone (to put it appropriately, given the context), if you expect him not to, you obviously don't watch the show! Even when he knows he *shouldn't* be doing any proverbial porking and bumping uglies (too much imagery yet, even given the context?), we can rely on him to do it anyway. When he has the opportunity to massage his man-root with Loretta's love-hole (how about now? Is it too much imagery now?!? Is nothing profane!?!), you can bet he does it – despite the fact that it means he is betraying Cleveland.

There's a lot to be gained from an exploration of these issues, but one thing that we *should not* take from such scenes is a picture of human action as fundamentally character-driven. Here, surprisingly, the most honest examples of the human condition on *Family Guy* are Meg and Chris: we simply cannot predict what they will do. Who expected Chris to go hip-hop?

> *Peter:* Nice job out there tonight, Chris. You wiped the floor with that towel.
> *Chris:* Yo! Did y'all check me when that hottie was all up in my Kool-Aid? I looked to break off a little somethin'-somethin'

but my crew gave me the 411 on that skank and she's all about the bling-bling.

Lois: What's wrong?

Peter: He's speaking in tongues, Lois! Our son is possessed! Meg, start at Psalm 41 and don't stop reading until I tell you! The power of Christ compels you!

[Chris screams]

("Peter Griffin: Husband, Father . . . Brother?")

Or what about this?

Peter: Where's Chris? I asked him to fill up the canteens an hour ago.

Chris: *[being carried away by ants]* Hey, Dad, look. I covered my back with honey, and now the ants are taking me home.

Peter: He does the same thing at home with Velveeta and cockroaches. If you turn the light on fast, they slam him into the fridge.

("Fore, Father")

Chris is inexplicable. Unlike Quagmire or Stewie, who are as predictable as they are lovable, Chris defies our attempts to understand him. We just don't know who he is. Chris is a near-perfect model of a *situationist* view of human action. Situationism maintains that the explanations of our actions have little to do with our character traits, and everything to do with the circumstances in which we find ourselves. Whether we're chatting hip-hop, turning twinkies into poo, hitting on our mothers, or becoming famous artists – our actions are explained not by our character, but by the situations in which we find ourselves. In school, notes are passed. On a camping trip, you get in touch with nature. Chris's actions cannot be accounted for on a traditional account of character – but we *can* account for his actions when we are sensitive to the contexts in which Chris is acting. Oh, yeah, and the same thing applies to Meg.[9]

Character As Bad Faith: The Existential Perspective

Also opposing the Aristotelian conception of character is existentialism, a philosophical and literary movement with its roots in 19th and 20th-century Europe. Existentialism emphasizes the fundamental freedom of human beings. Indeed, as French philosopher Jean-Paul Sartre (1905–80) bluntly puts it: "man is condemned to be free." To claim that our character determines our action – that we act the way we do *because* of our character – is simply to misunderstand what it means to be a human being. We *are free*, Sartre says, although we constantly run in fear from this astonishing fact. We run precisely because to face our freedom is to face the dread-inspiring fact that we are totally responsible for all of our actions ("once thrown in the world, [a human being] is responsible for everything he does").

As strange as it might sound, the existentialist view is that there is no solid link between who we are now, and who we were 15 seconds ago – or for that matter, who we might be 15 seconds from now. While Aristotle insists that our character explains our actions – that it connects us to both the future and the past – the existentialist simply rejects this view. To believe that we are determined by our character is to fall prey to what Sartre calls "bad faith." Bad faith names the human tendency to think of ourselves as being like other objects in the world – likes stones, of Pawtucket Beer, or the Drunken Clam. We tend to think of ourselves as having an essence that is in some way outside of our control. If I am fundamentally a pervert, I will simply giggity-giggity whenever I can. It's not my fault. That's just the way I am.

This is a paradigm case of bad faith. We ignore the fact that we are 100 percent responsible for who we are, and cast off our responsibility by appealing to things like character. In fact, the existentialist contends, character is just an illusion. Nothingness itself separates us from our past and our future. There is an unbridgeable rift between what we have done and what we are doing; between who we are now and who we hope to be. A proverbial abyss separates us from our past and our present, and this abyss is the very essence of our radical freedom. This freedom is the source of anguish – and our lives are the persistent attempt to deal with the anguish of our freedom. The appeal to character is just one form of fleeing in the face of the human condition, of avoiding the absolute responsibility we have for our actions, the meanings of things around us, and the values we use to guide our everyday decision.

Now, I'm not suggesting for a second that Meg and Chris are pillars of responsibility. I'm not even suggesting they're existentialists (what existentialist would sing about buying a rainbow, anyway?). What I am suggesting is that the anti-characters of Meg and Chris instantiate the radical freedom that according to the existentialist *defines* the human condition. Peter, Lois, and Quagmire *always* act in predictable ways. They seem almost determined to do so by the very structure of the universe. Their characters loom large in each episode of *Family Guy*, and we thus know exactly what to expect from them.

But Chris and Meg, as I have been insisting, just aren't like that. They are not defined by any particular essential traits. As such, they are much truer to the human condition than their sometimes-well-meaning relatives. While they may not be much to look at, they do remind us of something of crucial importance, and something we often forget: we are more complicated than any particular trait. When we reduce ourselves to some set of characteristics, we prove yet again that the freedom to be what we want is too much for us. In hiding from this freedom, we are strangers even to ourselves.

So, I say to hell with Brian and Stewie! To hell with Peter, Lois, and Quagmire! Let's rethink our favorite *Family Guy* folks in terms of the anti-character. Meg and Chris are a monument to anthropological honesty. They defy our easy characterizations, and can enable us to recognize all that is wrong (or at least a few things that are wrong) with our commonsense notions of character. Meg and Chris enable us to return to existential authorship – they force us to take responsibility for our actions without appeal to character. And they map up with the psychological data too, at least if you're as flexible as I am with it. That's enough for me. I've decided that Meg and Chris will be my favorite anti-characters. They're keepin' it real. All those other characters are just one trick ponies essentially defined by one or two gags that they must inescapably repeat.

And by the way, you just got *punk'd*. You know I love Stewie. That little maniac is funny as hell.

NOTES

1   The 'P,' of course, is silent.
2   What the deuce!?! No one told me there would be math in this book!
3   In other words, it's as easy as the ratio between the circumference and the diameter of a circle, most easily expressed as 22/7ths.
4   Are you still reading these notes?
5   Peter also mistakes a monkey for Meg at one point. When the evil monkey is pointing at Peter, and Peter is running in fear (he's in the midst of

a traumatic memory of a prostate exam), he calls the monkey "Meg," and insists that he stop pointing ("Stewie Loves Lois").

6　In other words, Cristobel is still Chris, plain and simple.

7　I trust you know the answer. And it isn't because he had a bad day.

8　The experiment is reported in A. M. Isen and P. F. Levin's "Effect of Feeling Good on Helping: Cookies and Kindness," *Journal of Personality and Social Psychology*, 21, 1972, pp. 384–8. For an excellent discussion of much of the situationist literature and its relevance to moral philosophy, I highly recommend John M. Doris's *Lack of Character* (Cambridge: Cambridge University Press, 2002).

9　I would provide some more examples of Meg, but let's face it, she's just not very important.

9

HE THINKS HE'S PEOPLE:
How Brian Made Personhood for the Dogs

DANIEL MALLOY

Hi? He's a dog!

Peter, "Perfect Castaway"

[R]ational beings are called *persons* because their nature already marks them out as an end in itself, that is, as something that may not be used merely as a means, and hence so far limits all choice (and is an object of respect).

Immanuel Kant, *Groundwork of
the Metaphysics of Morals*

Brian: Portrait of a Person

We all know the Griffin clan: Peter, the overweight, sexist clod of a patriarch, Lois, the attractive, high born mother, Meg, the eldest and for some reason most detested child, Chris, the burgeoning if awkward artist, Stewie, the megalomaniacal and sexually confused infant. And then there's Brian. We're accustomed to the idea that the dog is a member of the family, but Brian challenges us to take this idea to a whole new level. Brian is not just any old dog, after all. He's bright, articulate, well read and well traveled, witty and urbane, and certainly a good deal more intelligent than the oaf he calls his master. While any dog can claim *affection*, Brian has a claim to *respect*.

Brian sometimes faces degradation, as, for example, when Peter wants him to beg for a treat in "Brian: Portrait of a Dog." Clearly, the reason such treatment is degrading is that Brian is a person. Persons *as such* are entitled to respect. The term *person* is used somewhat loosely in everyday speech. Most frequently, it is taken to be synonymous with the term *human being*, but even our legal system rejects this use. Until the 20th century, human beings were not all considered persons. Most famously, the US Constitution held that African-American slaves were the equivalent of 3/5 of a person. Likewise, women were not recognized as persons in their own right, capable of flourishing apart from men, until quite recently. Even today the term *person* is applied in legal circles well beyond the bounds of humanity. Corporations, for example, are considered legal persons. That is, corporations, like other legal persons, are bearers of rights. Our use of the term, however, does not include dogs. So, in claiming that Brian is a person, we must ask ourselves, what is it that qualifies Brian? What is it that makes Brian a person where other dogs in the *Family Guy* universe (with the possible exception of Brian's cousin Jasper) are not? This is no small matter. The debates around abortion, euthanasia, cloning, stem cell research, and genetic engineering all hinge, in some way or another, on the question of personhood.

A variety of criteria are claimed to be definitive by different sides of these debates. Some claim that all *Homo sapiens* are persons, making personhood a genetic trait. Others claim the possession of a soul is what matters, or even the possession of rationality. So let's explore how each of these possible views of personhood is handled, implicitly or explicitly, in *Family Guy*. Then we can explore the ethical implications of Brian's personhood, both in terms of how he should be treated and in terms of how we can expect Brian to act.

Why Are We Listening To A Dog?

The indignities that have been inflicted on Brian because of his dogginess are manifold. He was taken from his mother, Biscuit, when his eyes were barely open. Biscuit subsequently died and was stuffed before Brian got the chance to reconcile with her ("Road to Rhode Island"). In "Screwed the Pooch," when he sued Carter Pewterschmidt for the right to see his puppies when they were born,

100

the judge granted his claim, but on a condition that would be expected of no human being: the judge ordered Brian to be neutered (this little experience may explain Brian's subsequent hostility to Bob Barker, whom Brian wishes would "just die already" in "Chitty Chitty Death Bang"). People who don't know Brian treat him like they would any other dog. There is no malice behind these assaults on Brian's dignity, and for the most part he takes them in his stride. It seems to be only when the people who should know better treat him like a dog that Brian gets upset.

Consider "Brian: Portrait of a Dog." This entire episode centers on the family, Peter in particular, forgetting that Brian is more than simply a dog. First, Brian is asked to compete in a dog show – if he wins, the family will be able to afford an air conditioner. So far, no problem. Brian has some objections to being in the dog show, but he concedes. We've all done things we'd rather not for the sake of our families; participated in meaningless ceremonies, been polite to people we can barely tolerate, and so on. To this point, Brian is being treated with the respect due to any person. But Peter crosses the line when he expects Brian to beg for a treat at the end of his perform-ance. This is the first assault on Brian's dignity (excepting the point when the ring announcer calls him "Brain Griffin"). The indignities continue as Brian is escorted home by a police officer and fined ten dollars for being out without a leash. Brian runs away after another fight with Peter. He is subsequently denied service at a convenience store and an Italian restaurant and turned out of a bus station; all because he is a dog. When he attacks a pedestrian, Brian is restrained and sentenced to death. Thanks to Peter, he is granted a hearing before the city council where, just a few lines into his opening statements, he is rudely cut off by one of the council members, who blurts out, "Why are we listening to a dog?"

Throughout this episode, the indignities Brian suffers are justified in the same way: Brian is a dog. Dogs are not persons, and therefore not entitled to respect. The implicit reasoning here is that in order to be a person, one must be human. A council member even concedes that Brian might meet other criteria for personhood, but in the eyes of the council, he lacks one necessary condition of personhood: humanity.

I am not going to argue that Brian is, in fact, human. Brian is a dog. There's no denying that. But I will argue that you don't need to be a human to be a person. As we've seen, legally speaking, humanity is not a requirement for personhood. Corporations are not human beings, or even biological beings, and yet they are regarded as legal persons. Likewise, not all humans are regarded as persons. It is only relatively recently that women and non-whites have (correctly) been granted the status of personhood. Children and the mentally ill are still, more often than not, denied personhood. They have some rights, but do not bear the full range of rights entitled to a person. So, even though Brian is a dog, this does not justify treating him as a non-person.

In the premier episode of *Family Guy*'s reincarnation on network television, "North by North Quahog," Brian faces another challenge to his personhood, this one with some explicit reasoning. After Peter and Lois leave for their second honeymoon, placing Brian in charge of the household, our hero has some trouble keeping the peace between Meg and Chris. After he tells them to settle down, Chris responds, "I don't have to listen to you! You're a dog! You don't have a soul!" The implication, of course, is that Brian is not deserving of respect, and therefore is not a person, because he lacks a soul.[1] There are two ways we could understand what Chris is claiming. On the one hand, we could interpret Chris as meaning that Brian is not human and therefore does not have a soul and is thus not a person entitled to respect. This is simply a variation on the argument discussed above, and is dealt with using the same reasoning.

The idea that only human beings have souls is actually a relatively new one – through the late Middle Ages it was believed that all living things had souls. What made human beings unique was the possession of a rational, immortal soul. This gives us the key to the second possible interpretation of Chris's argument. On this interpretation, Chris's claim is that Brian, as a dog, is not a rational being – the soul being the faculty of rational thought. Only in modern times, particularly in the philosophy of René Descartes (1596–1650), came the belief that only human beings had souls as such, identifying the soul exclusively with the faculty of thought itself. Descartes argued in his *Discourse on Method* that all of the functions formerly ascribed to the soul, which included all of the functions of life like eating and reproduction, could be explained mechanically. The only exception to this rule was thought.

But there's a problem. The only person I know for certain is thinking is me – with everyone else, I'm just guessing (based on some evidence). They may be thinking, or they may be very sophisticated machines designed to mimic thinking. The point is that it is impossible empirically to judge whether or not a given being has a soul. After all, one can't simply look and see if someone has a soul. Chris obviously believes that Brian does not have a soul simply because he is a dog – but this is not a sufficient reason. Does Brian behave like a thinking being? Certainly he does – in some ways, more so than the other members of the Griffin clan.

In arguing that Brian is in fact a person, I want to call on an ally who may seem out of place in this argument, the 18th-century German philosopher Immanuel Kant (1724–1804). For those unfamiliar with Kant, allow me to explain why he may seem an unusual ally. Kant developed an ethical theory that is notoriously difficult to apply to animals. That ethical theory, however, also centers on the concept and importance of the person. Kant's ethical theory is deontological, which means that it focuses on questions of duty. For Kant, all of our duties flow from a single moral law, called the categorical imperative. He gives a few formulations of this law, but we will only discuss one at the moment: "So act as to treat humanity, whether in your own person or in that of any other, always as an end and never merely as a means."[2]

On the face of it, this would not seem to help our discussion of Brian. The categorical imperative tells us to treat humanity in a certain way; it mentions nothing about dogs. However, Kant's use of the word "humanity" is not as narrow as we might believe. The term humanity, as it is used in Kant's formulation, is a placeholder for the idea of a being with a rational nature. Such beings with rational natures could include angels, extraterrestrials, and perhaps exceptional dogs. For Kant, what made a being a person was not membership in a particular species, but possession of the faculty of reason. To the extent that we can test for this faculty, Brian clearly has it.

Thus, Brian is a person so long as he is rational. If we accept this criterion, then it is immoral to treat Brian with disrespect simply because he is a dog.

Bad Dog!

Now that we have established that Brian is a person, we can discuss in greater depth what that means. Persons must be treated in particular ways. We can't treat fellow persons in the same way that we treat mere things. Kant's way of expressing this essential moral insight was that persons should be treated as ends in themselves, and never merely as means. Broadly speaking, we must acknowledge a person's goals as just as valid as our own and not interfere with the pursuit of those goals. When we treat someone as a means, rather than as an end, we do not acknowledge their freedom to pursue their own course.

Stewie provides us with a perfect example of treating a person as merely a means, rather than as an end. While staying with his grandparents, Stewie steals his grandmother's necklace and frames the maid for the theft. Why does Stewie do such a horrible thing? In his words, he does it to "provide a little after dinner entertainment" ("Road to Rhode Island"). Stewie violates his grandmother's right to her property and costs the maid her job and probably her freedom for his own entertainment. He uses both women as means for his own amusement without respecting them as ends. This points us to another way of formulating Kant's categorical imperative. We should only act on those maxims (reasons) that we can at the same time will to be universal laws – in other words, that everyone could act on. To paraphrase, we should only do things that we can at the same time rationally consent to everyone else doing. Kant illustrates this formulation with the example of a man who wants to lie in order to get a loan that he has no intention or ability to repay. What if everyone did this? Suppose we lived in a world where everyone lied all the time just to get what they wanted (I know, we do; just go with me here). If that were the case, then no one would believe anyone else – our would-be liar couldn't get his loan at all. This formulation makes us ask whether we would want everyone to act in the way we are acting. Would Stewie want someone else to frame him for a crime in the name of after dinner entertainment? Stewie is certainly strange – but this hardly seems likely.

To respect a person is simply to acknowledge them as a person; someone with their own hopes, dreams, desires, wishes, and valid reasons. To treat a person as an end rather than as a means might demand as little as not interfering with their plans. In Brian's case, he is often respected, in spite of his being a dog. The end of the episode "Brian: Portrait of a Dog" is one such instance. After having been barred from drinking from a water fountain earlier in the episode, Brian's path is cleared so that he can take a drink. In "The Thin White Line," Brian's family and friends hold an intervention. Now, on the face of it, this might not seem respectful: confronting a substance-abuser with the consequences of his actions in order to shame him into changing his ways is hardly an act of non-interference. However, the point of an intervention is not to force the substance-abuser into rehabilitation. It is to confront him with facts and let him make a choice. (If you've forgotten, Brian chooses rehab.) In another instance, Brian chooses to leave his family and seek his fortune in Hollywood ("Brian Does Hollywood"). The family, in spite of their feelings, stands aside so Brian can pursue his dreams.

As a person, Brian is entitled to respect in this sense. But isn't this just the "Golden Rule" (Do unto others as you would have them do unto you)? Are we giving Kant credit for something that isn't particularly new? The parallel to the Golden Rule is actually misleading. Telling so-called little white lies can be justified under the Golden Rule; for Kant's categorical imperative, however, lying is always wrong. To take an example from *Family Guy*, in the episode "A Very Special *Family Guy* Freakin' Christmas" a minor subplot concerns Lois and Brian. Lois gives Brian a Christmas sweater, which he hates. She insists that he wear it and Brian, rather than tell Lois how he feels about the sweater, concedes. By Golden Rule reasoning, Brian could be seen as doing the right thing: he wouldn't want Lois to tell him that she hated a gift from him, and so he pretends to like the sweater. Under the categorical imperative, however, Brian is not treating Lois with respect. He is presuming that she needs protection from the truth – in other words, Brian is treating Lois like a child. In another instance, Brian gives the family sugar pills that he claims are sedatives in order to calm them down. Under the Golden Rule, he is probably doing the right thing – under the categorical imperative he is not.

This example brings up the flipside of personhood. Along with Brian's rights as a person come certain responsibilities. Brian is not just protected by the categorical imperative; he must also strive to obey it. The duties he is owed correspond to the duties he owes. Aside from being the family pet, Brian is also frequently the family conscience. Although Lois plays that role in many episodes, she herself goes over the edge sometimes ("Breaking Out is Hard to Do," "Lethal Weapons"). In these cases, Brian steps up. At other times, Lois simply isn't around or isn't the first to find out about one of the family's infractions. When Peter convinces the Grant a Wish foundation that Chris is terminally ill in order to save "Gumble 2 Gumble" ("If I'm Dyin', I'm Lyin'"), Brian is the first to respond ethically. Upon discovering Peter's fraud, Brian responds, "My god, you're a monster." This role of family conscience makes sense, as Brian, more than just being a person, is usually a pretty good person, at least by the standards of the *Family Guy* universe. But even so, Brian is no saint. Let's look at some of Brian's duties under the categorical imperative and how he fulfills or fails to fulfill them.

You Want Me To Be A Crazy Animal?!

Brian is generally a good person. He tends to treat people, whether they are strangers, family members, or friends, with a degree of respect. But, like all of us, Brian has his moral lapses. Often, these lapses are responses to perceived slights. Brian, like many other booze hounds, can have a bit of a temper. In "Brian: Portrait of a Dog," Brian attacks a pedestrian after he has been severely mistreated and the pedestrian in question has called him a "crazy animal." A similar incident occurs in "North by North Quahog" when Brian and Stewie frame Jake Tucker by planting cocaine in his locker as revenge for Jake letting Chris take the fall for his vodka. These are two of the few occasions where Brian does something morally wrong to someone outside the family. These cases may seem somewhat ambiguous – there are mitigating circumstances in each. But, if we follow the categorical imperative, mitigating circumstances don't matter. What matters is intent. Brian intended to hurt the pedestrian, just as he intended that Jake Tucker would "get it," in the words of Black-u-weather meteorologist Ollie Williams. Another incident where Brian violates his duties to strangers is in the episode "The Thin White Line." Under the guise of carrying out his duties as a drug-sniffing dog, Brian assaults an airline passenger looking for cocaine. Brian's intent here is not to do his job and prevent drugs from entering the country, but to find cocaine for his own use, which the passenger does not have.

More often, Brian violates his duties to members of the Griffin family. This makes sense; Brian is, after all, the family dog. It's only natural that the majority of his interactions would be with the family. Let's focus on his interactions with two people: his best friend Peter, and his apparent nemesis Stewie. In Peter's case, Brian generally respects him and treats him as an equal, although he seems to find it difficult at times. Brian's most common form of disrespect toward Peter is simple condescension. In fact, one of Brian's first lines of dialogue in the series is "Peter, it's after seven and you still have your pants on. What's the occasion?" Later in that same episode ("Death Has a Shadow"), Brian hits Peter with a rolled up newspaper to admonish him for lying to Lois. Normally, Brian's acts of disrespect toward Peter are motivated in one of two ways. Either he is trying to get back at Peter for some perceived slight, as when he storms out of the house in "Brian: Portrait of a Dog" and "Peter's Got Woods," or he is in some way attempting to help Peter. The rolled up newspaper is just one example of this, and one of the better ones because in it Brian is trying to help Peter do the right thing. At other times, Brian disrespects Peter in the course of helping Peter carry out his own misguided plans. In "Peter, Peter Caviar Eater," for instance, Brian goes so far as to torture Peter in order to help him carry out his plans to blend in with Lois's well-born peers. Later in the same episode, Brian destroys one of Peter's most prized possessions, a *Star Wars* collector's glass, in an attempt to undo the damage he's done.

Brian disrespects Stewie in a variety of ways and for a variety of reasons. Often, the reason is simple revenge, as when Brian convinces Stewie that his immunization shots were, in fact, a mind control serum in "Fore Father." Brian's motivation in this case is to get back at Stewie for ruining his collection of first editions. (Stewie used them to make papier-mâché.) On another occasion, Brian allows Stewie to believe something he knows to be false (that Jolly Farm is real), by simply not telling him the truth ("Road to Europe"). Brian's reason for this omission is a good one: he knows Stewie won't believe him anyway, and so it's better for Stewie to see through the illusion for himself. In this case, Brian does the wrong thing, or at least a morally ambiguous thing, but apparently for the right reason. In yet another instance, Brian frames Stewie for urinating on the carpets

("Brian in Love"). In this case, Brian's reason is simply that he doesn't want to get blamed and, well, no one listens to Stewie anyway. (The eternal question of *Family Guy*: can anyone but Brian understand Stewie?)

Lastly, let's consider the duties that Brian is perhaps least likely to fulfill: his duties to himself. Kant's categorical imperative makes clear that we are not even allowed to treat *ourselves* with disrespect; we are to treat humanity (rational nature), whether in ourselves or others, as an end and never merely as a means. As rational beings, as persons, we owe respect even to ourselves. This is perhaps Brian's greatest failing – he often fails to respect himself. Consider Brian's single most prominent character trait, aside from being a talking dog: Brian is also a drunk. (We won't even mention his brief cocaine habit in "The Thin White Line.") One of his most memorable lines from early in the series attests to this: "Hey, barkeep! Whose leg do you have to hump to get a dry martini around here?" ("I Never Met the Dead Man"). Now, some might say that drinking alcohol as such is not an act of disrespect to oneself. This is perfectly true, provided we add the words, "in moderation." Moderation, though, is what Brian usually lacks, drinking to excess more often than not. Such over-indulgence is an act of disrespect because, as many of us know from harsh, blurrily remembered experience, drinking in excess leads to making a fool of yourself, if you're lucky. If you're unlucky, it leads to jail time and community service and having your license revoked, as it has for Brian on at least one occasion ("Brian Wallows and Peter's Swallows"). And then, there are the health hazards of excessive drinking. I'm not sure how dog physiology handles alcohol, but if it's anything like human physiology, then Brian's liver is not his friend.

Other instances of Brian's lack of respect for himself seem to stem largely from his dual status as both a dog and a person. Aside from causing problems for his human companions, this dual status presents something of a quandary for Brian himself. For instance, in "Screwed the Pooch," Brian is caught masturbating and attempts to apologize to Lois. Lois tells him it's all right, to which Brian responds that it is not, in fact, all right because "I should be able to control my baser instincts." And he should. That's part of what being rational is all about. But Brian isn't just rational. He's a rational dog. As such, aside from rationality, he has millennia of breeding that lead him to act in certain ways – ways that are not always for the best, for himself or those around him. Brian seems to acknowledge this conflict in the episode "Don't Make Me Over," when he apologizes for barking and growling at Dr. Diddy. He claims that the habit comes from his father, and he does everything he can to make amends. This, of course, is not an instance of Brian lacking self-respect – it merely illustrates the conflict between Brian's dogginess and his rationality.

In other instances, Brian does things that self-respecting humans would not, but dogs do. For example, he openly acknowledges that he "uses his tongue for toilet paper" ("Running Mates"). At the end of "Brian: Portrait of a Dog," he licks Peter's face (and then warns him that if he ever tells anyone about it, he'll kill him). He wants to sleep at the foot of Peter and Lois's bed and when he can't (because the space is occupied by James Woods), he sleeps outside their bedroom door ("Peter's Got Woods"). These are instances where Brian displays a lack of self-respect, but they may be forgiven him as he is simply playing out his doggy nature.

On at least two occasions, Brian uses the conflict of his dual nature to his advantage. First, in "Brian: Portrait of a Dog," Brian attacks a pedestrian, claiming he is just acting the crazy animal he's accused of being. Then, in "North by North Quahog," Brian scoots his butt across the Tuckers' carpet, a perfectly normal, if widely discouraged, dog behavior, as an act of revenge against Tom Tucker for his refusal to help get Chris out of trouble.

So far, we've focused on Brian's violations of his duties as a person because, well, they're generally funnier than his fulfillment of those duties. But it should be remembered that most of the time Brian is a good person and occasionally even the moral guiding light of the Griffins. When Lois becomes a kleptomaniac in "Breaking Out is Hard to Do," it is Brian who talks her into giving herself up and returning everything she's stolen. When Peter loses his job the first time in "Death Has a Shadow," it is Brian who counsels him to tell Lois rather than lie to her. When Peter returns from his time as a castaway in "The Perfect Castaway," it is Brian who sacrifices his own happiness for the sake of the family. But, just as often as Brian is the conscience of the family, he plays the role of Peter's accomplice. We have all had that friend, or, in some cases, been that friend, who would talk others into doing things they shouldn't. Peter is that friend for Brian. He is, in the words of the rehab clinic director from "The Thin White Line," Brian's X-factor. In that episode, Brian goes along with Peter in pulling a prank on a camp full of pregnant teenagers. In "Wasted Talent," he helps Peter drink himself silly looking for Pawtucket Pat's silver scroll; he goes along with Peter in trying the PermaSuds in the brewery, after they've been told not to. In "Death Has a Shadow," he helps Peter drop thousands of dollars from a blimp during the Super Bowl. He acts as Peter's accountant when Peter essentially enslaves the native village that Chris has been sent to help in "Jungle Love." He goes along with Peter's plans when he ruins Lois's production of the *The King and I* in "The King is Dead." He sticks by Peter in his failed attempt to secede from the US and annex Joe Swanson's pool in "E. Peterbus Unum." And, in spite of his objections, in "The Story on Page One" he helps Peter in his failed attempt to prove that Luke Perry is gay.

Hi? He's A Dog!

In the end, what does it all mean? Brian the dog is Brian the person. He has rights, like any other person (including, apparently, the rights of citizenship. Twice in the series, in "Death Has a Shadow" and "Don't Make Me Over," Brian makes comments about how he votes). His rights must be respected, although they frequently are not. Usually, as we've seen, this comes down to Brian being a dog. Sometimes, though, his rights are trampled on for the same reason the rest of us have our rights trampled. You don't have to be a dog to be disrespected. Stewie, in particular, seems to take a special joy in disrespecting Brian not because he's a dog, but simply out of dislike. In fact, Stewie seems to enjoy pointing out the fact that Brian is a dog as an act of disrespect in itself. Stewie frequently uses the word "dog" in the way that a white racist might use the word "boy." Brian's dogginess is no more a justification for disrespect than someone's race – he is still a person, a rational being deserving of respect. Nor is his species a sufficient reason for his lack of respect for himself or others. He is owed respect and owes it in return. As Peter says in "Brian: Portrait of a Dog," "All Brian's ever wanted is the same respect he gives us. Well, that and Snausages. He's mental for those Snausages."

NOTES

1 True fans of the show know that Brian does in fact have a soul. One scene in *Stewie Griffin: The Untold Story* shows us Brian in the after life, enjoying a drink with the likes of Kurt Cobain, Ernest Hemingway, and Vincent Van Gogh.

2 Immanuel Kant, *Groundwork of the Metaphysics of Morals*, trans. and ed. Mary Gregor (New York: Cambridge University Press, 1997), p. 38 (some changes in the translation).

PART III

HE-HE-HE-HE-HE. YOU EXPECTED MORE LYRICS, BUT YOU'RE GETTING LOGIC, COMEDY, AND THE LOGIC OF COMEDY

10

THE LOGIC OF EXPECTATION:
Family Guy and the Non Sequitur

JONAH P. B. GOLDWATER

Family Guy is known for its absurd, non sequitur humor. Philosophy is known for its sober and logical approach to reality.[1] Non sequitur is Latin for "does not follow." Logic, on the other hand, is the study of what must follow.[2] Non sequitur humor thus seems to be the very essence of the illogical.

So, it doesn't look like philosophy and *Family Guy* can be friends. But let's not be misled by first impressions. Although non sequitur humor may appear not to follow from what came before, the jokes are not completely random. Though what happens may often seem illogical, it is almost never alogical. A non sequitur is only non sequitur relative to a sequence – and it's only surprising relative to an earlier expectation.

Though no philosopher, Peter Griffin himself recognizes this principle. When following several soldiers out of the cover of the jungle, Peter emerges dressed as a clown, and says, "You're all stupid. See, they're gonna be looking for army guys" ("He's Too Sexy for His Fat"). Peter has created his own non sequitur based on the expectation of what is supposed to follow – namely, another soldier. There is both a logic and a psychology (a "psycho-logic") to this sort of humor. So let's investigate how philosophy and logic can work together to understand the *Family Guy* non sequitur – and also the structure of the universe, if we have time.

Robots, Paradoxes, and Explosions

What does logic have to do with philosophy anyway? Because philosophers cannot simply accept beliefs dogmatically, they have to make arguments – give reasons – for their beliefs. Often times this consists of appealing to other, hopefully less debatable beliefs, in which case the connections and relationships between all those beliefs become very important. The moral of the story is that philosophers must be able to evaluate these connections and relationships. The laws of logic are the rules of the game according to which the connections between beliefs are judged. And when one idea is connected to a previous idea logically – according to the rules – it is said to follow from that idea.

Philosophers have long been impressed by the power of the laws of logic. For instance, medieval philosophers often wondered whether logic's power was so great that it could even constrain God, who was assumed to be omnipotent. Perhaps even God was not capable of doing things that were logically impossible, like making a rock so large even God couldn't move it.[3]

Given the power ascribed to the laws of logic, philosophers have been intrigued by the power of the contradiction to apparently break these laws, and thereby stop logic in its tracks. But this, for once, is an interest that philosophers may share with the general public. Because robots are essentially logic machines, they seem particularly susceptible to the disruptive threat of contradictions. When Peter is appointed president of a tobacco company, he gets his own simpering yesman ("Mr. Griffin Goes to Washington"). Aggravated by the kowtowing, and knowing the yesman must agree with and compliment him, Peter sets a trap. When Peter says "I hate myself," the yesman responds quickly "I hate you too." Peter replies "but I'm the president," to which the yesman responds "The best there is." Peter's trap has worked, and he interjects "but you just said you hated me." The yesman is caught, and stammers "but not you, the president, the you who said you hated you, hate, love . . ." This contradiction makes the yesman's head explode and reveals him to be a robot. Elsewhere, Peter wonders if certain ideas might blow up his own head. "I got an idea. An idea so smart my head would explode if I even began to know what I was talking about" ("Lethal Weapons").

Unlike robots, our human lives are often less than logical. And that makes life, well, funny. Søren Kierkegaard (1813–55) wrote: "Wherever there is life, there is contradiction, and wherever there is contradiction, the comical is present."[4] He was not the only philosopher to recognize the link between the illogical and the comical. Ludwig Wittgenstein (1889–1951) "said that a philosophy book could be written consisting of nothing but jokes: these would be based on fallacies, category mistakes, and other confusions about the logic of different concepts and arguments."[5]

Similarly, but more technically, Arthur Schopenhauer (1788–1860) wrote: "It is possible to trace everything ludicrous to a syllogism in the first figure, with an undisputed major and an unexpected minor, which to a certain extent is only sophistically valid, in consequence of which connection the conclusion partakes of the quality of the ludicrous."[6] Wow. Are your sides splitting? Someone get this man a microphone. With a sense of humor like this, it may shock you to learn that Schopenhauer was one of history's great pessimists.

But humor is not entirely illogical. Logic concerns inferences, the thoughts that one should have as a result of a prior thought. Humor also relies on having a particular thought as a result of a prior thought; humor relies on inferences too. But often times the difference between a logical inference and a comical inference is that a logical conclusion is expected in a way a punchline (a comical conclusion) is not. Instead, a punchline is somehow opposed to the inference one should have had.[7]

Philosophers often insist that the study of logic is not the study of how the brain or mind actually thinks. Instead, logic represents an ideal way of thinking – the way people should think, in theory – as opposed to the psychology of how people actually do think, in practice.[8] It may be possible to accuse me of equivocating different senses of logic, or conflating what is logical and what is psychological. But to those who accuse me of equivocating and conflating, I follow Peter Griffin in his response to the drug counselor at the rehab clinic when she accused him of being a degenerate. Oh yeah, "well you're a fastizio. See? I can make up words too" ("The Thin White Line").

The Clam or the Town?

Part of the popularity of *Family Guy* surely stems from its novel forms of humor. But there's no use reinventing the wheel, especially with so much good TV on. So *Family Guy* employs a traditional approach to humor based on ambiguity. A word or phrase is ambiguous when it has more than one possible meaning. Because each of these meanings is the basis for making an inference or expecting a certain sequence of words or phrases to follow, ambiguity allows different logical sequences and expectations to develop at the same time. But we can typically only have one such expectation in mind, especially when we aren't on guard for other meanings. And by selecting one meaning, and not another, we create the opportunity for the unexpected. When what subsequently occurs is in fact different from what we expected – when we have the wrong expectation – the incongruity is often humorous.

That might have been a little abstract. So let's analyze some jokes. After a boozed up Peter reveals his talent for piano, Lois exclaims: "You can only play piano when you're drunk!" Peter then replies: "That's not true. I can also vomit, fall down, and make dirty calls to your sister when I'm drunk" ("Wasted Talent"). The joke is based on the ambiguity of *only*. Lois intended her comment to mean something like: "out of all the times that are, the only times you are able to play piano are times when you are drunk," and this is how we are to understand it as well. But Peter's reply suggests that he understands Lois as saying something more along the lines of: "when you are drunk, you are only able to do one thing, which is play the piano," to which Peter naturally objects. Here's a philosophical-sounding question: Does the sentence "really" mean one or the other? The sentence is ambiguous, and may mean either, or both. But because one is more "obvious" or "natural," for whatever reason, a joke is created when the expectation of the obvious is shown to be wrong, and the less obvious is shown to be right (which is funny, I tells ya).

Here's another example. When Peter gets his favorite high school teacher, Mr. Fargas, off his medication, Fargas leads his students in dropping endangered California condor eggs off the roof of the school ("Running Mates"). Lois exclaims: "Ohmigod! He's going to wipe that species off the face of the earth!" Peter replies: "No, Lois, the janitor will do that." Here, the ambiguity is between a metaphorical and literal sense of wipe, the selection of which changes the (ambiguous) reference of the pronoun *he*.

Remember, logically minded philosophers care about what inferences are allowable or available from any given statement. But depending on which interpretation of a statement one takes, different inferences are available. If the only time Peter can play piano is when he's drunk, we probably can't infer anything about his respiratory system. But if Peter can do exactly one thing when he's drunk, namely play piano, then we might worry that when he's drunk he will be unable to breathe, and someone should call an ambulance. Many philosophers at the beginning of the twentieth century thought almost every sentence in our everyday ("natural") language was somehow ambiguous, and therefore our natural language did not transparently or obviously let us know what inferences were genuinely allowable. This created a big job for logically minded philosophers, like Bertrand Russell (1872–1970), who felt that ideally, every sentence should be "disambiguated" so as to reveal its true logical skeleton. An entire notation was invented to aid in clarifying the difference between statements like "out of all times, just the drunk times" and "if drunk, only piano." This way, when writing in such logical notation, one could always avoid ambiguity, as well as insure only valid inferences. But it's not all as rosy (or as fun) as this sounds. If language were disambiguated, how could anyone make a joke? Clearly, this whole project of disambiguation was an attempt to undermine this basis of humor.

But philosophy and comedy aren't really on such opposite pages here as I've made it seem (you know, to trick you. Sucker. Also, everything I say is a lie. Except that. And that. And that ("If I'm Dyin', I'm Lyin'")).[9] The non sequitur does not follow at all, as its name demands, and so is in fact illogical. The non sequitur does not normally come out of nowhere. Instead, it relies on "reversing" a specific expectation of the audience. Instead of a hidden or ambiguous logic, the non sequitur involves doing precisely the opposite of the logical expectation. (Let's see Lord Russell try and ruin that.)

Staying Out of Character

Family Guy non sequiturs are commonly reversals based on character.[10] If acting in character is something of a logical consequence of
having that character, then acting out of character is illogical and a
basis for humor. But instead of simply acting out of character in any
old way, for comedic effect *Family Guy* often uses something more
like a role reversal, where one set of characteristics is exchanged
for an opposite, but so related, set. Like when the Supreme Court
Justices, surely (perceived to be) a paragon of seriousness and deco-
rum, put their newest inductee through a fraternity style hazing
ritual, complete with beer chugging and demeaning challenges of
dexterity involving the butt muscles, traffic cones, and a cherry
("Let's Go to the Hop"). Or the time when the pope, normally
assumed to have a character of joyous devotion to his religious
duties, is portrayed as a reluctant and lazy teenager, who needs to be
told that "the floor is not a hamper" and who grumbles about being
woken up early and forced to wear his "stupid hat" ("Road to
Europe"). Or when Grizzly Adams and Ben, the rugged outdoorsman
and wild beast, are portrayed as a bickering domesticated couple.
And of course there is Stewie, a baby, who instead of loving his
mother wants to kill her.

Stewie – a master of the non sequitur – aside from being a matricidal maniac, is also something of a popinjay, a grandiloquent dandy
who would feel right at home using delightful anachronisms like
popinjay, grandiloquent, and dandy. These characteristics are the
precise opposite of the expected characteristics of a baby. Babies, who
typically cannot even control their own bowels, are rarely haughty
and condescending. Yet when Stewie is being potty trained, he yells:
"Listen you, I'll use these facilities when I'm damn well ready! Until
then you shall continue to sanitize my crevice and be damn grateful
for the opportunity!" ("Brian in Love"). Babies, typically being pre-
verbal, are certainly not users of pompous and esoteric language. Yet
Stewie calls Lois a "contemptible harpy" ("Death has a Shadow"),
and rails against the denial of "The fruition of [his] deeply laid plans
to escape from that cursed ovarian Bastille" ("Death has a Shadow").
Babies, far from being dandies, excessively concerned with fashion
and appearance, are virtually unaware of whether they are nude or

not. Yet Stewie slaps his drama teacher "for wearing blue socks with purple pants" ("From Method to Madness") and refuses to face his rival, Santa Claus, with a wet diaper ("A Very Special *Family Guy* Freakin' Christmas").

Because these characteristics are typical for an aristocrat of many years ago, it's no surprise that Stewie sees himself as out of touch with his contemporaries. Stewie picks up the phone and immediately says, "Hello, operator? Hello? God, that's right, you have to punch in the numbers nowadays" ("Road to Rhode Island"); Stewie tries to give romantic advice to Meg's friend at Meg's slumber party: "Let's try some role playing. I'll be Mark. And you ask me out to the . . . box social or whatever the devil you children are doing these days" ("15 Minutes of Shame"). These sorts of jokes are not just "randomly" out of character, but involve acting out of character in a certain way – namely, the opposite of the obvious characteristics of being a baby.

But acting in character may be humorous as well. Roger Scruton (1944–) writes that in satire, "the action is so much in character that we cannot but laugh."[11] When Stewie says, "Uh you've reached Stewie and Brian, we're not here right now, uh, and if this is mom, uh, send money because we're college students and we need money for books, and highlighters, and ramen noodles, and condoms for sexual relations with our classmates" ("Brian Goes Back to College"), the simple listing of attributes is funny just because it aptly describes a kind of character. But one of the twists *Family Guy* makes on this idea is that often times statements or actions are indeed entirely appropriate for a character, but the character has been transplanted to the wrong body. When Death finds some frat boys dead from alcohol poisoning, he decides to drink their beer. He then stumbles towards the car moaning "aw jeez," and "oh, man, I hope I don't get pulled over" ("Wasted Talent"). Death then tells himself to "be cool" and "maintain," before chewing some gum to hide the smell of alcohol on his breath. This is completely out of character for Death, who is neither unable to hold his liquor nor subject to authority, but satirically in character for a frat boy.

The comedy of acting in character but out of body is best illustrated when Chris, trying to lose weight, stops swimming like a human, and starts leaping like a salmon, and is then caught and eaten by a bear – which of course is entirely in character for a salmon

121

("He's Too Sexy for His Fat"). The person is out of character, but the character is in character. This combines a role reversal (the illogical opposite of logical character expectation – Chris is no fish!) and satirical accuracy (bears do eat salmon!) in a satisfactory manner. (That's the funniest way I could think of to say that.)

Often times, rather than the reversal of an entire person's character, a *Family Guy* non sequitur consists of the reversal of a characteristic expected of a given scenario. No matter how exotic the scenes, or how perilous the situation, *Family Guy* characters never abandon their everyday relations and concerns. When trying to escape a gun-wielding hotel manager, for instance, Brian and Stewie stop to argue about which getaway car to steal based on various aesthetic and social criteria. Stewie rejects Brian's first choice of an SUV, saying "we're trying to elude someone, not driving to soccer practice." He then chooses a darker colored car because it won't "show dirt," even though for Brian "it's just so dark" ("Road to Rhode Island"). These are not appropriate fight or flight responses. They are choices reflecting a life of leisure, luxury, and status. Similarly, in the height of a dramatic life change, Brian finds Stewie's note informing the family he's run off to live on the fictional "Jolly Farm," as depicted on his favorite TV show ("Road to Europe"). The note includes a prolonged discussion about what to do about a sweater Stewie left on the bureau and has yet to return to the store, and maybe he left the receipt on the dresser, but perhaps the return policy has expired, but "if you make a fuss they'll at least give you store credit or something." In the context of running away and changing one's life, dealing with returning a sweater is inappropriately mundane. These are not random concerns in any significant sense of the term. They are simply unexpectedly and ridiculously mundane.

Another type of *Family Guy* reversal of expectation involves doing the opposite of various TV conventions concerning the pacing and duration of various events. Here's a list: Peter falls, clutching his shin and wincing in pain for an unbearably long time ("Wasted Talent"); Death laughs at Peter when Peter suggests that a lamp was Peter Griffin so Death would take the lamp away to the underworld ("Death is a Bitch"); Peter spooks Lois, she drops the glass, it breaks, and Peter laughs endlessly ("15 Minutes of Shame"); the TV executive beats a staff writer with a painting for suggesting novelty in a TV series ("If I'm Dyin', I'm Lyin'"); and, of course, Peter's epic fights with the chicken. (I could continue the list for an unexpectedly long time, but you get the point).

But I can't resist: Chris suspects his grandfather's hairy ears of being an "enchanted forest," which Lois flatly denies. We get a close up view, however, and find elves living in this enchanted forest of ear hair. The first elf says, "Let us run to the meadow and dance." The second says, "You first, I'm self-conscious" ("Holy Crap"). Instead of carefree magical elves, we find self-conscious, nervous, and awkward elves. Another non sequitur based first on a specific association with a pop culture phenomenon, then followed by character reversal, occurs when Meg and Lois each say "oh no, oh no," upon which the Kool Aid man bursts in with his catchphrase "oh yeah!" But instead of his typical boundless enthusiasm and self-assurance, he then backs out of the courtroom sheepishly and self-consciously ("Death Has a Shadow").

And Now For Something Completely Random

The species of illogical reverses of expectations discussed so far aren't the real coup de grace of the *Family Guy* non sequitur. We've been starting from a given basis from which comically to deviate. The most outrageous or random-seeming non sequitur gags are the ones that start with the phrases "Like the time I . . ." or "I haven't been this blank since I blankety blank." Not only do these jokes seem not to follow, they also simply don't seem to be the opposite of something. Instead they seem to come out of nowhere. But they don't. At least, not always.

These sorts of random jokes seem a classic example of a "stream of consciousness," a phrase coined by the philosopher and psychologist William James (1842–1910). A stream of consciousness may be a long series of a person's ideas or images, where what comes next may be only loosely linked to what came before, and is certainly not linked by any rules. It's clear that Peter and the show's writers have had many personal experiences linked through popular culture. In many seemingly random excursions into bizarro world, the scenario we witness is associated with some pop culture scenario (as in the Kool Aid case mentioned above).

Immanuel Kant (1724–1804), the last great pre-postkantian philosopher, believed that there were certain categories of thought through which minds must understand the world. There's something right about this. One's experiences and network of associated concepts color how one sees the world. Peter clearly sees the world as if filtered through the categories or concepts of television. This becomes literally true when he and Meg accidentally disrupt cable TV in Quahog. Peter misses watching TV so much that he walks around with a cardboard frame in front of his face in order to watch life as if it were on TV ("I Never Met the Dead Man"). And rather than for a more obvious reason, Peter doesn't want Death to stay at his house to convalesce because "how would we explain to it Mr. Roper?" ("Death is a Bitch"). Or the time when Peter is hoping for a big inheritance from Lois's relative, and as the lawyer speaks, Peter says excitedly: "c'mon big money, big money, big money, no whammy, no whammy, stop!" as if he were on the game show *Press Your Luck* ("Peter Peter Caviar Eater"). Because of his basic familiarity with that show, and because he finds himself in a scenario where he might get some free money, that's what pops up – that's his association.

The show's writers expect the audience to have shared many such connections with television and so join the fun of remembering a common culture. Schopenhauer wrote that "philosophy is the peculiar science in that it presumes nothing." By contrast, *Family Guy* clearly presumes a lifetime of immersion in popular culture to ground the associative links to their random jokes.

But I don't want to ruin all the fun. There are definitely some gags that seem pretty damn random. Like when Peter demands the station manager put "Gumbel to Gumbel" back on the air, and after a refusal, and a long silence, Peter wonders, "You gonna eat that stapler?" The station manager replies, "You can't eat a stapler." Before the words are barely out of his mouth, Peter asks, "Wanna split it?" ("If I'm Dyin', I'm Lyin'"). Or the time Tom Tucker calls Peter a "self-described Huguenot" ("Running Mates"). Or when Meg says: "The last time you left Dad alone, he turned the house into a giant puppet" ("Dammit Janet"). That's pretty random.

Some Final Forays Into Metaphysics

Philosophers tend to consider the universe a place of order and meaning. The ancient Greek philosophers saw the universe as a cosmic drama, often developing teleologically – towards an end, or for a purpose. Religions, especially eschatological[12] ones, see the universe the same way. Rationalism, a philosophical movement dominant in Europe in the 17th and 18th centuries, emphasized the rational order of the universe, where "thoughts and things" evolved in tandem.[13] Idealism, popular in the 18th and 19th centuries, held that the universe is dominantly mental, and so correspondingly ordered along the lines of thoughts. G. W. F. Hegel (1770–1831), perhaps the culmination of both rationalism and idealism, was ironically mostly incomprehensible. But in one of Hegel's more comprehensible dictums, he said "the rational is the actual, and the actual is rational," emphasizing the symbiosis of reason and the world.

What happens, and why, in such a reasonable world? The great rationalist Baruch Spinoza (1632–77) wrote: "It is of the nature of reason to regard things as necessary, not as contingent," and "in nature, there is nothing contingent."[14] That is, reason looks at the world and sees that everything has to happen – everything happens necessarily – because the faculty of reason sees the reason for everything happening. On the other hand, what makes an event contingent also makes it random. If an event is contingent, it might have been otherwise. And if something might not have been one way, it could have been another way, in which case it actually being one way rather than the other is arbitrary, or random. Another rationalist philosopher, G. W. Leibniz (1646–1716), championed the "principle of sufficient reason" – there had to be a, well, sufficient reason for everything.

Because having a philosophy is a sure way to get enemies, a school of philosophers called empiricists arose in the 18th century in order to oppose the rationalists. For these empiricists, like John Locke (1632–1704) and David Hume, (1711–76), the rational is not the actual at all. Hume in particular drew a strict division between the world of reason and ideas, on the one hand, and the actual world itself of facts, on the other. This meant that for Hume the perceived order and reasons for events was entirely a product of the mind (which for Hume mostly worked associatively, or subjectively, as described above), in which case the world itself, minus the imagined order, was a "mere succession," or just one damn thing after another, as the famous saying goes, without any actual logic or order to it at all. Sensing that this view lacked the grandeur and majesty of rationalism, William James (the stream of consciousness guy) wrote:

"The lowest grade of universe would be a world of mere withness, of which the parts were only strung together by the conjunction 'and.' "[15] In other words, an inferior sort of universe is one where this happens and that happens and then this happens and then that, where each thing is merely with or alongside the next, as opposed to being connected through reason. Existentialist philosophers in the 20th century, sensing this lack of connection to anything else, were lonely and smoked cigarettes, and thought that this lack of connection in the world meant there was no meaning or order to the universe, or at least to France. Instead, they thought everything was random and absurd.

I imagine one might suspect that the Quahog of *Family Guy* is such a world, where one thing happens, and then another, and then another, with no apparent order, reason or logic, and it's all just absurd.[16] But the universe of *Family Guy* is not simply a low grade one of "mere withness," as I've tried to show. It is not just one damn thing after another. Instead the humor relies on the expectation or assumption of a certain orderly progression to things. And the plot itself is typically conventionally straightforward, moving in an orderly, meaningful fashion, often times even with what the comedian Larry David calls "hugging and learning" at the end. In *Family Guy*, non sequiturs typically do not advance the plot; after a zany non sequitur, the scenario returns to normalcy. Why? Because *Family Guy* must reset our expectations at normal. For if everything were random, without any direct relation to what came before, there could be no expectation, and no presumption of logical consequence from which to comically deviate, in which case it would indeed be just one damn thing after another, which isn't actually funny. As Kierkegaard wrote, "If one proposed to make everything comical by means of nothing, it is clear at once that his comedy is nowhere at home, since it lacks a foothold in any sphere."[17] Even the most random humor relies on a logic of expectation, and *Family Guy* has taken this technique to new heights, employing the orderly universe as a support for their absurd antics, and enriching what might otherwise be a low grade universe indeed.

NOTES

1   Just as the slovenly liberal cop said when paired with the fastidious conservative cop, "I smell a sitcom!" ("To Live and Die in Dixie").

2   The Merriam-Webster dictionary defines logic as "interrelation or sequence of facts or events when seen as inevitable or predictable."

3   There are many tests that may challenge the idea of God's omnipotence. A modern variant of one is: can God microwave a burrito so hot that even he cannot eat it? (We owe this example, of course, to *The Simpsons*.)

4   Søren Kierkegaard, "Concluding Unscientific Postscript," quoted in John Morreall, ed., *The Philosophy of Laughter and Humor* (Albany: SUNY Press, 1987), p. 83.

5   John Morreall, "Introduction" to *The Philosophy of Laughter and Humor*, p. 1.

6   Arthur Schopenhauer, "On the Theory of the Ludicrous," quoted in Morreall, *The Philosophy of Laughter and Humor*, p. 55.

7   A popular theory of humor is called the "incongruity theory," which stresses that it is when something is incongruous that it is funny. Many philosophers have proposed different versions because it was realized that not all incongruities are funny. I believe the theory is somewhat off the mark. It typically does not account for the *congruity* – the close, almost logical, relationship a punchline must have to the set up in order to be funny, as I shall illustrate.

8   Though there is a "logic" to the jokes we will discuss, and I will speak of expectations as inferences, much humor also relies on the psychology (psycho-logic) of expectation, which might, strictly speaking, not be "logical."

9   Peter is employing a version of an ancient paradox, known as the Cretan's, or liar's, paradox.

10 *Character* comes from a Greek word meaning "to scratch, or engrave." Because characteristics are thought to be engraved on one's person just as marks are engraved or set in stone, *character* is a basis for assuming or expecting unchanging and consistent behavior.

11 Roger Scruton, "Laughter," quoted in Morreall, *The Philosophy of Laughter and Humor*, p. 162.

12 This word is just as dirty as it sounds.

13 "The order and connection of ideas is the same as the order and connection of things." Baruch Spinoza, *Ethics* (Princeton: Penguin), p. 35.

14 Spinoza, *Ethics*, pp. 20, 59.

15 William James, *Pragmatism* (New York: Dover Press, 1995), p. 60.

16 In which case Jerry the tobacco executive says: "Smoke!" ("Mr. Griffin Goes to Washington").

17 Søren Kierkegaard, "Concluding Unscientific Postscript," quoted in Morreall, *The Philosophy of Laughter and Humor*, p. 84.

127

11

WHAT ARE YOU LAUGHING AT (AND WHY)? EXPLORING THE HUMOR OF *FAMILY GUY*

ANDREW TERJESEN

Ken Tucker's review of the first volume of the *American Dad!* DVD in *Entertainment Weekly* was largely about *Family Guy*. Tucker doesn't think *Family Guy* is playing around – he thinks it's downright mean. "Both *Family Guy* and *American Dad!* are larded with cheap, mean humor that panders to audiences, letting them off the hook by implying that this is a parody of cheap, mean humor."[1]

I don't want to be mean, or support those who are, so we better get thinking about whether or not *Family Guy* is guilty of these accusations. We need to look at the *ethics* of humor. For example, is it morally wrong to laugh when Peter (misunderstanding Lois's objection to his plan to find a Native American high roller to pay one million dollars to sleep with her) says, "These people took 24 dollars for the isle of Manhattan. They have no idea what things are worth" ("The Son Also Draws")? Of course people *do* laugh at such remarks, but *should* they? Just like people do things they shouldn't, people laugh at things they shouldn't laugh at. To determine what we ought to laugh at, it will be helpful to consider in general what makes us laugh. Once we understand why things in general are funny, we can determine why particular jokes are funny. And once we determine why particular jokes are funny, we can figure out what it is we are laughing at and whether it's wrong for us to do so.

What Makes Things Funny?

Philosophers have proposed three main answers to the question: "Why is something funny?" The oldest answer – stretching back to

128

Plato (428–348 BCE), but most clearly expressed by Thomas Hobbes (1588–1689) – is the Superiority Theory. Hobbes describes humor in the following manner: "Sudden glory is the passion which maketh those grimaces called laughter; and is caused either by some sudden act of their own that pleaseth them; or by the apprehension of some deformed thing in another, by comparison whereof they suddenly applaud themselves."[2] So, according to Hobbes, we find something funny because it makes us feel better about ourselves – either because of something we did really well or because we see how others are inferior to us. When we see Peter struggling to answer the question "What color is a fire truck?" ("Petarded"), Hobbes would say that we laugh because we feel so much smarter than (and therefore superior to) Peter.

Sigmund Freud (1856–1939) gave a different answer to the question "Why is something funny?" According to Freud, we laugh because it helps us relieve our stress about uncomfortable topics.[3] Let's call this the Relief Theory. When we see the film used by Happy-Go-Lucky Toys for sensitivity training ("Women in the Workplace" produced in 1956), we laugh at the narrator's comments like: "Tell them how good they look every day – even if they're homely or unkempt" and "Nothing says good job like a firm open palm slap on the behind" ("I Am Peter – Hear Me Roar"). Freud would say that we find this funny because we have a lot of stress regarding how to conduct ourselves in the workplace (and in some cases because our workplace makes us uncomfortable because it has not recognized that times have changed since the 1950s).

But these theories don't explain why we find it funny when a National Geographic special on fire trucks features a fire truck hunting gazelles on the Serengeti ("Petarded"). For that we need the Incongruity Theory. Presumably we don't need to feel superior to a fire truck, and we shouldn't have any Oedipal hang-ups about them either. What's funny about the fire truck National Geographic special is that it doesn't fit with our expectations; instead it combines two things that don't go together. Immanuel Kant (1724–1804) summarizes Incongruity Theory well: "Something absurd (something in which, therefore, the understanding can of itself find no delight) must be present in whatever is to raise a hearty convulsive laugh. *Laughter is an affection arising from a strained expectation being suddenly reduced to nothing.*"[4] It may sound like Kant's description could fit

129

all humor. It certainly seems to explain the bulk of what goes on in *Family Guy* from Stewie's rendition of "Rocket Man" *á la Shatner* (". . . And the Wiener Is") to subtitles that aren't in English (beginning of "Let's Go to the Hop"). However, not everyone laughs because of incongruity. After all, racists finds a racist joke funny *because* it meets their expectations, and pratfalls can be funny even when they are telegraphed far in advance.

Our brief survey shows that there is no single, all-encompassing reason why we find things funny. This should not be surprising. Ask yourself – are buildings, people, and mountain vistas all beautiful in the same way? Obviously not. As we have seen, the three theories of humor are each well-suited for some examples but not others. Still, just because jokes don't all work the same way doesn't mean they have nothing in common. Humor has an important social function – things make us laugh for different reasons, but all that laughter has the same purpose.[5] As anthropologists have documented, humor is very useful in conveying social norms. But more on this later.

So – Why Are Parodies of Mean-Spirited Humor Funny?

For now, we'll assume that the writers of *Family Guy* aren't just pretending to do a parody of mean-spirited humor. (Later we'll actually show that it truly is a parody.) Given what we now know about why things are funny, what makes such parodies funny? It's unlikely that one particular theory of humor would apply to every example of a parody of mean-spirited humor. Fortunately, every theory of humor can be applied to such parodies.

Take, for instance, the following exchange about a beer commercial.

Announcer:	Pawtucket Patriot Beer. If you buy it, hot women will have sex in your backyard.
Lois:	Typical male fantasy – women drinking beer. I guarantee you a man made that commercial.
Peter:	Of course a man made it – it's a commercial, Lois, not a delicious Thanksgiving dinner.

("I Am Peter – Hear Me Roar")

130

According to the Superiority Theory, this is funny because it makes us feel better about ourselves. If this were actually mean-spirited humor, that would mean feeling superior to women. But this is a parody, so the person we're laughing at is anybody who would take it seriously. In other words, we feel superior to anyone who would hold such an extremely sexist view.

Consider another example. Lois decides to play video poker at the casino owned by Native Americans but only (in her words) "as long as you're not using it for fire water" ("The Son Also Draws"). We might laugh because we feel superior to Lois, but we might also laugh as a way of dealing with stress over race relations. Since it's a parody, our stress derives from the uncomfortable feeling we get knowing that there are still people who make such racist assumptions.

In many cases, the joke in a parody of mean-spirited humor will be at the expense of someone who is mean-spirited. In those situations, the Superiority Theory or Relief Theory would seem to apply. But there are some parodies that do not seem to fit this mold. Consider what Peter says to Cleveland after Peter learns of his African-American heritage: "I got no idea how to be black – except for not smiling when I get my picture taken" ("Peter Griffin: Husband, Father . . . Brother?"). The Incongruity Theory comes into play here. We expected Peter to say something really awful, but instead he invokes a far less obvious stereotype (or common one, it's not one I've heard before). In this case we laugh because Peter's racism defies our expectations.

One common thread through all of these examples is that the object of humor is the person who might make such comments, not the person the comments are about. With a parody of mean-spirited humor, we laugh at mean-spirited people, instead of laughing mean-spiritedly.

Why Is It Not Okay to Laugh at Mean-Spirited Humor, But Okay to Laugh at Parodies of It?

Aristotle (384–322 BCE) tells us virtue is determined by a thing's proper function.[6] So, virtuous (or ethical) laughter would be determined by the proper function of laughter. Although there are different theories as to why something is funny, all laughter seems to have the same function: it serves to indicate what should be avoided. After all, nobody likes to be laughed at. In many cultures, ostracism and ridicule have been used as social punishments. This continues in the modern world, definitely in high school and almost certainly beyond.

People's ethnicity, religion, and sex are irrelevant in determining their value as human beings. Presumably we all disagree when Peter says "Women are not people – they are devices built by the Lord Jesus Christ for our entertainment" ("I Am Peter – Hear Me Roar"). Instead, we would condemn such a statement and anyone who thinks such a thing. Since we judge such a belief to be one that we shouldn't hold, we should ridicule anyone who does hold that belief in the hopes of getting them to give it up.

Since parodies of mean-spirited humor target mean-spirited people we *ought* to laugh at the parodies. By laughing at them we are reinforcing the idea that no one should be like them. This is the proper function of laughter – establishing social norms – and so it is part of the domain of ethics. Which is not to say that all humor is ethical – after all, a society can adopt and enforce social norms (like slavery) that are clearly wrong. However, because humor works to shape our ideas of right and wrong, when it endorses ideas that are morally justified, we are doing the right thing when we laugh at it. On the other hand, mean-spirited humor is mean precisely because it ridicules someone for something that should not or cannot be avoided. We *shouldn't* laugh at people for being good people, because no one should be discouraged from being a good person. The most mean-spirited humor involves making fun of someone because of something they can't change (like a physical handicap). In those cases especially, it seems wrong to ridicule someone for being who they are. After all, they can't choose not to be handicapped – and if there is no choice, it is not the domain of ethics. Mean-spirited humor violates the proper function of laughter and therefore is unethical. Laughing at parodies of mean-spirited humor reminds us of these violations.

But, Can I Laugh At *Family Guy*?

We've established why it's okay to laugh at parodies of mean-spirited humor, but what we need to show now is that *Family Guy* is a parody of mean-spirited humor and not just pretending to be (as Ken Tucker alleges). This requires getting inside the heads of the *Family Guy* writers, which is no easy task (especially if you're not a font of 70s

and 80s trivia). Philosophers call this the Problem of Other Minds –
how do I know that you are a conscious creature as opposed to a
zombie? The most common solution, as explained by Bertrand
Russell (1872–1970), is that I see the similarities between your outward behavior and the behaviors I exhibit when I know that I'm
thinking. From these similarities, I conclude that you must be thinking what I would be thinking in the same situation. For example,
when I'm in pain, I scream and cry. You're screaming and crying, so I
infer that you're in pain. But what are the outward behaviors of
intending to do a parody – as opposed to *pretending* to do a parody?
Or to put it more bluntly, how do I act when I am sincerely making
fun of people who are mean-spirited and how do I act when I am
using it as an excuse to be mean-spirited?

Let's consider a controversial episode of *Family Guy*, "When You
Wish Upon a Weinstein." This episode (as the commentary on the
DVD notes) was not aired by Fox during the initial run of *Family
Guy* because Fox executives considered it anti-semitic. (It has since
been shown on Cartoon Network, TBS, and Fox – although with
changes.) "When You Wish Upon a Weinstein" centers around Peter's
attempts to get Chris bar mitzvahed in an attempt to make him
smart. In the episode, Peter sings:

> Lois makes me take the wrap
> Cause our checkbook looks like crap
> Since I can't give her a slap
> I need a Jew
> Where to find a Baum, Steen or Stein
> To teach me how to whine and do my taxes
> Though by many they're abhorred
> Hebrew people I've adored
> Even though they killed my Lord
> I need a Jew

In broadcast airings the line that was deemed most anti-semitic
has been changed to "I don't think they killed my Lord." In defending this episode, the writer (Ricky Blitt) takes two different
approaches. The first, which is probably the most common defense
for humor that could be deemed offensive, is that he himself is
Jewish and a number of Jews were asked for their opinions on the
episode. The problem with this approach is that it ignores the fact

that someone can be treated wrongly and not know it. Think of how someone can be poorly treated by people who they think are their friends. Does the fact that they don't object to being a doormat make it morally permissible?

The writer also says that those executives at Fox who thought it was offensive were not paying attention to the context of the song (and other comments that were seen as anti-semitic). In effect, they were not looking for the clues the writer left that he was *sincerely* making fun of anti-semites (as opposed to using the episode as an excuse to be anti-semitic). That the executives missed these clues is somewhat understandable, since the best parodies try to look as much like the thing they are parodying as possible and subtly exaggerate the things that they want to make fun of. It would not be a very funny parody if the words "CAUTION: THIS IS NOT AN ENDORSEMENT OF ANTI-SEMITISM" kept flashing on the bottom of the screen.

Instead, Blitt had to rely on less obvious clues (although honestly they are not that hard to miss) in the form of who is saying what. Most of the things that can be deemed anti-semitic come out of Peter's mouth (and the rest out of Lois's mouth). Seth McFarlane points out in the commentary on this episode that they had spent a season and a half establishing how stupid Peter was (only in a later episode ("Petarded") would this be officially documented). That a stupid person would say such anti-semitic things seems a strong recommendation against repeating them. By definition, an idiot is not someone to model your behavior after.

Even a casual viewer could easily realize that the anti-semitic comments were being made by a total idiot. Within the episode there are clear indicators that Peter lacks the basic reasoning skills we associate with good judgment. The whole reason Peter thinks he needs a Jew is because he used all of Lois's rainy day money buying volcano insurance. This insurance was sold to him in the following exchange:

Salesman:	According to my uncle, who's a real whiz with volcanoes, a volcano is coming this way.
Peter:	*[thinks]* I too have an uncle. *[says]* Come in.
	[Some discussion of the cost ensues]
Peter:	. . . I'm pretty sure we've never had a volcano either.
Salesman:	Well, don't you think we're overdue for one?
Peter:	Touché, salesman.

Here Peter commits an error in reasoning known as the Gambler's Fallacy – thinking that just because something hasn't happened yet, it is more likely to happen in the future. (Do you think the chances keep increasing that pigs will fly out your butt?) Moreover, when Max Weinstein gets Peter's money back, we find out that Peter signed a piece of paper that gave him no insurance coverage – it just said "volcano insurance" over and over and then at the bottom "He's signing it. He's signing it. I can't believe it."

Furthermore, when Lois accuses him of acting like a child for buying the insurance, Peter responds: "If I'm a child, then know what that makes you: a pedophile. And I'll be damned if I'm going to stand here and be lectured by a pervert." And the most obvious example of Peter's poor reasoning skills is the very premise of the episode – he thinks that converting Chris to Judaism will automatically make Chris smarter. This is another fallacy, thinking that just because two things are correlated that they must be causally related. (Most players on NBA basketball teams are over 6 feet tall – do you think joining an NBA team would make Regis Philbin 6 feet tall?) Peter's ignorance about Judaism is also evident – as he thinks that going to temple means going to something out of an *Indiana Jones* movie.

In determining who is the butt of the jokes in this episode, paying close attention to context is key. Lois also says some things that could be construed as anti-semitic. And while she is not portrayed as a complete idiot, she did marry Peter, which says something about her poor judgment. In addition, some attempts are made to correct Peter's anti-semitism. Take, for example, the following exchange:

Peter: . . . So you're saying I need a Jewish guy to handle my money.
Cleveland: Peter, not every Jewish person is good with money.
Peter: Well, yeah, I guess not the retarded ones but, but why would you even say that . . . for shock value? Geez Cleveland, there's edgy and there's offensive.

Cleveland seems a reasonable fellow and not very mean-spirited, and so it is out of his mouth we have a reasonable response to Peter's anti-semitism. It's worth noting that Peter's response also draws the line we did earlier – jokes that make fun of things people can't change are inappropriate. Even Peter accepts this principle. The difference is that he has a skewed perspective on what is intended as a joke and what is intended as a statement of fact.

Where Do *We* Draw the Line?

If Peter can understand the ethics of humor, but still misapply it, how can we be sure that we're not doing the same thing? After all, Peter thinks that Cleveland is joking because Peter thinks it's an undeniable fact that all Jews are good with money. One of the clues we look for in determining whether something is a parody is that it denies the obvious. It seems pretty clear that the show is not endorsing anti-Irish sentiment when it shows the exhibits at the Museum of Irish Heritage ("Peter Griffin: Husband, Father . . . Brother?"). And it doesn't seem to be endorsing anti-Christian sentiment when Mel Gibson falls off of Mt. Rushmore because (in Peter's words) "Christians don't believe in gravity" ("North by North Quahog").

But this subtle approach can only work if you're sure that everybody knows that what you're showing is not true. You don't have to look very far to find people who believe crazy (and false) things, for example, that a Jewish conspiracy controls the world and the Holocaust never happened. Knowing that such nutjobs exist, it would be wrong to provide them something to laugh at. That would be aiding and abetting their reinforcement of harmful social norms. For example, in the commentary on "When You Wish Upon a Weinstein," Blitt mentions a joke that was deemed too offensive. It was a parody of *E.T.* in which Peter discovers Max Weinstein in his shed after he rolled a ball in and it rolled back, followed by Peter rolling in a quarter that didn't return. In this case, we don't have the statement of an idiot; we have an action. And while one would like to think that the action is unbelievable, it did not have the proper context to indicate that it was a parody.

In using parodies of mean-spirited humor, one has an added responsibility to distance oneself from the ways in which people might use the parody as a way to get their anti-Semitic views past the Standards Board. "The Son Also Draws" provides a classic example of how this can be handled (and in a funny way using the "The More You Know" PSA style of 80s Saturday morning shows).

Stewie: Stupid, Greedy Savages.
Lois: Stewie, that's a terrible thing to say. This one particular tribe has lost its way, but most Native Americans are proud,

hardworking people who are true to their spiritual heritage. They are certainly not savages.

Stewie: Oh that's funny mother. Just this morning you said they were lazy like the dirty Mexicans. Just kidding. The Mexicans are a clean and industrious people with a rich cultural heritage.

Meg: Yeah, not like those dumb, gargantuan Swedes. Actually, the Swedes run the gamut from very short to very tall. And did you know that Sweden gave us the brilliant inventor Alfred Nobel.

Peter: Yeah, which is more than we ever got from those freeloading Canadians. Canada sucks.

On the commentary to this episode, Seth McFarlane mentions getting angry emails from Canadians about that episode (where there is no disclaimer). Of course, we have to wonder if these Canadian viewers were engaging in mock indignation, presenting a parody of those people who don't understand that jokes require context. (One can hear Peter saying, "Those silly Canadians – they're the funniest people in our country!" But not me, I'm smart enough to know the geography of Canada and wise enough not to further antagonize people who share an unguarded border with us. Unlike those can't-take-a-joke Norwegians.)

Now, one night watching an *In Search of . . .* or *Is It True?* marathon makes you realize that for every crackpot theory you can think of, there is someone out there who believes it is an undeniable fact. Does this mean that any attempt at a parody of mean-spirited humor is unethical – because someone will laugh at it for the wrong reasons? The trick here is not to focus on the fact that someone in an old bomb shelter believes it's true. Instead we need to ask ourselves how many people probably believe it's true. The more people believe it, the more we need to be careful how we frame our parody. It would probably be hard to come up with more than a handful of people who think that the Irish are an inferior race or that Christians are completely irrational. On the other hand, there are clearly large numbers of people who espouse anti-semitic ideas or assume that a young South Asian-American needs to be welcomed to this country. In those cases, one must tread more carefully, because the probability of someone missing the hint (because not all Jews are good with money) is greater.

For some people, it seems wrong to play the odds – any possible misunderstanding of what the joke is about is unacceptable. This was a concern Dave Chappelle had about his show – that people *might* be laughing too hard and for the wrong reasons at his skits – and it is one of the reasons he gave for canceling it in his *Actor's Studio* interview. Which raises the question – given the potential for abuse, why is it okay for people to produce this kind of comedy for public consumption? The short answer is that (1) this kind of humor does not cause racism to exist (so without it there would still be racist thoughts) and (2) without this kind of humor we lose a very effective way of not only making fun of racists (and therefore publicly disapproving of them), but also getting them to realize their own folly (as they laugh at Peter's stupidity and begin to realize what they are really laughing at). While it might go over some people's heads, it's not like our society is devoid of more straightforward condemnations of racism, sexism, or anti-semitism. If it were, then the context of this comedy would be very different – and even though the people who produced it might view it as a parody, there would be very little reason for the general audience to do so. Admittedly, this kind of humor requires a bit more thought than a simple pun or knock-knock joke, but that's what makes it more rewarding (and therefore a valuable addition to the repertoire of comedy).

Take that, Ken Tucker.

NOTES

1 Ken Tucker, "DVD Review: *American Dad* Vol. 1," *Entertainment Weekly* April 21, 2006.

2 Thomas Hobbes, *Leviathan*, edited by Richard Tuck (Cambridge: Cambridge University Press, 1991), Part I, Chapter 6, p. 43.

3 Freud explores this in his 1905 work *The Joke and Its Relation to the Unconscious* (London: Penguin, 2002).

4 Immanuel Kant, *Critique of Judgment*, translated by James Creed Meredith (Oxford: Oxford University Press), Section 54.

5 For another comprehensive view of humor that makes use of its function, see Simon Critchley's *On Humor* (New York: Routledge, 2002), although he sees the function of humor as being more about self-understanding than social control.

6 Aristotle, *Nicomachean Ethics*, translated by Terence Irwin (Indianapolis: Hackett Publishing, 1985), Book I, Chapter 7, p. 15.

12

THINKIN' IS FREAKIN' SWEET! *FAMILY GUY* AND FALLACIES

ROBERT ARP

If Liza Is Wrong, Then I Don't Want To Know What Right Is

In the episode "Peter Griffin: Husband, Father . . . Brother?" Peter shows Chris a family album. Believe it or not, one of Peter's relatives was a philosopher. Complete with shabby clothes, goatee, and hand rested under chin, Peter's relative is deep in contemplation when his wife asks, "Aren't you going to go look for a job?" The philosopher lifts his hand up in the air as if to make some profound claim, stares into the heavens, and responds, "Why?" The scene is hilarious – even to philosophers – because it plays on a stereotypical view of a philosopher. Philosophy is a useless endeavor for lazy people who just want to sit around doing nothing but contemplate why-questions.

However hilarious they might be, stereotypes can be harmful both morally and logically. The moral harm comes from assuming that "if one or a few are like that, then they must *all* be like that." Quagmire evidently had a couple of one-night stands, and now he seems to think that all women want sex (worse yet, sex with him!). The members of the KKK following Peter and Cleveland around in the episode "Death Lives" (Peter thinks they're ghosts) incorrectly think that all non-white people are wicked or subhuman. Think of all of the racism, sexism, ageism, and every other negative "ism" that results from people inappropriately jumping to the conclusion that "they're all like this or that." Recall Diane Simmons' claim, "Well, Tom, I just plain don't like black people" ("I Never Met the Dead Man").

The logical harm of stereotypes is that the conclusion one draws is not supported by the reasons given for that conclusion. The conclusion that "they're all like that" or "they all must have that same feature, quality, or characteristic" does not follow from and cannot be fully supported by reasons having to do with one or a few instances being "like that" or having the certain feature, quality, or characteristic. Sure, I've met my share of professional philosophers who sit around and do nothing, but I could never legitimately draw the conclusion that they *all* sit around and do nothing. In fact, contrary to popular opinion, the vast majority of professional philosophers either have jobs as professors or are looking for such jobs. Likewise, not *all* women want sex (especially with Quagmire), and to the dismay of the KKK not *all* non-white people are wicked. Stereotyping is simply bad thinking.

So, the scene depicting Peter's philosopher relative is hilarious for most people because of their incorrect perception of philosophers as lazy people, while I suspect it's hilarious for philosophers because of the absurdity associated with the flawed thinking. Logicians (people who study the principles of correct reasoning) have a term for the kind of bad thinking involved in our lazy philosopher example. They call it a fallacy and the thinking involved, fallacious reasoning. A fallacy occurs when we inappropriately or incorrectly draw a conclusion from reasons that do not support the conclusion.

Fallacious reasoning is all too common. Racists think that just because they have had a bad experience with a person of a particular race, creed, or color, then "they must all be like that." You might believe that since a famous person thinks that something is right or true, then it must be, the way Peter does when he makes the claim that "If Liza [Minnelli] is wrong [about the positive effects of taking "performance-enhancing" drugs], then I don't want to know what right is" ("Brian: Portrait of a Dog"). Instead of seeking to become an authority in a particular matter ourselves, we too often blindly accept what someone tells us as "The Gospel Truth" because we perceive them to be an authority concerning that particular matter. Think of the episode "Holy Crap" where Peter's dad, Francis Griffin, is introduced as a strict Catholic who thinks that masturbation is unnatural and evil just because the bishops of the Catholic church say so. Or, we might even conclude that all the dinosaurs died out

140

because Peter touched himself at night as a child, as the man at the museum tells Peter in the episode "Wasted Talent."

On reflection, we can see we're not justified in concluding that "they're all like that," it's true because Liza says so, masturbation is unnatural and evil (thank God!), or that the dinosaurs died out because Peter touched himself at night. In these cases, the conclusions that we draw do not follow from the reasons that are given as supposed support. In other words, these are all examples of fallacies.

Lois, Listen to Reason . . . and All of These God-Damned Definitions!

This chapter is a kind of lesson in logic. We're going to use *Family Guy* as a way to become better at reasoning ("what the deuce!?!"). To do this, we're going to have to get clear on some basic terminology (I know, you weren't expecting any homework). So here goes:

> Logic is the study of the principles of correct reasoning associated with the formation and analysis of arguments. An argument has two or more claims, one of which is known as the conclusion and it – the conclusion – is supposed to follow from and be supported by other claims known as premises.

Wow. Two sentences and four definitions. But we're really just giving names to some familiar things. Arguments pop up all the time – so we're constantly dealing with premises, conclusions, and their relation to each other. In "A Hero Sits Next Door," Joe and his family move in next to the Griffins. Peter reasons that Joe will make a great baseball player for Peter's company's team because he sees Joe's baseball awards. Peter's reasoning could be put into the form of an argument with two premises leading to a conclusion:

Premise 1   If Joe has baseball sports awards, then he is good at baseball.
Premise 2   If he is good at baseball, then he'll be good on my company's baseball team.
Conclusion   Therefore, if Joe has baseball sports awards, then he'll be good on my company's baseball team.

Where do our premises and our conclusion come from? How do we form arguments? Well, arguments are composed of claims, a

141

concluding claim (the conclusion) and at least one supporting claim (the premise). A claim is a statement, proposition, declarative sentence, or part of a declarative sentence, resulting from a person's beliefs or opinions, that communicates that something is or is not the case about your self, the world, states of affairs, or reality in general. (Try to say that ten times fast!) Claims are either true or false, and again, are the results of beliefs or opinions that people have concerning any part of what they perceive to be reality. We make our beliefs and opinions known in the form of claims. For example, "I am typing this chapter in a coffee shop" and "Cartoons, like *Family Guy*, are pictures" are claims that happen to be true, whereas "Peter Griffin was the 40th president of the US" and "Stewie is Meg's illegitimate crack-addicted baby" are false claims (although it's true that Peter was the first president of Petoria).

A claim is shown to be true or false as a result of evidence, which can take the forms of either direct or indirect testimony of your senses, explanations, the testimony of others, appeal to well-established theories, appeal to appropriate authority, appeal to definitions, and good arguments, among others. So, that I'm typing in a coffee shop is shown to be true by the direct testimony of my own senses, that cartoons are pictures is true by definition of a "cartoon," that Peter was president of the US is false because of the testimony of the senses of others and authorities, and that Stewie is Meg's illegitimate crack-addicted baby is false, presumably, because of paternity tests linking Stewie to Lois, among other forms of evidence. Some claims are difficult, or impossible, to show true or false with evidence. Claims like "God exists," "Abortion is always immoral," and "I have an immortal soul" would fall into this ambiguous category, and that's one reason why ideas, issues, and arguments surrounding these claims are considered "philosophical."

We appeal to evidence on a daily basis. In doing so, we are offering arguments with premises and conclusions. In "DaBoom" Peter thinks that his family should get into a bomb shelter in their basement for the arrival of the year 2000 because he thinks that Y2K will cause all kinds of computer malfunctions, leading to the launch of nuclear warheads and a nuclear disaster. If asked why his family should get into the bomb shelter, Peter's argument might look like the following:

Premise 1	Y2K will cause nuclear weapons to be launched in 2000, likely killing anyone not in a shelter.
Premise 2	The bomb shelter likely will keep us safe.
Premise 3	We should do what will likely keep us safe.
Conclusion	My family should get into the bomb shelter for the arrival of 2000.

Dinduction?

The argument we've just analyzed is a deductive argument. Deductive arguments are arguments in which the conclusion is meant to follow from the premises with absolute certainty. In other words, if all of the premises are true in a good deductive argument, then the conclusion is inescapable. We can extract a deductive argument from the episode "Wasted Talent." Before actually attempting to locate one of the winning scrolls for the Pawtucket Pete Brewery tour that has been hidden in a beer bottle, Peter and Brian probably thought along these lines:

Premise 1	If we drink this truckload of beer, then we'll find the scroll.
Premise 2	And if we find the scroll, then we can go on the brewery tour.
Conclusion	It follows that if we drink this truckload of beer, then we can go on the brewery tour.

Provided that the two premises are true, the conclusion absolutely must be true. There is no other conclusion that could possibly be drawn from these premises. In fact, you know exactly what the conclusion of this argument is before even seeing it, from looking at the premises alone.

But deduction isn't the only game in town. Inductive arguments ("what? More definitions? I think I need to take notes!") are arguments in which the conclusion is meant to follow from the premises with a degree of probability. In a good inductive argument, if all of the premises are true, then the conclusion is *probably* true – but only probably.

In "Wasted Talent" after Peter and Brian sneak drinks of Pawtucket Pete's forbidden "beer that never loses its carbonation," they start to float up toward the fan in the ceiling (much to their dismay as they think they will be killed by the fan's spinning blades).

143

Brian farts and notices that this release of gas causes him to descend away from the deadly fan in the ceiling. He then reasons that if Peter farts, he too will start to descend. Brian's reasoning might look like this:

Premise 1   I farted and then descended.
Premise 2   Peter is in a similar situation and is like me.
Conclusion   If he farts, then, it's likely Peter will descend too.

We can see that, given the premises, the conclusion probably or likely will be true, but not definitely. It makes sense to conclude that Peter will descend, given that Brian has descended. But the truth of Brian descending because of farting doesn't guarantee that, with absolute certainty or without a doubt, Peter *will* descend. It's still possible that Peter will not descend, so the conclusion is merely probable or likely. It just so happens to be the case that in the episode Peter does descend, but he needn't necessarily have descended. I just farted right now, but I'm not descending (although the other people in the coffee shop are moving. Now I can really spread out).

Consider anytime in a *Family Guy* episode where someone asks, "Remember the last time you tried doing something like this?" and then they show a flashback to that actual time where something embarrassing, hurtful, immoral, or just plain downright stupid has occurred. Usually this question is asked in reference to Peter as he is about to do something incredibly embarrassing, hurtful, immoral, or stupid. The idea is that if Peter engages in this activity, then it will have the same unfortunate outcome that it had the last time. The reasoning involved is inductive because the conclusion that "This time the unfortunate thing X will happen" is supported with a premise that relies upon a past occurrence where that unfortunate thing X has happened. But we can never know *for sure*, *for certain*, or *with absolute certainty* that the future will be just like the past, so we temper our conclusion by saying *it is likely that*, *it is probably the case that*, or *most likely* this or that will happen. Again, even if it's true that some stupid thing happened to Peter in the past, it doesn't follow with absolute certainty that the same stupid thing will happen to Peter in the future. In fact, in numerous *Family Guy* episodes the future becomes the present and the past, and the stupid thing that happened to Peter in the past *does not* happen to Peter again. So, the conclusion turns out to be false.

A Compelling Argument . . . You've Swayed Me, Woman

There are good arguments and there are bad arguments in both the deductive and inductive realms. A good argument, in either realm, is one where (a) the conclusion does follow from the premises and (b) all of the premises are true. If either one of these conditions is not met, then the argument is bad and should be rejected. In the deductive realm, that a conclusion follows from premises means that the argument is valid (it is invalid if the conclusion does not follow). When an argument is valid and all the premises are true it is called a sound argument. This will make it so that the conclusion absolutely, positively, without a doubt, is true, and this is a good thing! In the inductive realm, that a conclusion likely will follow from premises means that the argument is strong (it is weak if the conclusion likely does not follow). When an argument is strong and all the premises are true in the inductive realm, the argument is called a cogent argument. This will make it so that the conclusion most likely or probably is true, and this is a freakin' sweet thing too!

So we must always go through this two-step procedure of checking our own arguments and the arguments of others to see if (a) the conclusion follows from the premises (is the argument deductively valid or inductively strong?) and (b) all of the premises are true. If the argument fails to meet either (a) or (b) or both, then we should reject it, thereby rejecting the person's conclusion as either absolutely false or probably false.

For example, Brian and Peter's argument concerning the brewery tour probably is a bad one because Premise 1 seems false, given the information. It's not true that if they drink a truckload of beer, then they'll necessarily find the scroll. After all, there are probably numerous truckloads of beer. On the other hand, the farting argument was a good one. It was true that when Brian farted, he descended. And given this fact, along with Peter's similar predicament and bodily functions, Brian had a strong case for drawing the conclusion that Peter would descend as well. (Some guy just sat down next to me, so I'm going to fart again right now. Let's see if it works. Yeah, he's moving. That'll teach him.)

145

The Conclusion is Obvious: I Must Destroy All Vegetables!

Unfortunately, people will often try to convince us of the truth of claims in order to deceive us, or sell us something, or get us to vote for them, or become part of their group, or share their particular ideology. They will also try to convince us that a conclusion follows from a premise or premises when, in fact, it does not, kind of like what happens when we think that all philosophers are lazy and useless. As we've seen, deceptive arguments in which the conclusion doesn't follow from the premises are called fallacies.

One of the most common fallacies is hasty generalization. In a hasty generalization, a person incorrectly draws a conclusion about characteristics of a *whole group* based upon premises concerning characteristics of a *small sample* of the group. Most times, when we think to ourselves "they're all like that" in talking about anything – people, cars, philosophers, vegetables – based upon a small sample of the group we're talking about, we commit a hasty generalization. There is usually no way *definitely* to conclude something about the characteristics of an entire group since we have no knowledge of the entire group. The next member of the group we encounter may turn out to have different characteristics from members of the group we know thus far. Any form of prejudice and stereotyping, by definition, involves a hasty generalization. Consider the way Jews and African Americans are stereotyped, how Mexicans and philosophers are typecast as lazy, and gays are *all* flamboyant in *Family Guy*.

The writers of *Family Guy* play on people's hasty generalizations to make their points in episode after episode. In "A Picture is Worth 1,000 Bucks," Peter hastily generalizes that *all* of Chris's works of art will make lots of money, because *one* of his art pieces has made lots of money. Relying on this hasty generalization, he uproots his family and transports them to New York thinking they'll be rich and be able to live a New York kind of lifestyle: "My son here is gonna be the best thing to happen in New York since Mayor Giuliani had all the homeless people secretly killed." In the end, Chris's artwork bombs out! Unlikely as it seems, even Stewie sometimes commits the fallacy of hasty generalization. In "I Never Met A Dead Man," after being forced to eat his broccoli, Stewie assumes that all vegetables must be this bad and concludes that *all* vegetables must be destroyed. To recast a cliché: "One bad vegetable doesn't spoil the whole bunch."

Another common fallacy is the ad hominem. In this fallacy, someone concludes that a person's claims or arguments are false or not worth listening to because of premises that concern an attack on the actions, personality, or ideology of the person putting forward the claim or argument. In other words, instead of focusing on the person's issue, claims, or argument, one attacks the person (ad hominem is Latin for *to the man*). This strategy is used when we try to discredit a person's argument by discrediting the person. But notice, the person and the person's arguments are two distinct things – to attack one isn't necessarily to attack the other.

For example, in the episode "Running Mates" Peter smears Lois's good name by spreading rumors about her: "[Our children] deserve a school board president who doesn't leave her feminine ointments in the fridge next to the mustard. That was the worst sandwich I ever ate! She flosses in bed. She snores like a wildebeest. She freed Willie Horton. She nailed Donna Rice . . . [She] eats babies." People conclude, without even listening to her claims, that she must have nothing good to say, or that what she has to say is automatically false. What does Lois's personality – even if she was the biggest murdering, raping, *snoring* slut on the planet – have to do with the truth or falsity of the claims she makes about how to hold a civil office? The answer is: absolutely nothing! The conclusions that "she must have nothing good to say, or that what she has to say is automatically false" just do not follow from claims about her personality.

Here's another example. If Mayor West claims that smoking is wrong and wants to tell you why it is so, *and* he has a cigarette hanging out of his mouth when he is telling you this, you cannot conclude automatically that what he has to say is worthless or false. You could accuse Mayor West of being a hypocrite, but you cannot conclude that what he is saying is worthless or false without first hearing his argument!

An argument from inappropriate authority is just what it freakin' sounds like, incorrectly drawing a conclusion from premises based upon a non-credible, non-qualified, or illegitimate authority figure. The best way to avoid this fallacy altogether is to become an authority concerning some matter yourself by getting all of the relevant facts, understanding the issues, doing research, checking and double-checking your sources, dialoguing with people, having your ideas challenged, defending your position, being open to revising your position, and the like. But since we can't become authorities on everything, we need to rely upon others.

In the episode "Holy Crap," Chris's grandfather thinks that Chris is masturbating in the bathroom when, in reality, he just needs to go number 2. Grandpa Griffin claims that what he thinks Chris is doing (masturbating) is a sin and that Chris will go to hell for it. Now, what authority does Chris's grandfather have to make such pronouncements about who will go to hell or not? Is he a priest? You might say that anyone who knows Catholic church doctrine can become an authority on issues such as masturbation and hell. But if you investigate church doctrine, you can see that no human being – pope, priest, or layperson – can make pronouncements about who will go to hell or not. So Chris's failure to recognize this fallacy gets him to accept the idea that he'll go to hell if he poops/masturbates.

Jumping to Conclusions and Jumping for Joy That This God-Damned Chapter is Coming to a Close

So, now that we've gone through this little logic lesson, there's a couple of things to keep in mind. The most important thing is to not jump to conclusions. Remember that every single chapter in this book will kick ass. Why? Well, it's because this chapter kicks ass, of course. Even if this chapter *didn't* kick ass, all the others still would. Also, I wouldn't listen to anything that any university professor says because *you know* they're all liberal, closeted commie pinkos. Listen to George Bush, especially when it comes to military strategery, the teaching of Creation Science in public schools, and the fact that the Bible should be everyone's rulebook. That way, you'll definitely avoid the pitfalls of bad reasoning.

13

THE SIMPSONS ALREADY DID IT! THIS SHOW IS A FREAKIN' RIP-OFF!

SHAI BIDERMAN AND WILLIAM J. DEVLIN

Let's begin with a trivia question. What TV cartoon series focuses on a dysfunctional family of five? Hint: the members of the family include an overweight, dimwitted father accompanied by a stable and supportive wife (who he doesn't deserve), three children (an oddball son who doesn't seem to fit in, an under-appreciated daughter, and a baby), and, of course, a dog? If you answered *The Simpsons*, then you've just won a weekend in Springfield, USA. Until January 31, 1999 *The Simpsons* was the only correct answer to this question. But then Fox introduced America to *Family Guy*, a TV show that fits this description like Homer fits into Krusty's puffy clown pants. People who watch both shows cannot escape the almost embarrassing déjà vu: same characters, same kind of mischief, similar relationships between family members and between the family and the town, and similar plotlines. Both series have the same nuclear family structure. Both have a set of secondary characters, neighbors and friends (from Flanders, Moe, Lenny, and Carl, to Cleveland, Quagmire, and Joe) who contribute to plot developments. And both have peripheral characters who play a role in the functioning of society (from Mayor Quimby, Homer's boss Mr. Burns, and news-anchor Kent Brockman, to Mayor Adam West, Peter's one-time boss Mr. Weed, and news-anchors Tom Tucker, Diane Simmons, and Tricia Takanawa).

Family Guy mimics plotlines and backdrops from *The Simpsons*: life in a luxurious mansion, post-nuclear war survival, adventures in politics, dealing with obesity, drinking problems (including losing one's job due to such problems), enrolling in the witness protection program, and so on. The commonalities don't end there. At the philosophical level, both series address the same issues: the downfall of the nuclear family (challenging the parental role model, introducing the infant's world of purity, naïveté, and incapacity), the downfall of the social order (law enforcement as an arbitrary exercise of power, and the stupidity and humor of the social contract), the nature of reality (my mind versus other minds), information as power (the role of the media and news anchors), ethical standards, the play of language, *yada, yada, yada.*

In fact, these similarities are a big problem. *Family Guy* is a rip-off of *The Simpsons.* Let's be more specific about the charges: *Family Guy* is a fraudulent and phony series, lacking originality and creativity, and simply riding the successful coattails of an original cartoon comedy. Its creator, Seth MacFarlane, is lazy and unimaginative, simply stealing from Matt Groening and the writers of *The Simpsons.* None of this is lost on Groening and his writers, by the way. In *The Simpsons* episode "The Italian Bob," a picture of Peter is shown in a book of criminals under the charge of plagiarism (while a picture of Stan Smith of *American Dad!* is shown under the charge of plagiarism of plagiarism).[1] Peter is presented again in "Treehouse of Horror XIII," this time as one of the many, more rudimentary and shoddy, clones of Homer. Clearly, *Family Guy* doesn't have anything to add to the world of American animated sitcoms, which hasn't already been provided by *The Simpsons.* As *South Park*'s tin foiled sidekick, General Disarray, incessantly points out to Professor Chaos, "Simpsons did it!" And here, again, is the heart of the criticism: *Family Guy* is a bad work of art within the genre of animated sitcoms because most of its ideas are taken directly from another animated work of art.

It gets worse. When we take away the unoriginal qualities of *Family Guy,* we're left with only nonsensical back-stories that contribute absolutely nothing to plot or thematic development.[2] *South Park* made this point in "Cartoon Wars, Part I," an episode in which Cartman becomes irritated by the claim that his humor is similar to the humor of *Family Guy.* Cartman hates the comparison: "I am nothing like *Family Guy!* When I make jokes they are inherent to a story! Deep situational and emotional jokes based on what is relevant and has a point, not just one random interchangeable joke after another!" If we strip *Family Guy* of all it steals from *The Simpsons* we seem to be left with garbage – a chaotic mess of superficial, incoherent toilet humor.[3]

So why should we even bother with *Family Guy*? Why should *Family Guy* be the subject of an "and Philosophy" book? Before we dismiss *Family Guy*, we need to address more carefully the most philosophically pressing question about the show. Is *Family Guy* really a rip-off?

Indeed, what is a rip-off? If we think about this question within the context of art, we might say that every work of art is a rip-off of something else. A picture or painting of a chair simply rips-off a real chair. Rober Doisneau's famous 1950 photograph "Kiss at the Hôtel de Ville" is just a rip-off of a couple's kiss with a Parisian backdrop. But these are not really rip-offs; they're imitations. What about the posters and postcards we buy of Leonardo da Vinci's *Mona Lisa*? Are they rip-offs of the original? Again, these are not really rip-offs; they're copies. An actual artistic rip-off is a counterfeit, a fraud. A rip-off is a bad work of art because it lacks originality and creativity.

But is *Family Guy* really art? Are we giving fart jokes too much credit?

"From Method to Madness"

Three theories of art – representation, expression, and form – might allow us to say that *Family Guy* is art, fart jokes notwithstanding. According to the simplest version of the *representation* theory, x is an artwork if x imitates or represents something. Consider watching a performance of William Shakespeare's *Hamlet*, looking at an Ansel Adams photograph, and encountering the *Equestrian Statue of Marcus Aurelius* in Piazza del Campidoglio, Rome. We might say that in each case we witness a work of art precisely because each one essentially imitates reality. In these cases, each work imitates by re-presenting a certain aspect of the real world. Art, thus, is essentially a medium that captures something specific about life and the world by representing that specific feature within the work: *Hamlet* re-creates the concepts of revenge, death, and power, an Ansel Adams photo captures the beauty of nature, and the Marcus Aurelius statue re-creates the character of Aurelius in his stoic nobility.[4]

So according to representation theory *Family Guy* would be considered a work of art insofar as it re-presents, re-creates, or imitates life and the world. *Family Guy* involves two kinds of imitations.

151

First, the series imitates by representing the suburban life of a nuclear family of five. Second, the series imitates by doing things already done on *The Simpsons*. Thus, while *Family Guy* would be a work of art according to representation theory, it would be a bad work of art. It's a rip-off, stealing its perspective from *The Simpsons*.

But representation may not really tell us why *Family Guy* qualifies as a work of art. The drawings are not very realistic, nor are they meant to be. Just think of the misshaped heads, exaggerated chins, and disproportionate bodies. Representing reality doesn't seem to be what the show is about. After all, *Family Guy* features a dog who not only speaks, but attends college, drives a taxi, and has a drinking problem. Meanwhile, baby Stewie is a mastermind who speaks eloquently (with a very adult vocabulary), sings, dances, and creates advanced technological weapons with the intent of destroying his mother. The story lines don't represent life either: Peter creating his own country (Petoria), Brian's adventure in becoming a porn director, Stewie's quest to destroy Peter's sperm in a micro-size space ship, Meg being sold to the Goldmans, Peter's friendship with Death, and so on.

So let's apply a second theory of art to *Family Guy*. According to the simplest version of *expression* theory, x is an artwork if x is a medium for communicating feelings or emotions. The artist uses his or her work of art to express a certain set of feelings to the audience. Homer's *Iliad*, Picasso's *Guernica*, and Beethoven's Ninth Symphony are all works of art because each one is essentially a form of communication between the artist and the audience. Homer (the Greek poet, not the Simpson patriarch) expresses pride and glory in human struggle; Picasso communicates the horror and suffering of war; and Beethoven extends the feelings of love and tenderness.[5]

But as with representation, expression may not really tell us why *Family Guy* qualifies as a work of art. While many episodes of *The Simpsons* and *South Park* conclude with a feel-good moral of the story (they've "learned something today"), *Family Guy* makes no attempt to express a specific set of emotions. As Cartman points out, *Family Guy* doesn't coordinate its comedy so that it is deeply "situational and emotional . . . and has a point." Instead, the jokes are random and interchangeable, thereby disarming and detracting from any solid concept or emotion that can be communicated between the artist and audience.

Let's consider a third and final theory of art. According to the simplest version of *form* theory (or formalism), x is an artwork if x displays significant form. A musical piece displays its form by the interrelation of its parts or movements and by the interrelation of its melody, harmony, and rhythm. A painting displays its form through the interrelation of elements such as line, color, light, and shape. A work of literature displays its form through the interrelation of elements such as narrative technique, plot structure, and theme. So, whether we're considering Mozart's use of the string quartet in his chamber music, Mondrian's use of rectilinear shapes and solid colors in *Composition*, or Shakespeare's structuring of sonnets by iambic pentameter, works of *art* display significant form.[6]

But as with representation and expression, form may not really tell us why *Family Guy* qualifies as a work of art. We would expect the series to follow the form of the TV sitcom. We would expect a central theme to be presented in a developed plot, leading to a resolution. We would expect subplots and minor characters to reinforce the main plot and the actions of the central characters. But to the contrary, each episode of *Family Guy* is filled with miscellaneous and non-sensical back-stories. Rather than push the plotline along, this hodge-podge of cultural references becomes so random and far-fetched that it obliterates the traditional formal approach to a narrative.[7] *Family Guy*, then, doesn't fit the third candidate for a theory of art since it does not conform to the rules of the traditional narrative structure; rather, it openly and intentionally flouts them.[8]

"It's a Hic-a-doo-la World!"

So what makes *Family Guy* a work of art (assuming, of course, that it is)? Perhaps surprisingly, there is a way of understanding *Family Guy* as art in virtue of the fact that it is *difficult* to understand it as art. The key is a postmodern conception of art – one that challenges the idea that art has a definite essence.

As the philosopher Arthur Danto (1924–) explains, postmodern artists create works of art that intentionally do not fit any of the traditional theories of art. One of the reasons behind this intention is to make a statement about the identity of what makes a work of art, *art*. For the first time, the artists themselves raise the question "What

153

is art?" and, at the same time, challenge the philosopher's and art the-
orist's traditional answers, by creating works of art that do not fit in
the given theories of art's essence. For instance, Andy Warhol's *Brillo
Boxes* are simply Brillo boxes made of wood instead of cardboard.
John Cage's musical composition *4'33"* is a piece with 3 movements
that is performed *without playing a single note.*[9] Marcel Duchamp's
ready-made *Fountain* is a real urinal, while his painting *L.H.O.O.Q.*
is simply a remake of da Vinci's *Mona Lisa* with a moustache. All
of these artists and their works challenge the standard definitions
and approaches to art. According to Danto, such postmodern art
leaves philosophers and the philosophy of art with "deep questions
to consider, questions of representation and reality, of structure,
truth, and meaning."[10]

The philosopher Jean-François Lyotard (1924–98) points out that
this postmodern challenge is not confined to art museums. Rather the
world itself – contemporary culture – is postmodern insofar as it is
an eclectic collage of "anything goes" that "panders to the confusion
which reigns in the 'taste' of the patrons." In our postmodern world,
we experience a barrage of disconnected artistic aspects, from
McDonald's food, to Western movies, to Paris perfume.[11] These
artistic elements become so entrenched in our daily lives that they
blur the distinction between the appearance of the art world and the
reality of ordinary life.

The philosopher Jean Baudrillard (1929–2007) points out that the
postmodern world is defined by consumer culture and its reliance
upon electronic communications, which further blurs the line between
appearance and reality. With the dominance of televisions, radios,
computers, cell phones, fax machines, and so on, face-to-face interactions are diminishing while the "exchange of symbols" increases.
This new postmodern culture is a *hyperreality* (a society where reality
is the fast-paced interchange and play of images, symbols, and signs).
Now, technological forms of entertainment and information provide
the individual with a richer and more intense set of experiences
than those experienced in the mundane version of reality. As appearance and reality are no longer easily distinguished, the line between
original and copy begins to dissolve. Communication and interaction
in hyperreality are *simulations*, or imitative reproductions, of real
experience. The objects and content of experience are thus, at the
same time, both the original and the copy, or imitation.[12]

Following Danto, we can say that *Family Guy* doesn't fit into the traditional theories of art because it is challenging these definitions of the art of animated sitcoms. With its shoddy representations of reality, its pointless or absent themes, and its destruction of the traditional forms of narrative, *Family Guy* is a work of art that inherently raises the question "What is art?" and, at the same time, rejects the standard approaches as suitable, all-encompassing answers. Likewise, following Lyotard, *Family Guy* is an eclectic collage of "anything goes" that incorporates a wide variety of features of postmodern culture. While the references are too numerous to list, *Family Guy* incorporates allusions, satires, and homages to many different areas of late 20th century and contemporary culture. Considering the consumerism of the postmodern world, we see references from Trix cereal to Snausages dog treats, to the video game *Doom*, to Tag body spray; in music, from Hanson, to Billy Joel, to Kiss; in television, from *All in the Family*, to *Family Feud*, to *Murder She Wrote*, to *The Real World*; in film, from *Dirty Dancing*, to *Rocky,* to *Tron* (and many more besides). Even famous and infamous figures in contemporary culture – from Kevin Federline, to Stephen Hawking, to Ronald Reagan, to Osama bin Laden – are satirized.

Finally, *Family Guy* can be identified with Baudrillard's notion of hyperreality in the sense that the world of *Family Guy* is a world centered around simulations through images, symbols, and signs. Within this animated world, we find that Peter understands his world, and organizes his life by the hyperreality of television. His past is full of people from the world of television, whether it is Superman, the Kool Aid man, Wile E. Coyote, or Gilligan. Likewise, his present actions are determined and guided by the world of television. For instance, in "Brian Goes Back to College," Peter and his friends live their lives as if they were the A-Team. Or perhaps more significantly, Peter's religious life is shaped by the Fonz from *Happy Days*. The Fonz not only becomes his spiritual advisor ("The Son Also Draws"), but also becomes his god and idol, such that Peter builds a church to worship him ("The Father, the Son, and the Holy Fonz"). Peter becomes so deeply immersed in the world of television that even when he runs over the cable transmitter, preventing him from watching TV, he comes to see the "real world" as a slew of TV episodes, where he can "change the channel" simply by turning around or looking away ("I Never Met the Dead Man").[13]

155

But this hyperreality is not confined *within* the world of *Family Guy*; rather, it extends *beyond* this animated world. We find that the series itself challenges its own reality. For instance, in "Da Boom," the entire episode ends up being a dream in the mind of the character of Pam Ewing of the show *Dallas*, and thus becoming not only a dream of another television show's character but also a parody of *that* very show. The levels of "reality" within the extended world of television itself, thus collapses. This collapse even extends to the "real world" of the viewing audience. In "The Father, the Son, and the Holy Fonz," Stewie speaks directly to *us*, the audience, as he tells us to switch the channel from Fox to ABC and watch *Desperate Housewives* for five seconds so that we can understand his joke about the actress Marcia Cross (he even tells us that he'll wait for us). By presenting this postmodern hyperreality, both within the world of *Family Guy* and outside to the world of the audience, *Family Guy* helps to dissolve the division between reality and appearance.

Family Guy: The Postmodern Cartoon

If we see *Family Guy* as a work of postmodern art, then we should evaluate it by the same standards as we evaluate Warhol's *Brillo Boxes* and Duchamp's *L.H.O.O.Q.* The latter works of art aren't criticized as rip-offs. After all, there's nothing fraudulent or deceptive about them. Warhol was not stealing from the Brillo Manufacturing Company. Duchamp was not ripping off the *Mona Lisa*. Likewise, as a postmodern cartoon, *Family Guy* is not ripping off *The Simpsons* in the sense that it is trying to deceptively steal from the original contemporary American animated sitcom. In fact, it is quite the opposite approach. MacFarlane's *Family Guy* so obviously takes cinematic structures, storylines, and features from *The Simpsons* in order to make the point that any clear distinction between original and copy has dissolved. But the references and ideas from *The Simpsons* are only one facet of the postmodern, multi-featured world that is present in *Family Guy*. The series has become such a collage of various other television series, animated or non-animated, that it no longer makes sense to pinpoint *The Simpsons* as the work that is the influence of, and original to, *Family Guy*.

Ultimately, the charge that *Family Guy* is a rip-off must be dismissed, and ironically this dismissal can come from *South Park* and *The Simpsons*. In *South Park*'s "*The Simpsons* Already Did It!," Butters learns that he should not be concerned about whether or not *The Simpsons* did what he intended to do. As Cartman puts it, "Dude, *The Simpsons* have done everything already. Who cares?" Meanwhile, Chef points out that a skit from *The Simpsons* "Tree House of Horror VII" is taken from an episode of *The Twilight Zone*. Likewise, even *The Simpsons* acknowledges that there is no escaping the use of ideas from other shows in the world of animation. As Roger Meyers, Jr., the head of Itchy and Scratchy Productions, points out in "The Day the Violence Died," "Animation is built on plagiarism! If it weren't for someone plagiarizing *The Honeymooners*, we wouldn't have *The Flintstones*. If someone hadn't ripped off *Sgt. Bilko*, there'd be no *Top Cat*. Huckleberry Hound, Chief Wiggum, Yogi Bear? Hah! Andy Griffith, Edward G. Robinson, Art Carney."

While its peers can absolve *Family Guy* from the charge of being a rip-off, we have seen that the series is, indeed, *not* a rip-off since it is a postmodern work of art that intentionally tears down the distinctions between appearance and reality, original and copy, and uses the world of television to push this dissolution. So, sit back, relax, and enjoy the postmodern comedy *Family Guy*, knowing full well that you are not watching a secondary, unoriginal, and uncreative animated sitcom (as if you need us to tell you that). Giggity-giggity, giggity-goo.

NOTES

1   *American Dad* is an animated sitcom co-created by the creator of *Family Guy*, Seth MacFarlane. Thus, MacFarlane created Stan Smith by ripping off his own *Family Guy* character, Peter Griffin, which in turn is a rip-off of *The Simpsons*' character, Homer Simpson.
2   And even the introduction of nonsensical stories may not be terribly original, as such events already occur in *The Simpsons*.
3   The charge of *Family Guy* as being a rip-off or a poor work of art is not limited to *The Simpsons* and *South Park*. We find similar criticisms being presented in various magazines, from *Mad* to *Entertainment Weekly*, to even *The New Yorker*. Furthermore, several other animated artists vocally or artistically join in on the complaints – Kevin Smith and

David Mandel (creator and co-producers of *Clerks: The Animated Series*), Chris Ware (creator of the comic *Jimmy Corrigan: The Smartest Kid on Earth*), and John Kricfalusi (creator of the animated series *Ren & Stimpy*) have all lambasted Seth MacFarlane for being unoriginal and deceptive in his *Family Guy*. MacFarlane humorously responded to the charges from *South Park* in his speech to the graduating Harvard class of 2006, through the persona of Stewie: "The boys at *South Park* are absolutely correct: Those cutaways and flashbacks have nothing to do with the story! They're just there to be . . . funny. And that is a shallow indulgence that *South Park* is quite above, and for that I salute them."

4　For a further account on the theory of art as representation, see Plato, *The Republic*, translated by Allan Bloom (New York: Basic Books, 1991); Aristotle, *Poetics*, Books 1–3, found in *The Student's Oxford Aristotle*, Vol. 6, translated by W. D. Ross (Oxford: Oxford University Press, 1942).

5　For further readings on the theory of art as expression, see Leo Tolstoy, *What is Art?*, translated by Richard Peaver and Larissa Volokhonsky (London: Penguin, 1996); R. G. Collingwood, *The Principles of Art* (Oxford: Oxford University Press, 1938).

6　For a further discussion on the theory of art as form, see Edmund Burke Feldman, *Varieties of Visual Experience* (Englewood Cliffs, NJ: Prentice-Hall, 1967); Clement Greenberg, *Arts Yearbook*, No. 1 (1961).

7　This is one of the driving points of *South Park*'s episodes "Cartoon Wars", parts I and II, where a satire of *Family Guy* is shown as the children watch a fake episode of *Family Guy*, which includes three disparate and pointless cutaways that involve cultural references to David Hasselhoff, Mr. T, and William Shatner. In between these cutaway flashbacks, we find the main characters reiterating the main plotline, as if to suggest that the back-stories are such a digression that the audience needs to be reminded of the real narrative structure that is supposed to be present in the story. *Family Guy* is portrayed as being so absurd that *all* of the storylines are written by manatees who randomly select "idea balls" to put together overall concepts for the plot of each episode.

8　For a more detailed consideration of the three art theories we have considered, as well as others, see Noël Carroll, *Philosophy of Art: A Contemporary Introduction* (London: Routledge, 1999).

9　Cage simply records the sound of the world around him as his audience waits for a 'real' performance.

10　See Arthur Danto, "Art, Philosophy, and the Philosophy of Art," *Humanities* 4 (1983), pp. 1–2.

11   See Jean-François Lyotard, *The Postmodern Condition* (Minneapolis: University of Minnesota Press, 1984), p. 76.

12   See Jean Baudrillard, *Simulacra and Simulation*, translated by Sheila Faria (Ann Arbor: University of Michigan Press, 1994).

13   Notably, in the same episode, Lois's position towards Peter's addiction to television helps to sum up *Family Guy*'s case as postmodern art. Initially, she is proud of Peter moving away from TV, as she explains that he has "broken TV's hypnotic spell over us. Now we can see the world for what it is." Later, however, she repents, encouraging Peter to return to the hypnotic spell: "Oh, come on Peter, don't you miss TV just a little? The familiar stories, the broadly drawn characters, the convenient plot turns that bring a character around at exactly the right moment." This encouragement indicates not only the ubiquity of TV for Peter, but also implicitly jabs *Family Guy* itself, since it is exactly the opposite of her characterization of TV shows: *Family Guy* does not provide its audience with familiar stories, broadly drawn characters, or plot turns to help build character development.

PART #F
FAMILY PROBLEMS

14

IS BRIAN MORE OF A "PERSON" THAN PETER? OF WILLS, WANTONS, AND WIVES

MARK D. WHITE

Recent TV dads have not been the most impressive guys on the block. (If it were produced today, *Father Knows Best* would probably be named *Father Knows Squat*.) Consider two recent but classic sitcom dads, Tim Taylor from *Home Improvement* and Ray Barone from *Everybody Loves Raymond*. They're certainly not the brightest stars in their respective family constellations, constantly being corrected and reprimanded by their more sensible wives (and kids, and parents – everyone except the houseplants). But in the end, like most buffoon sitcom fathers, they show they have good hearts, and end up epitomizing family values no less than the last competent sitcom dad, Cliff Huxtable of *The Cosby Show*.

Cartoon dads, on the other hand, are usually not as virtuous but just as thick, and we need look no further for an example than Homer Simpson. Ah, Homer, how you have raised – or maybe lowered – the bar for TV fathers everywhere. But you have a challenger in the portly, bespectacled form of Peter Griffin, patriarch of *Family Guy*. Homer and Peter have many similarities, such as the obvious physical features, their much more sensible wives (by now a TV sitcom cliché), and their smart-aleck kids. There are differences, of course – for instance, Homer worships Grand Funk Railroad and Peter is a Kiss man all the way. (Although, as far as we know, Marge never slept with Mark Farner, and we all know about Lois and Gene.)

The most important difference by far is their pets. They both have dogs, but Homer's dog, Santa's Little Helper, is nothing like Peter's

163

dog, Brian. In fact, as we shall see, Brian is more of a person than Peter is. To make the case, we'll focus on a classic article by philosopher Harry Frankfurt (1929–), perhaps better known for his recent bestseller *On Bullshit* (probably the only philosophy book Peter or Homer would ever look at).[1] In the classic article, "Freedom of the Will and the Concept of a Person," Frankfurt argues that certain features of one's desires are more important than biology or species in qualifying one as a "person." In fact these features of desires are even more important than the choices one makes.[2] While we're on the topic of choices, we'll explore the broader area of philosophy known as *action theory*, which examines how people make decisions and act on them. We'll also see what we can learn about when good people make bad decisions. (You can probably guess we'll be talking about Peter a *lot*.)

You're Freakin' Nuts, Pal!

So exactly how does Frankfurt define personhood? What is it about desires that separates persons from mere beasts (even human ones)? Frankfurt separates desires into two types: the most basic desires are what he calls *first-order desires*, and they are just what you and I usually think of as desires. Lois wants to sing in a nightclub (or basement), Stewie wants Lois dead (or worse), Brian wants martinis (and Snausages), and Peter wants to watch TV (that's it, just watch TV). These are all first-order desires. All people have first-order desires, as do all higher animals (Brian isn't the only dog that wants to sniff a butt once in a while).

Many philosophers think that such desires provide the fundamental motivation behind everything we do, above and beyond all other influences on our behavior (more on this later). This may be true even if your first-order desires conflict. In "I Never Met the Dead Man," Peter wants to help Meg, but also wants to watch *Star Trek*, so he has to make a choice, saying, "Sorry, Meg. Daddy loves you, but Daddy also loves *Star Trek*, and in all fairness, *Star Trek* was here first." Quagmire has a thing for the ladies (culminating in stalking Lois in the bowling alley restroom in "Blind Ambition"), but also wants to remain in Quahog (after getting caught), and so he lets the other guys help him with his problem. Brian wants to eat chocolate

164

after being neutered, but worries that it will make him fat ("Screwed the Pooch"), and so on.

In each case, one of the desires will determine the chosen action, implying the other will not. But this doesn't mean the other desire goes away. Even if Brian eats the chocolate, part of him still wishes he didn't so he could keep his, ahem, girlish figure. Even if Quagmire keeps away from women, he still wants to – well, you know (giggity-giggity). In Frankfurt's terminology, whichever desire we actually follow is our *will*, and the will is absolutely crucial to personhood.

Introducing The Wanton (Peter, Please Stand Up)

Nothing I have said so far differentiates persons from non-persons, much less human beings from animals. All of them have first-order desires, perhaps even conflicting ones, and we can certainly call their choice their will in Frankfurt's sense.[3] In his view, the difference between persons and non-persons comes down to the ability to reflect upon and judge one's will, or to have desires regarding one's desires.

But how do you have desires about desires, especially if your desires conflict? We have to imagine another type of desire, not a desire to do or get something, but a desire to have a certain desire (funny as it sounds). Frankfurt calls this a *second-order desire*, and this is our first step towards defining what it is to be a person. A second-order desire is a desire to see a certain first-order desire be followed.[4] We have these all the time – for instance, I often say, "I want a donut, but I don't *want* to want a donut." A person trying to quit smoking may say that she wants a cigarette, but she doesn't *want* to want a cigarette. We often have two conflicting first-order desires, and we can also have a second-order desire that ranks one first-order desire over others. For example, Brian wants chocolate, but doesn't *want* to want chocolate. Quagmire doesn't *want* to want to be – well, Quagmire – and so on.

To Frankfurt, wanting to want something, or having second-order desires, is what makes somebody a person. In contrast, he uses the term *wanton* to refer to someone who does not have second-order desires. Wantons are like animals, blindly following their impulses without reflecting upon them. This is not to say that a wanton does not have competing first-order desires, and does not struggle to

165

choose between them, or is not rational when making such a choice. It just means that he does not have any higher criterion to help judge and choose between them – he does not want one desire to "win out" against the other. A person, on the other hand, does – she wants to see one desire determine her action, whether it actually does or not. So even the smoker who doesn't *want* to want a cigarette, but ends up having one anyway, is a person.

Frankfurt uses the example of two heroin addicts. (We'll meet them again later when we discuss another philosopher's writings – I wonder if they have someone particular in mind?) One of them wishes he were not addicted, but still regularly succumbs to his addiction. He is a person in the sense we have defined here, because he wants heroin, but he doesn't *want* to want heroin. The other has no opinion regarding his addiction, and just blindly follows his desire to get high – he is the wanton. The two addicts may act similarly, in that they both inject heroin, but their thought processes are much different. The person regrets his actions because of his second-order desire not to want heroin, and the wanton does not, because he has no second-order desires (at least, not concerning his heroin addiction).

Brian Reflects, Peter . . . Well, Peter Just Farts (And Giggles)

In the episode "Brian in Love," after seeing a therapist (a moonlighting Jack McCoy?) about a recent string of "accidents" on the carpet, Brian realizes that he is hopelessly in love with Lois, Peter's wife. He finds himself flirting awkwardly with her, misinterprets her innocent gestures as similar affection toward him, and loses his temper when Stewie gets kisses from Lois (purely to torment Brian, of course). More importantly, Brian realizes pursuing this love would endanger the special friendship he enjoys with Lois – he reflects on his passion for Lois, and decides that he does not want to have this desire any longer. Brian, therefore, is a person in the sense of the word we have laid out – he has a second-order desire to not have his first-order desire for Lois. (Of course, he does give in to his first-order desires somewhat and marries Lois in "The Perfect Castaway," though the marriage was never consummated – not even Fox would touch that, at least not until *American Idol* releases its evil spell on the American public.)

Then we have Peter – do I even have to explain why Peter is a prime example of a wanton? I grant you, Peter is a passionate man, for he loves many things – TV, sex, TV, beer, TV, Kiss, and TV. He has many desires, but all of them are first-order desires. We have no evidence that he has second-order desires – that he reflects on his wants, and would like for some of his wants (rather than others) to determine his actions. In "I Never Met the Dead Man," after he knocks out the town's cable TV transmitter, Peter wears a TV cut-out strapped to his waist so everyday life appears to be on TV. This is clearly obsessive behavior (who would have thought?), but Peter never seems to consider what his overwhelming desire for TV does to him or his family. Even when he eventually gives up TV to spend time with his family, he has simply switched one first-order desire for another, without any judgment between them that would show a second-order desire.

Using Frankfurt's terminology, it would seem that Brian, the dog, is more of a person than Peter, the human being. If we define "person" biologically, this is ridiculous, of course. But using Frankfurt's criteria for personhood, Brian is the person, and Peter is the wanton. We can characterize other *Family Guy* characters in these terms too. For instance, Stewie has a maniacal devotion to world domination and Lois's demise, but never seems to reflect on the absurdity of these goals, so he is a wanton (though, to be fair, most infants would be). Meg and Chris, although older and (slightly) more mature than Stewie, also show few signs of second-order desires, and therefore are probably wantons also. But the adults of Quahog fare much better: Cleveland's tranquility and serenity may reflect a second-order desire to avoid conflict, even after he finds out his wife Loretta slept with Quagmire in "The Cleveland-Loretta Quagmire." And yes, even Quagmire has occasion to reflect on his obsession with sex, and so qualifies – we must reluctantly concede – as a person!

This is not as detached from common experience as it may seem. Don't many of us treat our pets like persons (though not because we attribute second-order desires to them)? Some guys even treat their cars like persons, and I'm sure Quagmire has a few inflatable toys that he treats like persons. And just as we often treat animals like

167

persons, we sometimes describe certain human beings as animals, either because they are brutally cruel (like serial killers) or severely brain-damaged. So even in common language, the word "person" does not always refer to biology.

Freedom of the Will[5]

Frankfurt identifies *freedom of the will*, another feature of persons, as related to having second-order desires. Someone has freedom of the will when they can control their first-order desires according to their second-order desires. For instance, I have a first-order desire to eat a donut, but a second-order desire not to. Since my will is what I actually do, then freedom of the will implies that I can control what I do in accordance with my second-order desires, and I won't eat a donut. (I may eat a cruller instead, but HEY – I didn't eat a donut! Philosophers can be very literal when they want to be.)

Now, Frankfurt doesn't claim that true persons have freedom of the will all the time, or even some of the time, but only that they *may* have it. For instance, take the example of the two heroin addicts. The person, the one who reluctantly fed his addiction, is capable of freedom of the will (though he obviously doesn't have it when he succumbs to heroin). Now compare him to the addicted wanton, who just blindly feeds his desires, and has no opinion about addiction. He obviously has no freedom of the will, but more importantly, freedom of the will is not even a possibility with him, because he does not care one way or another what his will might be.

Let's get back to Brian and Peter. If Brian can't keep from acting on his feelings for Lois, he may not have freedom of the will. But at least he can *conceive* of having freedom of the will, because he has the second-order desires necessary to understand such freedom. Peter wouldn't even imagine having or not having freedom of the will, because he has no second-order desires about which first-order desires he wants to act upon. For example, he wants to watch *Who's the Boss?*, so he watches *Who's the Boss?*, and he never reflects on his desire to watch *Who's the Boss?* His will is to watch the hilarious hijinks of Tony Micelli, and since he has no second-order desires regarding his will, we can't conceive of Peter having freedom of the will. (Though he does have taste in TV programs.)

168

You're Weak, Brian – Weak!

Now that we've elevated Brian to personhood, let's knock him down a few pegs. (Ok, it was Stewie's idea, I admit.) Brian recognizes his obsession with Lois is wrong, but let's say he still gives in to it. Using Frankfurt's terms, his will is not as he would choose, so he lacks freedom of the will (though it is still a possibility for him). To use a more common term in philosophy, we can also say he shows weakness of will.

Since this term uses a slightly different sense of "will" than Frankfurt's, let's define it this way: someone shows weakness of will when he acts against his better judgment. Here, "will" means the ability to choose actions according to your best judgment, rather than other actions with their own attractions.[6] Dieting is a great example – I show weakness of will when I eat donuts, though I know donuts are bad for me. If my will were stronger, I would be able to resist the all-too-real temptations of the donut, but when I am weak . . . well, you know the rest (*burp*).

Philosophers since Aristotle (384–322 BCE) – who used the term *akrasia* to describe weakness of will, though he may have just said "ah, crazy" and someone wrote it down incorrectly – have struggled to explain acting against one's better judgment. ("Ah, crazy" apparently wasn't good enough – sorry, Aristotle, better luck next time.) After all, if we decide that one course of action is best, and we believe that it's the right thing to do, and it's in our power to do it – then why don't we do it? Of course, if we're not sure it's the right thing to do, or if we just can't do what we think is best, it's understandable to do something different. But if we're sure it's the right thing to do, and we can do it, then why don't we do it?

The most puzzling thing about weakness of will is not just the fact that it's so hard to explain, but that it's just so common! All of us struggle with desires we'd rather not give in to, whether it's for donuts, cigarettes, or leering at lesbian cheerleaders romping at the mall water fountain. Sometimes we convince ourselves that what we want to do (but don't want to want to do) is really the best thing to do – "I should eat a fifth piece of cake at this party, or I'll offend the host," or "I should watch these cheerleaders make out, or I'll hurt their self-esteem." But that wouldn't really be weakness of will – we just manipulated our judgment to fit our impulsive desires, a case of self-deception.[7] When I say weakness of will, I mean cases in which we truly know doing something is not the best choice, and we do it anyway.

Hold the phone – isn't such action just plain old irrational? It would be very easy to say that and be done with it, but it would label so much behavior as irrational that the term would lose any value it has as a description (or a condemnation). But we can't reject the accusation of irrationality out of hand – we are talking about an action that was taken freely and intentionally, but against our best judgment. If that's not irrational, then what is?

But maybe the action wasn't "freely and intentionally" taken. (It's almost like I meant to use those exact words in the last sentence, isn't it?) Maybe I intended to pass on the donut, but I ate it anyway – did I change my intention, or did I act against my intention? If I did act against my intention, was my act even free, or did something control me? Maybe something possessed me to do it – the baker from the donut commercials, Stewie's mind-control device, or Paris Hilton? (OK, she's why I eat Carl's Jr. burgers, not donuts.)

Let's Welcome Back . . . Our Heroin Addicts! (Applause)

Maybe this entire discussion is off track. What if actions taken out of weakness of will aren't irrational at all, but the very example of rationality? That's what philosopher John Searle (1932–) claims in his book *Rationality in Action*, in which he argues that philosophers have gotten rationality and weakness of will wrong all these years.[8]

Most philosophers believe that desires and beliefs completely determine action. If Quagmire wants to be happy, and he believes that servicing female prison inmates on conjugal visit days is the best way to achieve happiness, then he will do it, end of story. (Giggity giggity giggity.) To do otherwise would simply be irrational – in fact, rationality is often defined as making decisions consistent with your desires and beliefs (however perverse they may be). According to this definition, cases of weakness of will are clear examples of irrationality – I desire to eat well, I believe that the best way to eat well is to give up donuts, but I eat donuts anyway.

But Searle disagrees, and brings back our favorite heroin addicts to prove his point. He says that this theory of action applies more to heroin addicts and animals than human beings. A dog (not Brian, of course) wants to smell bad, he believes that rolling in that steaming pile of goo is the quickest way to smell bad, so he rolls in the goo. Likewise, the heroin addict wants to get high, he believes that heroin is the most effective way to get high, so he shoots heroin. Predictably, Searle regards blindly following your desires and beliefs to be an unflattering picture of decision-making and action.

So what is missing from the standard picture, according to Searle? Just a little thing called free choice, or what philosophers call agency. The standard theory of action is an example of "psychological determinism," which holds that mental factors such as desires and beliefs wholly determine someone's decisions and actions. If our actions are completely determined by our desires and beliefs, then we cannot really choose our actions – we have no agency. (The problem gets worse if we recognize how little choice we have over our beliefs and desires, but don't get me started!)

Searle says that true rational choice occurs in "gaps" in the decision-making process, jumps in the chain of mental events that cannot be modeled. In other words, once we have weighed all of our desires and beliefs, we make a choice which may follow from the desires and beliefs and may not, because that final choice was made in a "gap" in the deterministic process. This gap represents free choice or free will, and is necessary in Searle's view for true rationality to exist.

By flipping the usual idea of rationality on its head, Searle says that weakness of will is evidence for, rather than against, rationality. The fact that we can take actions against our better judgment shows that we are not slaves to our judgment, which serves in mostly an advisory capacity.[9] True choice is above and beyond judgment, though understandably, judgment usually wins in the end. But nothing can explain why bad choices are made – whatever happens in the gap is unknowable, being the result of free will.[10] (I can hear Peter now: "Lois, I'm sorry I blew up the house, but you can't expect an explanation – I did it in the gap! Heh-heh!")

Searle's idea is closely related to volitionism, as described by another leading philosopher, R. Jay Wallace (1957–).[11] Wallace also criticizes the standard theory of action, which he calls the "hydraulic conception," because it compares the various influences on decision-making to opposing forces in physics, with the greatest force being the "winner." Like Searle, Wallace emphasizes the lack of true agency in this model, and instead suggests that "rational agents are equipped with a capacity for active self-determination that goes beyond the mere susceptibility to desires and beliefs," a capacity that could be called willpower.[12] He also emphasizes that choice is something that we do, not something that happens to us, like the standard model of choice would imply. In other words, the standard model leaves no room for persons – just their desires and beliefs. (And even without his chiseled physique, Peter's desires and beliefs alone would be just as scary!)

Of course, recognizing the existence of a will makes weakness of will a lot easier to understand. (At least we don't have to ask "weakness of what?" anymore.) Though Searle regards weakness of will as evidence of rationality, it is still usually a bad thing, representing an inability to follow the recommendations of your own judgment and instead succumb to sudden impulses and temptations. If we recognize willpower as a person's ability to stick to her judgment, then strength and weakness of will become truly meaningful concepts. If I give in to donuts too often, my will is weak, but if I start succumbing to them less (without being influenced by higher prices, less opportunities to get them, and so on), then my will has gotten stronger – not perfect, but less weak than before.

"Are We Done Yet? *Star Trek* Is On . . ."

Perhaps criticizing Peter Griffin for not having an elaborate structure of desires is like shooting fish in a barrel, I admit. And no one will deny that Brian is some dog (even without having an unbelievably literate spider to point it out in writing, like she did for that decidedly unspectacular pig – that's Stewie's gripe, not mine). But more than just pointing out that Brian is smarter than Peter, these observations gave us a chance to explore the concept of personhood, which goes above and beyond species, as well as related concepts in action theory, such as rationality and weakness of will. If nothing else, we've provided Brian with arguments to convince his many – and I mean many – human female conquests to give him a chance. (Just don't tell Quagmire – he doesn't need any more encouragement.)

172

NOTES

1 Harry G. Frankfurt, *On Bullshit* (Princeton: Princeton University Press, 2005).
2 Harry G. Frankfurt, "Freedom of the Will and the Concept of a Person," *Journal of Philosophy*, 68 (1), January 14, 1971, reprinted in Frankfurt's *The Importance of What We Care About* (Cambridge: Cambridge University Press, 1988), chapter 2.
3 Frankfurt's use of the word "will" is somewhat controversial; we'll discuss that later.
4 To be accurate, Frankfurt makes a distinction between simple second-order desires, a desire to have a desire but not necessarily a desire to see it satisfied, and second-order volitions, in which you do want the desired desire satisfied. The difference is not important for us, and even Frankfurt dismisses the simple second-order desire pretty quickly, so I will refer to the more common case as a second-order desire.
5 "Will? Which Will?" Peter asks, then says, "Hey, did I ever tell you about that time I went clubbing with Will Farrell in New Jersey and we bumped into Paris Hilton and that janitor guy from *Scrubs*?"
6 If a person's second-order desires reflect their best judgment, then the discussion of weakness of will that follows closely parallels what we said about Frankfurt above. (Isn't it nice when everything comes together – kind of like an episode of *Who's the Boss?*)
7 David Pears calls this *motivated irrationality* in his appropriately titled book, *Motivated Irrationality* (South Bend, IN: St. Augustine's Press, 1997).
8 John Searle, *Rationality in Action* (Cambridge, MA: MIT Press, 2001).
9 This is similar to the description of two aspects of the will by Immanuel Kant, the famous 18th-century philosopher, who distinguished between *Wille*, which recommends action based on morality, and *Willkür*, which is responsible for actual choice. For more on this reading of Kant (which Kant scholars do not universally agree upon, believe it or not), see Lewis White Beck, *A Commentary on Kant's Critique of Practical Reason* (Chicago: University of Chicago Press, 1960), pp. 176–81.
10 I'm not even touching the topic of free will versus determinism, a much broader metaphysical issue. For more on this, see Robert Kane, *A Contemporary Introduction to Free Will* (Oxford: Oxford University Press, 2005).
11 See R. Jay Wallace, "Three Conceptions of Rational Agency," *Ethical Theory and Moral Practice*, vol. 2, 1999: 217–42, also available in Wallace's *Normativity and the Will: Selected Essays on Moral*

    Psychology and Practical Reason (Oxford: Oxford University Press, 2006), chapter 2.

12 R. Jay Wallace, "Normativity, Commitment, and Instrumental Reason," *Philosopher's Imprint* 1 (3), (www.philosophersimprint.org/001003), 2001, p. 2 (also available in *Normativity and the Will*, chapter 5). Another philosopher, Richard Holton, holds that "the agent's decision is determined not just by the relative strength of . . . the desires and the intentions. Rather, there is a separate faculty of will-power which plays an independent contributory role" ("How Is Strength of Will Possible?", in S. Stroud and C. Tappolet, eds., *Weakness of Will and Practical Irrationality*, Oxford: Oxford University Press, p. 40). Finally, to see how your humble author works these ideas into economics, see "Does *Homo Economicus* Have a Will?" in B. Montero and M. D. White, eds., *Economics and the Mind* (London: Routledge, 2007), chapter 9.

15

THE EGO IS A HOUSEWIFE NAMED LOIS

ROBERT SHARP

Babies don't talk. This is a simple claim, an obvious point, but it bears repeating whenever we watch a television show that features a talking baby. Oh, dogs don't talk either, except in cartoons. Should babies and dogs actually try to communicate, say by gurgling or growling, their language would be very basic. Simple ideas might be conveyed, but nothing as complex as "I plan to take over the world," or "Whose leg do I have to hump to get a drink around here?" In a cartoon such as *Family Guy*, however, babies and dogs *do* talk. Why is this? In part, the goal is to create humor. Having a baby speak like an educated adult is funny because it is an unusual role reversal. But I propose another possibility. I propose that Baby Stewie and Brian the dog could be seen as aspects of Freud's model of the human mind. More specifically, Stewie and Brian represent the id and the super-ego respectively, both of which are competing for the attentions of the family's ego, who just happens to be a housewife named Lois.

Freud Shows the World How to Go Mental

At the turn of the 20th century, Sigmund Freud developed the process of psychoanalysis, a psychological approach to curing mental illnesses. At first, his work rested on a distinction between conscious and unconscious[1] thought, phenomena most evident when analyzing dreams.[2] Later, however, Freud realized that this distinction was not subtle enough to capture the various types of thoughts humans can

175

have. And good thing he did, or we may have lost the basis of the comedic conflicts between Stewie and Brian! Conscious and unconscious parts of the mind have no clear way of speaking to one another, unless some intermediary is present. Yet, Freud still sensed that some sort of communication was taking place, since people often did things that they would not consciously choose to do. He thus prepared a new model of the mind, one that consisted of three major aspects: the ego, the id, and the super-ego.

This new model did not give up the idea of conscious and unconscious thoughts. That distinction was included in each part of the new model. The ego, which is the self-identifying aspect of the mind, has both conscious and unconscious areas (Freud, p. 630). In other words, we are not always fully aware of what we think about ourselves. I may identify myself as a husband, a professor, and a fan of *Family Guy*, while not realizing that unconsciously I also have doubts about my abilities to be a good father or son. These unconscious identities might still affect my approach to life, even though I am not aware of them. In extreme cases, they might even undermine the other roles that I consciously identify. Part of the goal of psychoanalysis is to bring out these repressed feelings, allowing me to confront them and overcome them.

The ego is the part of the mind that we most easily identify in ourselves. When you think about who you are, you are reflecting on the ego (by using the ego, oddly enough!). However, Freud claims that there are two other parts of the human mind. The first is the id, that part of the mind that pursues pleasures, especially primal, physical pleasures. It wants to sleep and eat and have sex. According to Freud, "the ego seeks to bring the influence of the external world to bear upon the id and its tendencies" (p. 635). The id ignores consequences, pushing for its desires to be fulfilled at any cost. The ego checks those desires by recognizing the limits of the world. As Freud explains, "ego represents what may be called reason and common sense, in contrast to the id, which contains the passions" (p. 630). We all know how strongly the passions can pull us, but common sense tells us that we cannot always give in to this pull. So in the episode "The Thin White Line" Brian's id leads him into cocaine addiction, while his ego sends him to rehab. When we lose the common sense the ego can provide (say, by getting drunk) or we never have it

176

(say, by being Peter Griffin), the damage the passions can cause is often irreparable.

Luckily, the ego is not the only force that conflicts with the id. Freud claims that we also have a super-ego, or ego-ideal, which gives "permanent expression to the influence of the parents" (p. 642). Our feelings of guilt, whether conscious or unconscious, often come from the super-ego's reminders of what our parents would think. This is why Lois is so concerned that Peter is setting a bad example for their children when he gets liposuction in the episode "He's Too Sexy for His Fat." Our parents are our first external role models. Both directly and indirectly, we learn what is acceptable through our relationships with our parents. If they do not set a good example, our super-ego can lead us astray. Usually, the super-ego identifies more with the parent of the same sex. So boys identify with their fathers, creating a morality based on masculinity, while girls identify with their mothers, creating a morality of nurturing. Yes, Freud was a bit sexist in how he saw these roles, but in either case the healthy development of the super-ego marks the transition from selfish infant to maturing human being. An unhealthy super-ego might lead us to build a Church of the Holy Fonz in order to identify with our father's religious lifestyle.

While Freud presents id, ego, and super-ego as conflicting aspects of the mind, he also resists making harsh distinctions between the three forces. The mind is a unit, with different parts that can be separated for the sake of analysis. We can compare the mind to a family (an apt analogy for our purposes!). A family can be divided into parts, such as mother, father, son, daughter, baby, and dog. However, when considering what the family does *as a family*, we can still see it as a unit that has satisfied some of its parts and not others. If the son gets kicked out of the scouts (as Chris does in "The Son Also Draws"), the father might drag the whole family with him in an attempt to reinstate the son. The rest of the family may protest (including the son himself!), but the controlling figurehead can exercise his authority to force the trip anyway. The ego is like that figurehead, the final decision maker in the mental process. Or at least it should be; in some cases, the ego is overcome by the id or by repressed forces. That is when mental health breaks down, just as the family is likely to break down without strong leadership.

So a Woman, A Baby, and a Dog All Go into a Brain . . .

In the case of *Family Guy*, Lois plays that strong leadership role. She is thus best suited to play the part of the ego in our analogy. While Peter sometimes gets his way, it is often temporary. Lois is usually right, and at some point Peter usually figures this out in classic American sitcom style. The wife is the boss. She is the ego of the family. Lois is grounded while still being capable of being frivolous. She is complex in a way none of the other characters are, and she is more aware of the external world and its demands. Remember that the ego balances the id by making a reality check (Freud, p. 636). A strong ego can stop the id from recklessly pursuing pleasure. The id knows nothing but its own desires, but the ego knows what will work and what won't. Lois plays this ego role with most of the family, but in particular with baby Stewie.

Stewie is a classic example of the id at work. He pursues his own pleasures at every turn, never caring about what the fulfillment of his desires might mean for other people. He seeks to take over the world, not in order to better it but simply to get whatever he wants. In "Brian Does Hollywood" Stewie plans to take over the world by using a mind control device. He takes the device onto the set of *Kids Say the Darndest Things* but is foiled when Bill Cosby takes the device as part of his zany routine. In "I Never Met the Dead Man" Stewie creates a weather machine that will eliminate broccoli from the world, with no regard for the consequences. His plan is to create a hard freeze that will destroy all broccoli. He even taunts his broccoli: "Mother says you're very good for me, but I'm afraid I'm not good for you!" Of course, Stewie doesn't care about how his freeze would devastate the world. He simply wants to destroy his nemesis. This is classic id behavior. It does whatever it can to fulfill its own desires. Luckily, Lois is there to stop Stewie, even when she is not fully aware of what he is doing.

However, Lois is not Stewie's only foil. He also must face the super-ego of the family, Brian the dog. Brian is the closest thing the show has to a moral compass. He is well educated, having attended Brown University, we are told ("Brian Goes Back to College"). He also clearly identifies with the people who nurture him, in this case Lois and Peter. Brian sees himself as human in many ways and can be found sipping martinis and babysitting Stewie. At one point, he even fights for his civil rights not to be treated like property ("Brian: Portrait of a Dog"), showing his connection to morality and the super-ego. In many ways, he has more family responsibilities than either actual parent and is often the only one aware of Stewie's plans. When the baby (the id) goes too far, Brian takes charge and tracks him down, as when Stewie decides to search for the fantasy land in his favorite TV show ("Road to Europe").

A similar relationship is sometimes shown between Brian and Lois, symbolic of the super-ego's ability to keep the ego from succumbing to the demands of the id. In "Breaking Out Is Hard to Do," Lois turns to a life of shoplifting. Apparently, it is the thrill of stealing that appeals to her, not the money. She is subject to her id, until Brian steps in and reminds her that stealing is wrong. She gets caught anyway, since our super-ego cannot save us from facing the external consequences of our actions. Nevertheless, you can bet that any time you see a dog lecturing a housewife, some sort of symbolism is happening. In this case, the symbolism is classic Freud.

In fact, even subtleties within these interactions among Lois, Stewie, and Brian do a good job of showing the relationship among the ego, id, and super-ego. For example, we know that Stewie not only speaks but does so in a very adult way. Yet, somehow Lois rarely understands what he is saying. This fits the relationship between id and ego. The id has impulses, but they are raw and cannot be expressed in a way that the ego could really understand. At one point, Stewie blurts out in frustration: "God, do you people understand every language except English" ("Love thy Trophy")? So the battle wages on without any real communication. The id certainly knows it is being restricted, but the ego does so without ever directly confronting the id. There is no way for the ego to reason with the id; the id has no reasoning capability that would enable it to stop pursuing its desires.

The super-ego, on the other hand, is better understood by the ego, since it is the ego-ideal. Lois often seems to look up to Brian, and she understands what he is saying. They even get married when Peter is lost at sea ("The Perfect Castaway"). Brian's motives are partly to support the family (he understands obligation), but he also has a crush on Lois, which I will discuss more in a moment. In many ways,

179

Brian makes a better father than Peter. One might argue that he fills that role even when Peter is present. He takes care of the children, especially Stewie, who would otherwise be without true supervision. This is an odd relationship when we think of it in terms of a dog watching a baby, but if we consider it as the super-ego battling the id, the relationship becomes much clearer. Stewie is wary of Brian, the only one smart enough to understand Stewie's goals. He does not actually respect Brian, since the id respects nothing other than its own desires. However, he does recognize that Brian is as much his foe as Lois is.

Of course, Stewie and Lois are not always enemies, anymore than Stewie and Brian are. There are times when she does exactly what Stewie would do in the same situation, as when she plots revenge against the schoolmates who humiliated Meg ("And the Weiner Is . . ."). This fits with Freud's theory, since the id cannot be completely ignored by the ego without disastrous results. Occasionally, we must give in to the id so that our repressed thoughts do not begin to outweigh our conscious ones. So when Lois believes she has found evidence that Chris murdered his teacher's husband ("Fast Times at Buddy Cianci Jr. High"), she involves Stewie in the attempt to cover up the crime. As the id, Stewie is used to doing whatever is necessary to get what he wants. Sometimes Lois needs this ability in order to protect her family (and, by extension, herself). This is one mean mama when riled!

Overall, though, Stewie rarely gets his way. Something always foils him. Usually his failure is the result of unrealistic perceptions of the external world, a classic condition of the id. Only the ego is fully in touch with reality. Even the super-ego is an idealized state, one that gets its view of the world from the ego. Lois ultimately has as much control over Brian as she does over Stewie. They need the ego to survive, so for all Stewie's talk, he cannot actually kill Lois. Perhaps that is why he admits that "it's not so much that I want to kill her; it's just, I want her not to be alive anymore" ("Fifteen Minutes of Shame"). Lois is a natural barrier, a force of nature from Stewie's perspective, one that remains indifferent to his demands while still providing a steady source of nurturing for him, whether he likes it or not. Ultimately, Lois manipulates both Stewie and Brian with very little effort, despite remaining oblivious to their conflicts (which, after all, are unconscious to her!).

"Damn you, vile woman! You've impeded my work since the day I escaped from your wretched womb." (Stewie Griffin)

Part of the ease with which Lois is able to maintain power over the rest of the family can be attributed to Freud's Oedipal Complex, which is especially evident in Stewie and Brian. The Oedipal Complex is one of the more famous ideas that Freud introduced. It rests on the idea that children wish to take the place of the parent of the same sex in order to be the exclusive lover of the parent of the opposite sex. In other words, a son will wish to marry his mother while a daughter will wish to marry her father.[3] If the idea seems odd to you today, it was even more startling when it was first proposed, since almost no one took seriously the idea of infant sexuality that was the basis of Freud's idea.[4] Freud linked common infant behaviors to human sexuality, viewing things like thumb sucking or bed wetting as proto-sexual acts related to masturbation. Of course, they are not conscious sexual activities, which is why people had not yet linked them to sexuality. But according to Freud, cases in which such activities continued beyond the normal length indicated some sort of flaw in sexual development.

Stewie is not old enough to have these flaws yet. He is just a baby, so we might have a hard time detecting any sort of sexual development in him. However, we can still detect elements of the Oedipal Complex. Stewie's aggression toward Lois is borderline obsessive. He claims to want her dead and tries to hurt her in various ways. While this might be seen as hatred, it could also be interpreted as misguided attempts to get her attention. We've all seen little boys on the playground who chase or hit little girls that they like because the boys have no idea how to properly deal with their feelings. The episode "Running Mates" strengthens this interpretation. Stewie misses Lois when she is gone. He claims that he needs a foil for his plots, but we know that Brian would serve that role equally well. Most likely, he misses his mommy. He even seems to soften a bit without her presence and is clearly glad when she finally comes home.

Brian's Oedipal Complex is even clearer, especially in the episode "Brian in Love." In this episode, Brian is caught peeing on the floor. He sees a psychologist (and even sits on a couch in stereotypically

Freudian fashion!), who tells him that he is obviously in love with Lois, who is his figurative mother. Brian resists this interpretation at first. After all, Lois is not only his mother but also the wife of his best friend, who is also a sort of father (yes, it's very complex!). But Brian is a reasonable man . . . I mean dog. He eventually accepts this possibility and decides to confess his feelings to Lois. After discussing the situation, they decide to remain friends.

The episode clearly plays on the feelings of guilt that Brian must face as part of overcoming his Oedipal Complex. All of his feelings in this episode are repressed. The most likely reason for that repression is that his own ego could not accept the taboo feelings; taboos are a common reason for repressing our desires. So strong was this repression that Brian could not even recall peeing on the floor. His own ego had completely denied that the incident had ever happened. Brian confesses (both to others and to himself) only after being caught in the act. In the end, his super-ego reminds him that such a relationship is unacceptable, and he and Lois are able to work through the issue by talking about it. Without that resolution Brian is unable to overcome his problem. The discussion with Lois is a classic case of the ego being made aware of the repressed feelings and overcoming them with relative ease at that point. The only truly hard part of this Oedipal crisis was coming to terms with its existence. After that, the problem works itself out.

The incident also reinforces the connection between Brian and the super-ego. According to Freud, the super-ego is "the heir of the Oedipus Complex," meaning that we learn about boundaries largely from the proper resolution of the Complex (Freud, p. 643). Taboos, such as incest, are unknown to very young children, but as they learn their proper place, as child and not lover, they begin to understand the boundaries that they must honor. When a son resolves the Oedipal Complex, he is able to complete his identification with the father. However, he is also able to understand how he is different from his father, especially how his relationship to his mother is different. The mother is his father's lover, not his own lover. The boundary of the taboo of incest is created and it is one of our earliest lessons on morality and the restrictions that we must place on our actions.

Brian clearly understands these restrictions, not only before the incident but after. His proper resolution of the Oedipal Complex reaffirms his relationship with Lois rather than ruining it. We know, of course, that the feelings do not completely go away in this case, since he still wishes to sleep in the same bed as Lois when they are later married. Still, the problem is not recurring for the most part. Brian and Lois remain friends, and any hidden animosity Brian held toward Peter seems to fade away as soon as the conflict is resolved.

However, the Oedipal Complex is not limited to just a moment of sexual confusion. Its effects last the rest of our lives. At a pivotal point in our development, we learn what it is to be a man or woman. We also learn what society expects of us. Usually, this results in taking on a masculine or feminine role as we identify with the parent of our own sex. This would explain why Chris cheers for his father instead of his mother when the two are competing in "Running Mates." It also explains his confusion and pain in the episode "And the Wiener Is . . ." where Peter begins to resent his son for having a larger penis. Similarly, when Lois and Meg go on Spring Break together in "A Fish Out of Water," Meg tries to outdo her mother by showing her breasts to the crowd.

These identifications are not limited to the children either. Peter is constantly trying to impress his father by identifying with him in various ways. In the episode "Holy Crap," Peter consistently sides with his father, even when he shouldn't (as when his father attacks Lois for being a Protestant). He finally kidnaps the pope, his father's idol as a Catholic, in order to get an endorsement. The plan fails, but the attempt shows a son trying to connect with his father. In "The Father, the Son, and the Holy Fonz," Peter even starts his own religion so that he can become more like his father. Apparently, Peter is incapable of being Catholic, but he is willing to try anything to identify with his father. He develops the Church of the Fonz, the only religion he can truly embrace. In a touching scene, his father even joins the faith.

Here we see a failure to identify with the parent of the same sex, a failure that can have several consequences according to Freud. For example, Freud proposes that religion itself may be "a substitute for a longing for the father" (p. 643). In the Fonz, Peter sees a role model that he can identify himself with, creating a bond that he does not have with his real father. This gives him something to aspire to, something better than himself. Peter finds such substitutes everywhere, from the teacher that taught him how to dance in "Running Mates," to Gene Simmons of Kiss. According to Freud, a failure to create such identifications can even lead to homosexuality because a person may identify too closely with members of the opposite sex (p. 292). Perhaps some sort of slip in the normal development of sexuality would explain the character of Quagmire, but that would require a book in itself!

Sometimes a Cartoon is Just a Cartoon

When applying a theory like Freud's to something as complex and comedic as *Family Guy*, analogies will always be imperfect. For example, my theory that Brian represents the super-ego might be countered by examples such as the time that he wipes his butt on a neighbor's carpet in order to get revenge ("North by North Quahog"), though one might argue that sometimes revenge *is* the right thing to do. In any case, the comparisons work remarkably well overall. Brian *is* the most clearly moral member of the family. Stewie *is* the most clearly id driven. Lois provides the balance, the focal point of both characters' attentions. For different reasons, or perhaps the same reason in a different form, both Brian and Stewie are obsessed with Lois. They are also rivals, just like Freud's rival forces of super-ego and id. Again, Lois is the battleground for their war in many ways, as Stewie struggles to be free of her suppressing influence and Brian struggles to influence her actions.

I have no idea how many of these connections are intentional, but I am convinced that the writers are familiar with Freud's work. The episode "Brian in Love" is enough to prove that. But even beyond that singularly Freudian episode, there are clear indications that the writers understand the dynamics that exist between parent and child. Chris and Peter connect, while Peter is barely aware that Meg exists. Peter's own father is distant, causing Peter to struggle with how to get his attention. Freud anticipates all of these features of the common family, except perhaps Brian the dog. But then, there's no real explanation for a sophisticated, well-educated, articulate mutt.

NOTES

1   Today we tend to use the word 'subconscious' instead of 'unconscious' in order to distinguish such thoughts from the state of being asleep or knocked out.

2   See, for example, section 10 of Freud's essay "On Dreams" in *The Freud Reader*, edited by Peter Gay (New York: W. W. Norton, 1995), pp. 165–6. Further page references will be cited in the text.

3   In the case of a girl, the term 'Electra Complex' is often used, though not by Freud. Freud did, however, admit that boys and girls experience the Complex in very different ways (see *The Freud Reader*, pp. 671–6).

4   Freud points this out in his essay on "Infantile Sexuality" in *The Freud Reader*, p. 259.

16

THE LIVES AND TIMES OF STEWIE GRIFFIN

TUOMAS MANNINEN

Time to Travel . . .

Despite its apparent impossibility, time-traveling is a recurrent plot device in popular culture, especially in movies. The allure is easy to understand. Who wouldn't like to go back to a past moment and, armed with the knowledge of how things will turn out, try to make things different? But regardless of the allure, going back in time and changing things is an impossibility.[1] If I could go back in time to change some things more to my liking, then this would effectively prevent me from undertaking such a journey in the first place. But why is this so?

Time-travel plays an important role in the *Family Guy* movie *Stewie Griffin: The Untold Story*. In the year 2035, Chris is happily (?) married to Vanessa, who schemes to put Peter and Lois in a retirement home.[2] Lois sternly disapproves of Vanessa, despite her earlier motherly advice on girls to Chris ("Find a girl who smokes. Remember: if she smokes, she pokes"). Lois sees an opportunity to improve things in a blast from the past in the form of infant Stewie, who traveled into the future with Stu, his older self. Lois knows that Stewie is due back in his own time, and she agrees to help her darling son to return to his time on two conditions. First, Stewie must prevent Chris from marrying "that bitch Vanessa." Second, Stewie has to promise that Lois never ends up in a retirement home. With his characteristic homicidal glee, Stewie agrees. He interrupts Chris's wedding to Vanessa with extreme prejudice (and an RPG launcher). Vanessa is blown to pieces and, thus, her marriage to Chris is preemptively annulled.

But wait: if Chris and Vanessa never married on the account of Vanessa's being blown away (and effectively being killed) then Lois could not have made the request to terminate her daughter-in-law, and Stewie could never have been asked to carry out the request (not that he wouldn't have done it of his own volition, as suggested by his earlier remark: "Let me tell you something, 'Nessa – a bullet sounds the same in every language, so stick a freakin' sock in it!"). As this scenario contains a contradiction (Lois, unhappy with her daughter-in-law Vanessa, commissions Stewie to assassinate her *and* Lois never having Vanessa as her daughter-in-law), it can be argued that time-traveling into one's past is impossible. Yet not all philosophers agree.

Many metaphysicians (philosophers who focus on the ultimate nature of reality, including time) have argued that the impossible time-traveling scenarios are useless in that they do very little to show that time-traveling as a whole is impossible. But time-traveling scenarios (such as Stewie's future-sister-in-law-cidal journey) are not useless, for they can help us understand the nature of time and the conditions that restrict possible time-travel.

"What the Deuce?" (or: What is Time-Traveling?)

The philosopher David Lewis (1941–2001) defines time-traveling as traveling in which there is a discrepancy between time and time.[3] With ordinary traveling, the duration of the journey equals the time elapsed between the departure and the arrival of the traveler. But this is not so with time-traveling. For a time-traveler the time between departure and arrival is not equal to the duration of the journey. If the time-traveler's journey lasts, say, 10 seconds, the traveler could reach a time 30 years into his future (as happens to Stewie when he hitches a time-ride with Stu, his older self from the future); or the time reached could be 2,000 years into the past (as happens with Stu's vacation to see Jesus in person). Thus, a journey amounts to time-traveling if the duration of the journey does not equal the time elapsed between the moment of departure and the moment of arrival of the traveler. Although this gives just the bare bones of what time-traveling is, and it leaves a host of questions unanswered, it does give us the basic idea.

But does the basic idea even make sense? What comes before can't come after what came after, because then it wouldn't come before! To make sense of this, we need to distinguish between the *personal time* of the time-traveler and *external time*. One way of thinking about these notions is in terms of frames of reference.[4] The personal time of the time-traveler is time as the traveler perceives and measures it (by whatever means are at her disposal); the external time is independent of the time-traveler and her perceptions. Personal time is not just the subjective time-experience an individual has. If it were, then most of us (especially as students) would have experienced time-traveling, say, in cases where the passage of time seems to slow down to a crawl (like during a boring lecture). (Can Peter really still be wincing about his scraped knee? Can this chicken fighting scene really be lasting this long? And how many verses are there left to Peter's victory tune, "Shipoopi"?)

Paradoxical results follow from the definition of time-travel we have been considering when we compare it to facts about the nature of reality. To see and understand this, we need to make a few (widely held) assumptions. (Drum roll please):

(A1)   There is only one actual world, and only one timeline of events.

(A2)   A time-traveler who travels into the past is not constrained in what she can do at her destination.

(A3)   Our understanding of the nature of causality is (by and large) accurate.

(A4)   The time-traveler is subject to the same kind of causal dependencies as every other (non-time-traveling) person is.

Keeping these assumptions in mind, let's now fill in our sketch of time-traveling.

Doing Things, Stewie's Way

We assumed that a time-traveler would be able to interact with the environment at her destination in the same way as non-time-travelers. But is this really so? For time-traveling to be a genuine possibility (instead of just an academic one), the time-traveler would have to be able to survive, to use her senses, and to move around. These things appear unproblematic, but what about more significant interactions? Can we tell what interactions turn out to produce contradictions? If the traveler kills other individuals (as in Stewie's visit to Chris and Vanessa's wedding), we readily see the paradoxical results following.

Problem, the first: The grandfather paradox

The grandfather paradox (first introduced and defused by David Lewis) purports to show the impossibility of time-travel. Consider this *Family Guy* version of the paradox: in the year 2035, Stewie promises Lois that she will not end up in a retirement home in her old age. Now, given Stewie's matricidal tendencies, together with the time-traveling technology at his disposal, it would hardly be a stretch to imagine a scenario where Stewie travels to a time when Lois has not been conceived, and attempts to kill Carter Pewterschmidt, Lois's father. He would thereby fulfill his promise to Lois in a way she didn't anticipate but which would be quite fitting for Stewie's diabolical genius. If Lois is never born, she will never end up in a retirement home.

But there's a problem with such a plan, ingenious though it may be. If Stewie kills his future biological grandfather, then his mother will not be born and, consequently, neither will Stewie. Initially, it seems that this state of affairs entails a contradiction: if Stewie travels back in time, he could kill his grandfather. But at the same time, Stewie could not kill his grandfather.[5]

We can use this paradox to formulate some conditions on what a time-traveler can do if time-travel is possible. First and foremost, if we consider the causal chain of events in this imaginary scenario, we see that they form a self-defeating loop. Prior to traveling back in time, there are certain conditions that need to be true of Stewie. Most obviously, he has to exist. If we accept that past events cause future events (and not vice versa), we see that a necessary condition for Stewie's existence is that his mother existed (even if Stewie is reluctant to admit this).[6] In turn, a necessary condition for the existence of Lois is that her father – Stewie's maternal grandfather – existed and had children. Thus, Stewie's attempt to kill his maternal grandfather before Lois is born is bound to fail.

Of course, Stewie's journeys through time never threatened Carter Pewterschmidt's well-being (at least, not explicitly). But they very well could have. Following David Lewis's argument, Stewie could not have killed Mr. Pewterschmidt before Lois was conceived. In any attempt to do so, Stewie's grand-patricidal intentions would have been foiled. A world in which time-traveling is possible has to be a world in which odd coincidences crop up every time the time-traveler is about to do something that would leave a necessary condition for the time-traveler's very being unfulfilled.

We can now formulate a general condition for the consistency of time-travel into the past: if time-travel into the past is possible, the time-traveler can do nothing in the past that would impede her chances of embarking on the journey. For this reason, Stewie's killing Vanessa on Lois's request is an impossibility (both metaphysical and logical). Lois can ask Stewie to murder her daughter-in-law only if she *has* a daughter-in-law (which we can assume would have happened, had Vanessa not been blown to smithereens at the altar). In all such cases, the journey is possible only if the attempt to change the past will fail.

Problem, the second: Second time around

Another, stronger reason why all time-travel scenarios that involve attempts to change the past are inconsistent is that they commit the so-called *second-time-around fallacy*. This idea is proposed by Nicholas Smith as follows:

> There can be no first time around of a set of events with the time-traveler absent, followed by a second time around of the *very same events*, with the time-traveler playing a role: for either there is not a second time around; or else the second time around is a genuinely distinct series of events, to be involved in which is to *avoid* rather than *change* the original series of events. To see this, consider that to say that an event (for example, [Italy's winning the FIFA World Cup in 2006]) both did and did not occur, *simpliciter*, is to assert a contradiction.[7]

So the basic idea is that the time-traveler cannot change the past without it being a different past.

But even if the time-traveler cannot *change* the past, what about *affecting* the past? No, that won't work either because affecting the past amounts to the same as changing the past. In *Stewie Griffin: The Untold Story*, Stewie is horrified by the bleak future he will one day have. (Consider, for instance, Stewie's complaint to Stu: "I can't believe this. This is the future. Wait a minute! Everything looks the same. I say, where are the monuments to me? Where are my legions of followers? I thought I would be absolute ruler of the world by now!" Still, an even bigger letdown for Stewie is seeing Lois in the year 2035: "She's still alive? What the hell, man?!") Stewie plans to go back in time (from the future he has witnessed), and prevent his earlier self from having the near-fatal accident at the pool: "It seems that there is only one thing to do. I must return to the past to ensure I never have the close call with that lifeguard tower in the first place." But Stewie fails to realize that he cannot change past events.

In order to travel back to an event in the past, that event must be identical to the one we want to travel back to. (If it isn't identical, after all, it'll be a different event!) But here's the problem: if the time-traveler arrives in the past, it *won't* be identical to the first time the traveler was there (after all, he's only *now* traveling back in time for the first time). This means that time-travel is actually logically impossible. The time you travel to (where you are) is actually not identical to the place you wanted to go (where you were not already).

But is this enough to close the possibility of time-traveling? Couldn't the time-traveler be bound by a different set of causal laws than the rest of us? Certainly, this is logically possible. David Lewis explicitly assumes this to be the case in a world in which time-traveling is possible.

There is, however, a serious problem with this possibility. It violates our assumption (A4) above: we assumed that the time-traveler is subject to the same causal laws as everyone else. However, if it turns out that the time-traveler is bound by the same causal laws as everyone else, and that *everyone's* actions are governed by fatalism, this is not at all what we would expect. Fatalism is the idea that all actions are predetermined – "fated" – to occur. For instance, we typically assume that there was no necessity involved in your (the reader's) choice to pick up *Family Guy and Philosophy* from the shelf at your bookstore. Granted, now that you are reading this essay, it is safe to say that you did pick up the book, and so it is a necessary fact that you did pick up the book *in your past*. But if fatalism is true, then *you could not have chosen otherwise*, appearances to the contrary notwithstanding. (You were in the bookstore, looking at *Family Guy and Philosophy*, thinking "Any s#!* passes for philosophy nowadays" before reaching for the book. You look over, and see the title of Harry Frankfurt's book *On Bullshit* a few shelves over. But there's nothing you could have done. You the reader were destined to pick up *Family Guy and Philosophy*, even if you harbor strong resentment towards the series.) It may turn out that our understanding of the world is flawed and that we are governed in our actions by fatalism, but more is needed to establish that this is so than our mere fancy of retaining the possibility of time-traveling.

Here an objection could be raised. Why should we assume that there is only one set of causal laws that applies to time-travelers and non-time-travelers alike? It appears that to hold such a view amounts to a prejudice in favor of the ordinary. Our ordinary experiences, which show that causal connections run from the earlier to the later and not vice versa, may well be mistaken. Nevertheless, these experiences cannot be dismissed off-hand in order to salvage the inconsistent stories about time-travel into the past, and give wings to the fancy of time-traveling.

"You see . . . my time manipulator employs axioms from the quantum theory . . . ," or: The Quantum Model of Time-Traveling

Even if the model of reality we have considered doesn't leave room for time-traveling, there is still another model for us to consider. The arguments against the possibility of time-travel hold *only if* there is just one universe and one time-line. Despite the fact that this is the simplest model of reality, it is not the only possible model.

David Deutsch and Michael Lockwood endorse a multiple-universe approach to time-travel that is based on discoveries in quantum mechanics and, at first blush, seems to completely avoid our difficulties. In their essay "The Quantum Physics of Time Travel," Deutsch and Lockwood argue that the difficulties discussed above are purely academic, for they rest on a view embedded in classical physics.[8] This classical view, according to Deutsch and Lockwood, badly misconstrues the nature of time. An interpretation of time based on quantum mechanics not only postulates the existence of closed time-like curves (although only on submicroscopic levels) but allows time-travel using them. As they say:

> If something physically can happen, it does – in some universe. Physical reality consists of a collection of universes, sometimes called a multiverse. Each universe in the multiverse contains its own copy of the neutron whose decay we wish to observe. For each instant at which the neutron might decay, there is a universe in which it decays at that instant. Since we observe it decaying at a specific instant, we too must exist in many copies, one for each universe.[9]

If we consider one of the time-travel stories resulting in inconsistency in the single universe model, we find that these inconsistencies are seemingly avoided if the multiverse view is true.

> Suppose that [Stewie] embarks on a "paradoxical" project that, if completed, would prevent [his] own conception. What happens? If the classical space-time contains CTCs [closed time-like curves], then, according to the quantum mechanics, the universes in the multiverse must be linked up in an unusual way. Instead of having many disjoint, parallel universes, each containing CTCs, we have in effect a single, convoluted space-time, consisting of many connected universes. The links force [Stewie] to travel to a universe that is identical, up to the instant of [his] arrival, but that is thereafter different because of [his] presence. So does [Stewie] prevent [his] own birth or not? That depends on which universe one is referring to. In the universe [he] leaves, the one [he] was born in, [his] grandfather did marry [his] grandmother because, in that universe, he received no visit from [Stewie]. In the other universe, the one whose past [Stewie] travels to, [his] grandfather does not marry that particular woman and [Stewie] is never born. Thus, the fact that [Stewie] is traveling in time does not constrain [his] actions. And it turns out, according to quantum mechanics, that it never would.[10]

Deutsch and Lockwood argue that their model eradicates not only the problems with ostensibly self-defeating causal chains (such as are involved in the grandfather paradox), but also the problems associated with second-time-around fallacy, and the worries of fatalism entering the picture.

But a question remains: is this really time-travel? Let's take a closer look at the quantum model. Using the above example, let's call the universe in which Stewie was born, universe A and the one to which he travels, universe B. So Stewie travels with Stu from the year 2005_A to the year 2035_B and gets a glimpse of his own future (never mind for the moment where Stu originally came from – there are a plenty of letters left in the alphabet). Dismayed by the fact that he is not ruler of the world and that Lois is still alive, Stewie chooses to go back in time and prevent the chain of events that led to this unhappy future. But can Stewie go *back* to 2005_A? This would lead to contradiction, as it would commit the second-time-around fallacy. Rather, what happens is that Stewie travels back to 2005_C where he tries to prevent the close call with the lifeguard tower at the pool. If Stewie were successful, then come 2035_C Lois may well be dead and Stewart Gilligan Griffin may well be the absolute ruler of the world. But this is hardly time-traveling! Stewie's actions in his destination do not change the events in his past. He only changes things for someone who bears a striking resemblance to him. Thus, Stu (in 2035_B) is right not to gorge himself with ice cream, or to tear up a parking ticket, just in case. Stewie's actions in his destination (which is 2005_C) would have no bearing on how things are in 2035_B.

"Enough of this! I must complete my time machine!"

So, there may be no inconsistency in maintaining that Stu lives a successful life in 2035_A and Stu does not exist in 2005_C. After all, the two universes are similar, but not identical. Let's complicate things a little bit more: it can be argued that in order to avoid the second-time-around fallacy, it has to be the case that in the C-universe, 2005 *is* present and the events after 2005_C have yet to occur.

> Suppose . . . [Stewie] travels to 1001_B. It follows that either: (i) the post-1001 events have already occurred in B or (ii) they have not. If (i), then the events of 1001_B are being *revisited*, in a sense, since 1001 in that universe will be a time (as it is in our own) that is past. If this is the case, however, then [Stewie's] presence in 1001_B already entails a contradiction. . . . But this is precisely the kind of contradiction that motivated the multiverse theory in the first place, so (ii) must be the case: the events after 1001_B (relative to B) cannot have yet occurred. . . . We can state as a principle that to time-travel on the multiverse theory there must be for every time a universe at which that time is present. This is, of course, a peculiar thing to suppose, but it is hardly more peculiar, I submit, than the supposition that the theory of the multiverse itself is true.[11]

So, traveling from the year 2035$_B$ to the year 2005$_C$ does not amount to traveling *back* in time, but traveling *across* time-lines, across universes. The "past" of the B-universe is, in fact, simultaneous with the present of the A-universe. Now, in order for traveling across different universes to amount to time-travel, these universes must be full of identical things. Stewie$_A$ has to be identical to Stewie$_B$ (and ditto for everything else). But given that the two universes are different (because they are *two* universes, dammit!), it makes little sense to say that they are full of exactly the same things. So, the multiverse view can't account for time-travel either.

"I'll not stand idly by while you abrogate my plans. You shall rue this day. Well, go on! Start ruing!"

So what follows from all this? Could the possibility of time-traveling be salvaged after all? Could Stewie carry out Lois's request to stop Chris from marrying Vanessa and thereby save Lois from the retirement home? Will I, the author, have to start ruing the day I foiled Stewart Gilligan Griffin's plans by pointing out the logical and metaphysical inconsistencies in them? And do I intend to keep on asking rhetorical questions? The answer to all these questions must be given in the negative. Stewie is stuck with Lois in 2035, and I won't be ruing any time soon. Although it may turn out that our understanding of the world is inaccurate, and that ours is a world in which time-traveling is possible, we currently have no reason to think that our ordinary beliefs are mistaken. Perhaps Stewie the time-traveler should start ruing, as his megalomaniacal and matricidal plans are sure to be foiled by the year 2035, and there's nothing that little hellion can do about it.[12]

NOTES

1   Possibilities and impossibilities come in different flavors. Things can be logically possible: this means that the thing (whatever it is) does not contradict the laws of logic. Things can also be physically possible, that is, they do not violate the known laws of nature. So the statement "It is raining cats and dogs," if taken literally, expresses a physical

impossibility (given the known facts about precipitation, and the fact that condensed water vapor never produces an outpour of canines or felines), but this is logically possible. Metaphysical possibility falls between these two: something is metaphysically possible if it does not contradict more fundamental metaphysical claims (say, about causation). Unless otherwise indicated, this is the sense in which I discuss possibility in this essay.

2   Here it should be noted that *Family Guy* often lampoons popular culture, and the movie is no different in this. The account of time-traveling presented in *Stewie Griffin: The Untold Story* should not be understood as an attempt to provide a consistent time-traveling story, but to ridicule the ubiquitous time-traveling stories appearing elsewhere in popular culture, from *Star Trek* to *Terminator* to *Back to the Future*, and so on. *Family Guy*, instead of shying away from inconsistencies, embraces them. Yet the movie is valuable in that it may help us understand what possibility for time-traveling would entail, and it is in this sense that I discuss the movie.

3   David Lewis, "The Paradoxes of Time-Travel" in *Philosophical Papers*, vol. 2 (New York: Oxford University Press, 1986), pp. 68–9.

4   For further discussion, see Lewis (1986), pp. 69–70. Normally (that is, in non-time-traveling cases), these two time frames coincide. In the case of time-travel, the traveler's personal time frame is separated from the external time frame, and moved into the past, relative to the moment of departure. As for *how* this is accomplished (that is, whether by a DeLorean equipped with a flux capacitor, by a portal called the Guardian of the Forever located in a remote planet, or by a wristwatch-sized device that Stewart Gilligan Griffin purchases from Quahog Time Travel, Inc.), I will not address in this essay.

5   Lewis (1986), pp. 75–6.

6   Lois's well-being is a necessary condition for Stewie's existence, but it is by no means a sufficient condition. It is certainly conceivable that Lois had never met Peter Griffin (cut to a scene of the Pewterschmidts breaking out the champagne in celebration) or that they would have settled for just having two children. (As Lois explains to Chris: "It's been so long since I qualified for the Olympics. No, I wasn't in the Olympics. I got pregnant with Meg and couldn't go. Now I'm pro-choice.") So from Lois's well-being alone, it does not automatically follow that she gives birth to Stewie.

7   Nicholas J. J. Smith, "Bananas Enough for Time Travel?" *British Journal for the Philosophy of Science* 48 (1997), p. 365.

8   David Deutsch and Michael Lockwood, "The Quantum Physics of Time-Travel," *Scientific American* 270 (March 1994), pp. 68–74.

9 Deutsch and Lockwood (1994), p. 72.

10 Deutsch and Lockwood (1994), p. 73. I have taken the liberty of modifying the example to fit our discussion.

11 John Abbruzzese, "On Using the Multiverse to Avoid the Paradoxes of Time Travel," *Analysis* 61, no. 1 (2001), p. 37.

12 This chapter draws from an earlier paper of mine, "The consistency conditions for time-traveling," presented at the University of Iowa Graduate Student Colloquium and at the Iowa Philosophical Society Annual Meeting of 2003 at Grinnell College, Iowa. I wish to thank my audiences for their input. I am particularly indebted to the following people: to Jeremy Wisnewski, the editor of this volume, for his helpful comments; to Timo Siltala for useful discussions on time-traveling (and on *Family Guy*); and especially to my wife, Bertha Alvarez Manninen, for reading various drafts of this chapter, for suggesting numerous improvements, and for tolerating my watching *Family Guy*.

17

KIERKEGAARD AND THE NORM (MACDONALD) OF DEATH

ADAM BUBEN

It's truly remarkable how often Death appears on *Family Guy*. After all, death is usually a serious issue, not a comedic goldmine. Aside from the two episodes that feature the hooded, scythe-wielding Death (we'll use a capital 'D' when we're talking about the character), "Death is a Bitch" and "Death Lives," there are numerous episodes in which Death shows up briefly to great comic effect.[1] For example, in "I Take Thee Quagmire," Death says he has Celine Dion tickets, and jokes, "I'm not gonna kill her, I'm just gonna watch her die on her own." Death then looks for approval in the form of a "high-five," but when one guy obliges, the poor sap actually drops dead. While this depiction of a personified Death (originally voiced by Norm MacDonald, and subsequently by Adam Carolla) that one can joke with (or date, or take to the Gap) may make for entertaining television, some philosophers, like Søren Kierkegaard (1813–55), might claim that this sort of entertainment impedes a proper understanding of, or relationship with, death.

In his *Three Discourses on Imagined Occasions* (1845), Kierkegaard dedicates an entire discourse, "At a Graveside," to explaining how "the thought of death gives the earnest person the right momentum in life and the right goal toward which he directs his momentum."[2] Bad news for *Family Guy*, Kierkegaard speaks against, among other things, metaphorical depictions of death, including personifications, which hamper the individual's appropriate and important fear of death by diluting death's frightening nature (TDIO, pp. 79–81, 98–9).

But Kierkegaard isn't just a party-pooper. Unlike so many philosophers, Kierkegaard actually has a sense of humor (of what it's about, *and* of what's funny). So let's look carefully to see if he can get the joke and if we can learn something. Perhaps *Family Guy*'s (Norm of) Death, comically portrayed, can actually echo Kierkegaard's scathing critique of our everyday norms of death.

Kierkegaard on Death

From the time of Socrates (469–399 BCE) and the flourishing of Greek thought up to the present day, death has been an object of philosophical inquiry. Epicurus (341–270 BCE), for example, argues against the appropriateness of fearing death when he states, "So death, the most frightening of bad things, is nothing to us; since when we exist, death is not yet present, and when death is present, then we do not exist;"[3] and the French philosopher Jacques Derrida (1930–2004) claims, in an interview, "All of my writing is on death . . . If I have one goal, it is to accept death and dying."[4] Several key philosophical treatments of death, including Epicurus', are the targets of ridicule in Kierkegaard's "At a Graveside," and as it turns out, this ridicule provides some of the reason to believe that Kierkegaard might be critical of Death in *Family Guy*.[5]

Writing in 19th-century Denmark, Kierkegaard recommends thinking earnestly about death for guidance on the road to living as a true Christian. He describes three basic aspects of the earnest thought of death, and thus, three basic and, unfortunately, widespread ways that an individual (or in this case, a television show) can fail to keep death in mind in the right way.[6] First and foremost, when considering death, an individual must consider only his or her own death and not death in general, or death as the human condition (TDIO, pp. 73–5). There may be a time and a place for such general inquiries, but when the issue at hand is the relationship of death to one's own life, both death as a concept and the deaths of others are irrelevant (TDIO, pp. 86, 89).[7]

Second, one's own death is a certainty that will take place at an uncertain time (TDIO, pp. 75, 91). These brutal facts aren't ones we're eager to remember, but we must. Although it may feel as though my own death isn't on the horizon or is at least only off in the distant future, this feeling obscures the reality of my existence (TDIO, pp. 79, 91, 100–1; JP, v.1: 717).

Third, there's an appropriate fear of death that must be maintained (TDIO, p. 81). Unless one maintains this fear, one might fail to appreciate one's life, and thus possibly fail to realize the benefits for one's life of being aware of the other aspects of the earnest thought of death (TDIO, p. 98; JP, v.1: 713).

According to Kierkegaard, a person who earnestly thinks about these aspects of death will live a life focused primarily on *how* she lives rather than on *what* she accomplishes. The certainty and the uncertainty of death teach us that time to accomplish goals (the *what*) can't be guaranteed, but, thankfully, dedicated striving (the *how*) requires no amount of time (TDIO, p. 96). And because my life might end at any time, it's absurd to worry excessively about *what* I might accomplish in the future. With this mindset, many of life's concerns about *what* one is doing are revealed as merely "incidental" (TDIO, p. 96) to the truly important concerns of *how* one lives.[8]

"For if humanity discovers I'm no longer lurking in the shadows, the consequences will be dire": Kierkegaard on Death in *Family Guy*

It shouldn't be too hard to find examples of Death apparently failing to encourage his fans to think earnestly about death. In fact, at first glance it seems harder to find a single example of Death portrayed in a way that Kierkegaard would approve of.

In Death's first appearance ("Death is a Bitch"), he sprains his ankle pursuing Peter and is unable to carry out his duties while recovering on the Griffins' couch. Because no one can die, a glorious *Family Guy*-style chaos ensues around Quahog. There are two problems with this tale of Death, given Kierkegaard's account. First, though death can't be avoided, Death has been avoided, and by an overweight family man no less. Second, while death might come at any time, Death can't come until non-existent ligaments heal up. Even though this story is too outlandish to be taken seriously, it does nothing to help its viewers keep the certainty and the uncertainty of death in mind. In fact, the episode might actually encourage viewers to put off worrying about death until a time when death seems more likely. To believe that there's time to kill before death will come is, unfortunately, a sure sign that one has failed to learn Kierkegaard's lesson. And without this lesson, one might not make the all-important distinction between incidental concerns about *what* one is doing, and potentially meaningful concerns about *how* one is living.

Moving on, Kierkegaard believes that death itself is indefinable and inexplicable (TDIO, pp. 85, 96). One's impending encounter with death is something to be treated with the utmost seriousness and even an appropriate sort of fear. Death, however, in several episodes of *Family Guy*, boozes it up at a frat house, endures mom-nagging, and complains that Lois should've made his cocoa "with milk, not crap" ("Death is a Bitch"). In discussing death as indefinable and inexplicable, Kierkegaard means to emphasize the unknowable nature of death and the insecurity or fear that comes with this inability to know. When *Family Guy* personifies death, the unknowable becomes very familiar and this familiarity allows us to repress the fear that is a natural part of thinking about death. Indeed Peter becomes so unfazed by Death that he states: "I'm not afraid of anything, I laugh in the face of Death. See HAHAHAHA" ("Death is a Bitch"). Lacking an appropriate fear of death, Kierkegaard believes, a person might come to fear life more than death, or at least lose an appreciation for life. Without such an appreciation, a person might withdraw from the activities of life, long to die, or maybe even take his own life. An appropriate fear of death helps a person preserve a life in which death's lessons can be applied. As Kierkegaard says, "Earnestness does not scowl but is reconciled with life and knows how to fear death (TDIO, p. 88).

Instead of viewing death as one's personal encounter with the ending of one's own particular existence, *Family Guy* treats death more like a mere fact of human existence. For example, "Death Lives" depicts Death as the clipboard-carrying harvester of human life. This understanding of death as the general scourge of humanity is what Kierkegaard criticizes Epicurus for when he states: "it is still only a jest if he contemplates death and not himself in death, if he thinks of it as the human condition but not as his own" (TDIO, p. 73). Since the purpose of a particular individual's thinking about death is to alter that particular individual's life, Kierkegaard believes that our relation to our own individual death, and not humanity's relation to death in general, is what matters. Because Death doesn't appear as a subject of personal significance, but as a common problem for everyone, *Family Guy* doesn't seem to encourage its fans to think about death in the appropriate way (*I'm* not everyone, after all!). At no point are we drawn out in the way we should be (Reader: *you will die*).

But does this all mean that *Family Guy* is the source of a shallow life? Or is Kierkegaard just a stick-in-the-mud? Can't he appreciate a good fart joke? Actually, as we'll see, Kierkegaard thinks serious matters can make use of the comic (CUP, pp. 87–8). So maybe there's hope for *Family Guy* after all.

"Yeah, I know I should find this ironic, but really, I'm just bored as hell": Kierkegaardian Comedy in *Family Guy*'s Death

In Kierkegaard's *Concluding Unscientific Postscript to "Philosophical Fragments"* (1846), he discusses, at length, the nature of the comic.[9] Kierkegaard believes that comedy, if understood properly, performs the valuable service of illuminating the unfounded and thoughtless assumptions that individuals make about the character and meaning of their existences and daily activities.[10] With his understanding of comedy in mind, we can reinterpret Death in *Family Guy* as a concerned attempt to point out, albeit in an exaggerated way, how ridiculous it is to approach death in the way Kierkegaard believes most people do (JP, v.1: 717).

Near the end of *Postscript*, Kierkegaard claims to have "a more than ordinary sense of the comic and a certain capacity for making ludicrous what is ludicrous" (CUP, p. 622). He makes this claim to justify his role as a comic writer or "humorist."[11] The comic, you see, can be found wherever there's contradiction (CUP, p. 514) and the role of a comic writer is to speak up when there's something contradictory or ludicrous in the relation between the way things are and the way things should be. The mere presence of contradiction isn't sufficient for comedy though, Kierkegaard points out, since tragedy might also be found wherever there's contradiction (CUP, p. 514). What distinguishes the comic contradiction from the tragic is the absence of pain, or rather, the possibility of overcoming pain. Kierkegaard states: "The law for the comic is very simple: the comic is wherever there is contradiction and where the contradiction is painless by being regarded as canceled, since the comic certainly does not cancel the contradiction (on the contrary, it makes it apparent)" (CUP, p. 523). But what could be so painful about contradiction?

As a very basic pattern for painful contradictions, consider this: if a contradiction can be found between my actual existence and my ideal existence, pain arises when I become aware that I am not living up to this ideal (Barrett, pp. 129–30). When a comic depiction makes such a contradiction apparent to me, however, it can relieve the pain by demonstrating that there's a way out of the contradiction (CUP, p. 516) even if an appropriate positive action isn't immediately obvious. Simply put, by making certain actions or ways of thinking seem silly in relation to other possibilities (a strength of *Family Guy*), comedy can alleviate the pain of contradiction by demonstrating what not to do.

For example, when the Griffins send Brian, the dog, to pick up Stewie in Palm Springs rather than go themselves, and trouble predictably arises, the negligent parents among us are provided with a not so subtle hint that negligent parenting ought to be avoided ("Road to Rhode Island"). Comedy, for Kierkegaard, is capable of not only making us aware of contradictions, but also in doing so, actually helping us to avoid these contradictions and the pain they can cause. He claims that satire, a particular expression of the comic, is "oriented toward healing" (CUP, p. 515), but it's probably fair to say this about comedy, as he understands it, in general.

So now with Kierkegaard's sense of the comic in mind let's reconsider our earlier examples. To begin with, the case of Death's sprained ankle is a great example of death depicted in such a way that the certainty and uncertainty of death are seemingly forgotten. If one considers this situation carefully, however, its absurdity should only help demonstrate the contradiction between the reality of death's certainty and uncertainty, and any treatment of death that ignores this reality. For instance, the nonsensical idea that Death, an entity without ligaments, could be temporarily out of commission due to a sprained ankle allows us to see the mistake in treating death as though it might not come at any time. Since Death in this situation

203

can be seen as a comic symbol of the foolishness of failing to remember the certainty and uncertainty of death, it's doubtful that Kierkegaard would condemn this particular instance of Death in *Family Guy*. In fact, how could Kierkegaard reject this example when he derives a similar lesson from a comic story about another failure to take the certainty and the uncertainty of death seriously (CUP, p. 86)?

Moving on, it's only on a superficial level that the ridiculous personification of death in *Family Guy* seems to be the sort of thing Kierkegaard blames for making death less frightening. The comic contradiction, which is easily identifiable in this personification, is this: despite the fact that death is indefinable and inexplicable, Death is very precisely defined and explained as a fairly friendly human-like character that just wants "to fit in" ("Death is a Bitch," "*Family Guy* Viewer Mail #1"). The ridiculousness of Death is precisely what makes him valuable for identifying and dodging this contradiction in our lives. By making Death such an absurd character, *Family Guy* points out how silly the personification of death can be, and thereby suggests the mistake in using personification to become comfortable with death. Because the relevant contradiction might be harder to identify in less outlandish personifications of death, such as Brad Pitt's peanut butter sucking death character in the movie *Meet Joe Black*, it's more likely that Kierkegaard would see a threat to the maintenance of an appropriate fear of death in such a serious personification. Instead of viewing Death as yet another example of the far too common attempt to repress, through personification, what Kierkegaard sees as an important fear of death, we can view Death as a caricature of other attempts to use personification to repress this fear (CUP, p. 517). Brad Pitt's got nothing on Norm MacDonald.

The final problematic issue for Death is his portrayal as a general human concern, rather than as *your* concern. The contradiction present in this comic depiction is of course that while death is a very personal matter, Death isn't. Because death is often treated about as personally as Death is in *Family Guy*, there's also a contradiction between the very personal nature of *your* death and the very impersonal way you might treat death in general. Just as in the consideration of the other two points of contention, the absurdity of the way in which Death is presented is what makes him so helpful in identifying this contradiction and avoiding it in our lives. In comparison with thinking about the end of your personal existence, it's pure frivolity to imagine a robed skeleton showing up to check another human off of his list of things to do. Death, on this interpretation, is a comic character with the power to repel his viewers from what Kierkegaard would claim is the stupidity of approaching one's own personal death with a general idea of death in mind.

This is the End

Because its excessive irreverence and flippancy in pointing out contradictions could distract viewers from learning the important lessons of becoming aware of these contradictions, we might be concerned about the effectiveness of some of the comedy in *Family Guy* (CUP, pp. 282, 292, 519). This concern does not seem warranted in the case of Death, however. For the thoughtful viewer, Death is an absurd portrayal of erroneous and superficial, yet widely held, beliefs or ways of thinking about death. When one thinks about death as Kierkegaard recommends, these mistaken ways of conceiving death can be avoided. By embodying these mistakes, the ridiculous presentation of Death in *Family Guy* also allows us to notice and avoid the silliness of thinking about death improperly. Viewed in this manner, Death is a Kierkegaardian parody aimed at correcting us when we think about death in the wrong way. In exposing certain norms about our everyday thoughts of death as problematic, Death's Norm supports earnestly thinking about it.[12]

NOTES

1   There are also several episodes, in which we don't see Death at all, that still include death as a theme, or have something to do with death in the title. In fact, despite dealing very little with death, the first three episodes of the series have either "death" or "dead" in the title, and the fourth is called "Mind Over Murder." Much like our lives, *Family Guy* seems to have death hanging over it from the very beginning.

2   Søren Kierkegaard. *Three Discourses on Imagined Occasions*, translated and edited by Howard V. Hong and Edna H. Hong (Princeton:

Princeton University Press, 1993), p. 83. Subsequent citations from this work will be given parenthetically in the text as: TDIO, page #.

3   Epicurus, "Letter to Menoeceus." In *The Epicurus Reader*, translated and edited by Brad Inwood and L. P. Gerson (Indianapolis: Hackett Publishing, 1994), p. 29.

4   *New York Times Magazine*, January 23, 1994. Cited by Iain Thomson, "Can I Die? Derrida on Heidegger on Death," *Philosophy Today*, Vol. 43, No. 1/4 (spring 1999), pp. 29–42.

5   His reaction to earlier treatments of death, however, isn't all that makes Kierkegaard's account important in the history of philosophy. The tremendous impact of this account on existentialism (the branch of philosophy that deals with the nature and significance of human existence) and European (primarily German and French) philosophy of the twentieth century definitely adds to its significance. In particular, the influence of "At a Graveside" on Martin Heidegger's (1889–1976) famous presentation of death in *Being and Time*, guarantees Kierkegaard's account of death a place among philosophy's most noteworthy treatments of the subject. See Michael Theunissen, "The Upbuilding in the Thought of Death: Traditional Elements, Innovative Ideas, and Unexhausted Possibilities in Kierkegaard's 'At a Graveside.'" In Robert L. Perkins, ed., *International Kierkegaard Commentary*, *Three Discourses on Imagined Occasions*, Vol. 10 (Macon, GA: Mercer University Press, 2006), pp. 321–58, esp. pp. 327–47.

6   It is particularly appropriate for those involved in the creation of a television show to keep death in mind, since many shows are often in danger of cancellation. In fact, *Family Guy* faced its own death when it was canceled after its third season. Thanks to public outcry and impressive DVD sales, however, *Family Guy* discovered that there really is life after death and it looks a lot like season four. But this is a matter best taken up in *Family Guy and Philosophy* volume two (we should be so lucky).

7   Kierkegaard makes similar statements about death in his journals. See Søren Kierkegaard. *Søren Kierkegaard's Journals and Papers*, vols. 1–7, translated and edited by Howard V. Hong and Edna H. Hong (Bloomington: Indiana University Press, 1967–78), vol. 1, 721. Subsequent citations from this work will be given parenthetically in the text as: JP, volume #: entry #).

8   If it's not entirely clear at this point how Kierkegaard's Christian-oriented take on death could be relevant for *Family Guy*, all one need do is understand that although Kierkegaard is addressing an aspiring Christian reader, there's nothing about his account of death that's inherently Christian. The earnest thought of death only allows one to

realize the value of focusing on *how* one lives, and while this, one might think, is the most important realization for one who wants to be a Christian, this realization alone doesn't make one a Christian. Because Christianity doesn't hold exclusive rights to matters of *how* we live, Kierkegaard's existential focus on the *how* of living might have relevance for non-Christians as well. This is what leaves room for both Heidegger's account of death and Kierkegaardian interpretations of Death in the clearly non-Christian *Family Guy*. See Søren Kierkegaard, *Concluding Unscientific Postscript to "Philosophical Fragments,"* Vols. 1 and 2. Translated and edited by Howard V. Hong and Edna H. Hong (Princeton: Princeton University Press, 1992), p. 1: 610. Subsequent citations from this work, all of which are from volume 1, will be given parenthetically in the text as: CUP, page #).

9 Kierkegaard writes *Postscript* under the pseudonym Johannes Climacus. Although Kierkegaard's use of pseudonyms is a complicated matter, he often does this in order to present important ideas that may not be representative of Kierkegaard's fully formed positions. In the case of comedy, however, there's no reason to think that Kierkegaard and Climacus would disagree, and so, for the sake of clarity, it seems possible, even though not entirely appropriate (CUP, p. 627), to attribute the consideration of comedy found in *Postscript* to Kierkegaard.

10 Lee Barrett, "The Uses and Misuses of the Comic: Reflections on the *Corsair* Affair." In Robert L. Perkins, ed., *International Kierkegaard Commentary*, vol. 13 (Macon, GA: Mercer University Press, 1990), p. 135. Subsequent citations from this work will be given parenthetically in the text as: Barrett, page #; Søren Kierkegaard. *The Humor of Kierkegaard: An Anthology*, edited by Thomas C. Oden (Princeton: Princeton University Press, 2004), pp. 17–19, 24–5. Subsequent citations from this work will be given parenthetically in the text as: Oden, page #.

11 Kierkegaard actually makes important distinctions between comedy and humor (CUP, p. 521). In fact, he seems to claim that humor and irony are the two key varieties of the comic (Barrett, p. 125). There's some ambiguity, however, in the proper use of these terms and their relations to each other (Barrett, p. 129). One significant commentator on the comic in Kierkegaard even goes so far, I think incorrectly, as to equate comedy and humor (Oden, pp. 24–5). Despite obvious disagreement on how these concepts fit together, the portrayal of Death in *Family Guy* would most likely fit Kierkegaard's understanding of irony better than his understanding of humor. Even so, in order to avoid the confusion of both this disagreement, and the complex roles that irony and humor play in Kierkegaard's understanding of the stages of human

existence, it seems best to focus on the less technical term "comedy" in trying to account for Death.

12 I would like to thank Kelly Becker, Andrew Burgess, Haley Glover, Kristopher Konrad, Joseph Levy, Maureen Sergel, and Iain Thomson for their very helpful comments on an early draft of this chapter.

APPENDIX
Everything You Ever Needed to Know About Meg Griffin, as Compiled by the Contributors

WHAT THE DEUCE!?! THEY'RE REAL! (MOST OF THEM, ANYWAY)

Robert Arp currently is a visiting professor at Florida State University. He continues to publish in philosophy of biology, philosophy of mind, and popular culture. He edited the *South Park and Philosophy* book in this series. He thinks thinkin' is freakin' sweet!

Shai Biderman is a PhD candidate in philosophy at Boston University. His primary research interests are philosophy of literature and film, existentialism, and contemporary continental philosophy. His recent publications include several papers on reasonability, revenge, and determinism, as well as writings on Kafka, Nietzsche, and Heidegger. Since Shai tickled his brain with a pencil, he is unable to do math.

Adam Buben is a graduate student in the philosophy department at the University of South Florida. His primary interests include Kierkegaard, the samurai, and the philosophy of death. This is his second publication, but it is probably the first (and only) one that anyone will ever read. He spends his free time hanging around the bay, trying to pick up the giggity, giggity girls with his atrocious Quagmire impression, and writing silly *Family Guy* essays when he should be thinking about his dissertation.

William J. Devlin is a doctoral candidate at Boston University and a visiting lecturer at Bridgewater State College and the University of Wyoming. His philosophical areas of interest are the philosophy of science, truth, the philosophy of art, and existentialism. He has written papers concerning philosophy in relation to cultural series and films, such as *Lost*, *The Prisoner*, *South Park*, and *Star Trek*. In his spare time, he is an aspiring pupil of Glenn Quagmire. Thus far he has learned basic pick up lines, the joy of watching *Wings*, the ability to withstand mace, that Taylor Hanson is not a woman, and how to say ALLLRRIIIIIGGHT!

P. Sue Dohnimm does not exist, you silly rabbit.

Stephanie Empey is completing a doctoral degree at the University of California, Riverside. She would tell you more about herself if she weren't so busy with that bitch, motherhood. As things stand, she is trying to prevent her teenage son, Arrow, from attacking the editor of this volume for claiming that he invented the catch-phrase "Snap!"

Jonah P. B. Goldwater is an adjunct lecturer at Baruch College and a PhD candidate at the Graduate Center of the City University of New York. He is the author of his grocery list, and he has a firm handshake.

David Kyle Johnson is currently an assistant professor of philosophy at King's College in Wilkes-Barre, PA. His philosophical specializations include philosophy of religion, logic, and metaphysics. He also wrote a chapter in Blackwell's *South Park and Philosophy*, and has forthcoming chapters on *The Office*, *Quentin Tarantino*, *Johnny Cash*, *Batman*, and *Battlestar Galactica*. He has taught many classes that focus on the relevance of philosophy to pop culture, including a course devoted to *South Park*. (A class devoted to *Family Guy* is in the works.) Litigation is currently pending in David Kyle Johnson vs. Fox Studios; Kyle has sued Seth MacFarlane and Fox because, very clearly, Stewie is based on Kyle's childhood.

Sharon M. Kaye is an associate professor of philosophy at John Carroll University in Cleveland, Ohio. Her area of specialization is medieval philosophy. She has conducted extensive first-hand, in-depth, deliciou – *ahem* – delicate empirical research on all seven of the deadly sins.

Daniel Malloy is an adjunct assistant professor at Appalachian State University. He recently defended his dissertation on the critical theory of Herbert Marcuse at the University of South Carolina and has published articles on Hegel, Horkheimer, Adorno, Foucault, Leibniz, and Spinoza. Like his idol, Brian, Daniel has humped more than one leg for a dry martini and is always on the lookout for a midget with some gin.

Tuomas Manninen is a lecturer in philosophy at Arizona State University West. He received his PhD in philosophy from the University of Iowa in 2007. His research focuses on contemporary analytic metaphysics, theories of personhood, and Wittgenstein, and he has published articles on these that almost feel like they were written by a real philosopher. He chose a career in philosophy after realizing that it pays better than a bid on world domination. In his spare time, he hopes to complete a machine to control the global environment in order to rid the world of broccoli, and just like his dissertation, it is going to be a few sprinkles of genius, with a chance of doom.

Shaun Miller teaches in the philosophy department at Weber State University and has written a thesis on love and sex relating it from sadomasochism to soul mates. While he's constantly thinking about love and sex, he's wondering why people just won't let their inner Giggity come up to the surface. As a part time job, he works as a janitor at James Woods High School. By the way, what *was* the deal with Superman throwing the saran wrap "S" to the guys in black? What was *that* all about?

Jerry Samet is the pen name (and also, as it happens, the real name) of an associate professor of philosophy at Brandeis University. His main area of interest is the philosophy of the mind. The present essay is the opening salvo in what promises to be a full-frontal scholarly assault on the philosophy of the mindless. His scholarly ambitions understandably leave him no time to pursue hobbies or normal human interests.

Robert Sharp teaches medical ethics at the University of Alabama, where he educates students in the proper use of shrinking, sperm-destroying vessels. His personal research ranges from value theory to existentialism to philosophy of literature, especially Peterotica novels. In the process of contributing to this book, Robert asked both the editor and the publishers for more money. When they refused, he snuck into their houses and rubbed his butt on their carpets. He never saw the cameras and now serves community service by chasing "leafers" out of Quahog.

Andrew Terjesen is currently a visiting assistant professor at Washington and Lee University teaching classes in moral philosophy and the history of philosophy. He had previously taught at Austin

College (which is about as close to Austin, TX as Quagmire is to a committed relationship), Duke University, and the Thomas Griffin Memorial Annex of the Quahog Unemployment Office. Although he has done some things he is not proud of to stay in philosophy (what? you think we still have enough in the budget for a cutaway this late in the book? – those manatees don't work cheap dammit!), writing this essay fulfills the dreams of that young college student who wandered into his first philosophy class after a long night of "frenching Kermit." (Otherwise he would have taken that first biology exam and not ruined his chances for medical school.) He hasn't been this personally fulfilled since the time he taught Billy Zabka to do a Pinter play. (Look, just use your imagination – to get you started, Zabka was the main bully in *Karate Kid*.)

Raymond J. VanArragon is an assistant professor of philosophy at Bethel University. He has published articles in philosophy of religion, and is co-editor of *Contemporary Debates in Philosophy of Religion* (Blackwell, 2004). Though he claims not to take offense at *Family Guy*'s irreverent humor, witnesses report seeing him cringe on occasion while he watches the show.

Mark D. White is associate professor in the Department of Political Science, Economics, and Philosophy at the College of Staten Island in New York City, where he teaches courses combining economics, philosophy, and law. He co-edited the book *Economics and the Mind* (2006), and has written many articles and book chapters on economics and philosophy. Like Peter, he continues the search for the perfect-tasting suppository.

J. Jeremy Wisnewski is an assistant professor of philosophy at Hartwick College. He is the author of *Wittgenstein and Ethics: A Defense of Ethics as Clarification* (2007), and numerous articles in moral and political philosophy, philosophy of the social sciences, and other Very Important Areas. In addition to being addicted to *Family Guy*, Wisnewski also smokes crack, does heroin, abuses yard gnomes, jumps out of airplanes, and makes up lies to tell the world about himself. Wisnewski invented the slang use of the word "Snap!" (or so he claims), along with the number 7.

INDEX

Index